Giles

29.95

# High-Speed Memory Systems

# High-Speed Memory Systems

A.V. Pohm

O.P. Agrawal

Reston Publishing Company, Inc., Reston, Virginia
*A Prentice-Hall Company*

**Library of Congress Cataloging in Publication Data**

Pohm, A.V.
  High-speed memory systems.

  Bibliography: p. 229
  Includes index.
  1. Computer storage devices.  I. Agrawal, O. P. (Om P.).
  II. Title.
TK7895.M4P63 1983    621.3819′5833    82-21515
ISBN 0-8359-2835-7

© 1983 by
Reston Publishing Company, Inc.
A Prentice-Hall Company
Reston, Virginia 22090

All rights reserved. No part of this book may be
reproduced in any way, or by any means, without
permission in writing from the publisher.

10  9  8  7  6  5  4  3  2  1

Printed in the United States of America

# Contents

*Preface* ix

Chapter 1    HIGH-SPEED COMPUTER MEMORIES    1

     1.1   Introduction   1
     1.2   The Spectrum of Memories and Techniques   3
     1.3   Past and Present High-Speed Hierarchies   9
     *Problems*   16

Chapter 2    BASICS OF BUFFERED (CACHE) MEMORIES    17

     2.1   Introduction   17
     2.2   Basic Ingredients of a Cache Memory   18
     2.3   Cost and Performance Effectiveness   19
     *Problems*   22

Chapter 3    DESIGN OF CACHE MEMORY SYSTEMS    23

     3.1   Introduction   23
     3.2   Buffer Partitioning   26

3.3 Swapping Algorithms 27
3.4 Comparative Performance 33
3.5 Multimodule Main Memories 39
3.6 Effective Cycle and Access Times 50
*Problems 51*

**Chapter 4 HIT RATIOS AND FACTORS THAT AFFECT THEM 57**

4.1 Analytical Models 57
4.2 Hit Ratio Dependence on Block Size 65
4.3 Buffer Filling and Cold-Start Miss Ratios 68
*Problems 74*

**Chapter 5 MEMORY HIERARCHY ORGANIZATIONS 75**

5.1 Introduction 75
5.2 Multiple Buffered Modules 75
5.3 Coherence of Cache Information 79
5.4 Organization of a Multiple Cache-Processor System 81
5.5 Bus Performance in Servicing Multiprocessors 90
5.6 Optimizing Three-Level Hierarchies 92
5.7 Sample Cache Design for a Multiprocessor System 97
5.8 Virtual Memory Systems 103
*Problems 117*

**Chapter 6 ERROR-CORRECTING CODES AND RELIABILITY FOR HIGH-SPEED MEMORIES 119**

6.1 Introduction 119
6.2 Error-Detecting and Error-Correcting Codes 119
6.3 Reliability Analysis 127
6.4 Impact of EDAC Codes on Memory System Reliability 136
6.5 Commercial SBEC Circuits 139
*Problems 142*

Contents

**Chapter 7**    **HISTORICAL SURVEY AND EVOLUTION OF CACHE SYSTEMS**    145

    7.1   Introduction   145
    7.2   Large Cache Systems   161
    7.3   Other Cache-Related Studies   181
    7.4   Cache for Minicomputers   189
    7.5   Memory Management and Cache Support for Microprocessors   212

*References*   229

*Index*   237

# Preface

This book has been constructed to be a useful teaching instrument for advanced undergraduates and first-year graduate students. It is also intended for computer professionals who are involved in the design of memory systems.

The emphasis is on basic principles and studies. Although memory technology changes rapidly, the principles behind good design remain relatively static. Consequently, the book emphasizes the underlying concepts and techniques that a designer needs to carry out an effective design. Basic studies that developed the experimental groundwork for the analytical tools have been summarized both to demonstrate the validity of the theory and to provide design parameters.

The book starts with a relatively brief historical introduction in Chapter 1 and then proceeds to a simple illustrative example of a cache memory in Chapter 2.

Chapters 3 through 6 fully develop the theory and design of high-speed cache memory systems. In Chapter 5 a brief design is given for a multiple minicomputer cache system. A short discussion is also given on paged memory systems and their relation to cache memory systems.

The final chapter more fully explores the historical development of cache memories and shows the impact of memory hierarchies on a great variety of systems.

A.P. Pohm

O.P. Agrawal

# High-Speed Memory Systems

# Chapter 1
# High-Speed Computer Memories

## 1.1 INTRODUCTION

Within a scant three decades, computer systems have grown from simple conventional von Neumann machines to highly complicated, virtual time-sharing systems. This growth has brought profound changes in the organization of both the processors and the memory systems and has also placed an enormous demand on the speed and capacity of the memory systems. Figure 1.1 illustrates the growth in the speed and capacity of high-speed memory systems over the last three decades. This continuing development in the computer field has given birth to four generations of computers and, in the last decade, to the microprocessors. Microprocessors have been produced that occupy picoacres of silicon real estate, dissipate milliwatts, cost a mere $10 to $1000, and yet have the same or better capability than the giant machines of three decades ago.

    The tremendous progress achieved during this short time can be best illustrated by comparing one of the pioneer main computers with one of the recent types. UNIVAC 1, introduced commercially in 1951, had 1000 words of memory; each word consisted of 12 alphanumeric characters plus parity), a total of 84,000 bits of internal memory. This is less than the 16,000 bytes (128,000 bits) or more of memory found in many microprocessor systems available today, and compares very unfavorably with the 512K bytes to 1M bytes of memory found in some minicomputer

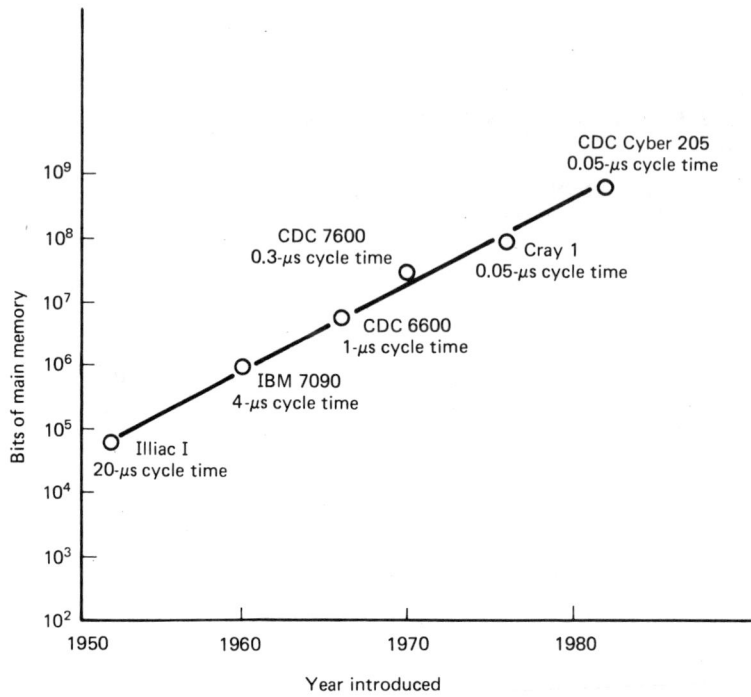

**Figure 1.1.** Growth of Largest Computer Main Memories.

systems and the 4M to 8M bytes of main memory capacity of the super-large main-frame systems. Tables 1.3 and 1.4 illustrate the memory capacity of some of the microcomputers, minicomputers, and large main-frame systems available. It is interesting to compare the $20/character cost of UNIVAC's memory with today's microprocessor and minicomputer semiconductor memory cost, on the order of 2¢/character, a reduction of about 3 orders of magnitude in the cost. In the large computer field, ILLIAC IV (introduced in 1970) has a main memory capacity of 33 million bits, with an access time of 120 nanoseconds (ns) (and cycle time of 240 ns), an improvement of about 500 times in memory capacity and an improvement of 900 to 1000 times in memory speed.

This rapid progress in memory systems has been necessarily associated with the processing power of the computers. Within the last three decades, the processing power of the computers has increased by a factor of 10 every 5 years.

In spite of these improvements in both processors and main memory systems, there has often been a persistent and severe mismatch between the speed of processors and that of main memory. This persistent gap has limited the performance of most computer systems to a value set by the speed of the main memory. Hence there has been a constant need to improve the main memory to obtain better throughput.

Progress in the computer industry generally has been guided by the principle of "better performance with minimum cost" and has resulted in a variety of innovative techniques for improving the performance of the computer system. These innovations can essentially be divided into the following two categories:

    **1.** Improving performance by increasing component speeds.

    **2.** Improving performance by architectural innovations.

Since the basic components are one of the limiting factors, the performance of the computer can be increased by using the fastest components available. However, the speed of the components is limited by the technology and the state of the art, and a point of diminishing return is always reached in speeding up the individual components. Hence this method loses its appeal and necessitates increasing computational throughput by some other means. Another way of improving the speed is to improve the speed with which elementary operations such as addition, multiplication, or division are performed. However, studies by Winograd [w6] have indicated that most computers operate within a factor of 2 of the theoretical limiting speed for addition and a factor of 3 of the limit for multiplication. Hence, larger speed increases are not to be found by this approach either, and this has necessitated improvement of computational throughput by architectural innovations in processors and memory.

Approaches of interest in the area of improving memory speed and capacity have been the following:

    Memory interleaving
    Memory hierarchies and virtual memory
    Development of bigger and faster memory chips
    Cache memories

The techniques involving cache memories and memory hierarchies are the ones to be more fully examined in the following material.

## 1.2 THE SPECTRUM OF MEMORIES AND TECHNIQUES

During the brief history of electronic computers, performance improvements in the computers have been associated with the improvements in memory capacity and speed. Over the last three decades, the memory

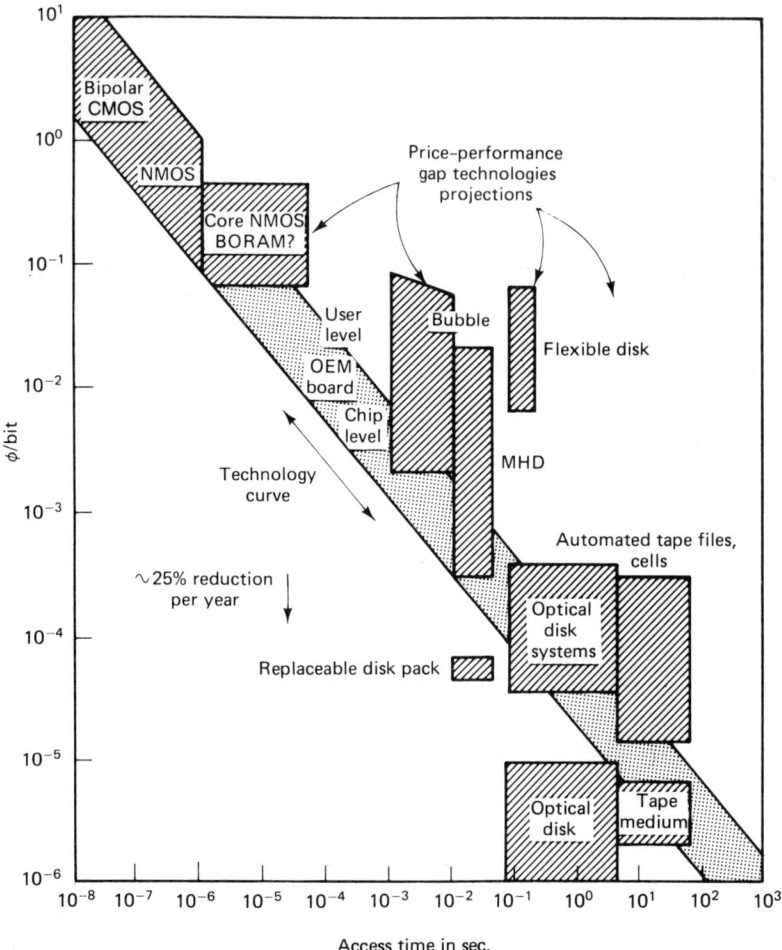

**Figure 1.2.** Cost and Speed of Various Memories.

capacity in the largest systems has increased from 1,000 to 8 million words and cycle time has been reduced from 20 ($\mu$s) to as little as 10 ns. However, even with improvement in technology, fast memories are more expensive than slow ones. As a consequence, it is more cost effective to have a hierarchy of memories with the smallest, shortest access time memory located physically close to the processor. The hierarchy is matched to the requirements of the central processing unit (CPU). Figure 1.2 illustrates cost and performance for various types of memories as of 1982.

As the memory capacity for a system increases, large storage modules are required. This, unfortunately, results in larger physical packages,

## 1.2 The Spectrum of Memories and Techniques

longer wires, and greater signal propagation delays. Even though single memories have increased in capacity and speed, their progress has not been able to keep pace with processor requirements. In large modern systems, it is not unusual for the processor access time to be more than twice the basic storage cycle time. For example, in IBM 360 model 95 with a flat film memory of 120-ns cycle time and 60-ns access time, the machine access time to 128K 64-bit words is 180 ns.

Use of a properly designed storage hierarchy in the memory system is one method of resolving this conflict between size and speed requirements. It provides an average access time only slightly larger than that of the small fast memory, but an amount of storage equal to the capacity of the large backing store. The idea of a storage hierarchy, in one form or another, has been an important concept for computer systems from the very beginning.

A memory hierarchy is a memory system consisting of at least two memories of differing speed and size. Typically, the first memory (near the processor) has a fast access time and a higher cost per bit. Because of this cost, the capacity of this fast level is made small to optimize system costs. The second level of memory technology is selected for its low cost per bit and necessarily has longer access and cycle times.

The use of a hierarchy is coordinated by software or hardware or by system software so that the overall characteristic of the memory system approximates the access of the fast technology and the low cost per bit of the slow technology. An example of an user-managed hierarchy is a core and disk overlaying system; an example of a system of software-managed hierarchy is a core and disk demand paging system; a prime example of a hardware-managed hierarchy is a bipolar cache and core memory system.

Computing systems have always included some form of storage hierarchy. Even simple calculators employ a two-level hierarchy consisting of internal registers and external keyboard entry data. This multiple hierarchy exists because of the cost of storage devices. If the storage device with the fastest access time were also least expensive, then a system would employ a single level of memory. Because of the lack of such memory devices, the requirements of high performance, yet low cost, are best satisfied by a mixture of technologies combining expensive high-performance devices with inexpensive lower-performance devices. Such a strategy is often called a *hierarchical storage system* or *multilevel storage system*.

The storage hierarchy exists, basically, to enhance the cost effectiveness of the system by integrating the characteristics of dissimilar memories, trading access time and cost. For the storage hierarchy to be cost effective, there must be substantial performance improvements. This implies that different levels in the memory hierarchy must have significant technical differences. One cannot achieve a sufficiently high performance-to-cost differential between a small and a large memory when both employ the same technology and similar access time. Table 1.1 shows the range of performance and cost characteristics for typical, current storage technologies, divided into roughly six performance levels. Although this table is a very simplified summary, it does illustrate that a spectrum of devices exists that spans over six orders of magnitude in both cost and performance.

A major design goal of an efficient storage hierarchy system is to provide the required amount of information to the processor at the speed of the fastest memory.

During the early days of computing, the main memory size was quite small (by today's standards), and a large fraction of program development time was devoted to the *overlay problem,* that is, deciding how and when to move the information between the main memory and auxiliary memory, and inserting proper commands in the main program to do so. These commands and procedures were, however, relatively straightforward, amounting to dividing the program into a sequence of segments that would overlay each other. Developments of efficient overlay techniques, however, necessitated complete familiarity by the programmers with the internal working of the machine; thus, a large amount of the programmer's time was spent worrying about the internal details of the machine, rather than solving the problem at hand. The arrival of high-level languages and algorithmic source languages in the mid-1950s, however, eased the programmer's task considerably. These languages enabled the programmers to construct large programs with relative ease and to be concerned more with solving their problems than with worrying about machine details. However, as the complexity of the programs grew, so did the magnitude of the overlay problems. In fact, roughly 25% to 40% of programming cost was attributed to solving overlay problems. Also, it was realized that poor overlay strategies could significantly affect program operating efficiency. With the increase of storage size, efficient overlay strategies and storage hierarchy became more important. Also, since the programmers were shielded from the internal details of the computers, it became increasingly difficult to persuade them to design efficient overlay strategies. This in turn resulted in a need for larger main memory capacity.

The need for executing large programs in small memory spaces thus motivated the development of both hardware and software mechanisms for moving information *automatically* between main and auxiliary memory. Two solutions emerged for automatic storage allocation and gave birth to the principle of *static* and *dynamic* storage allocation strategies. The static approach presumed the predictability of program behavior and

Table 1.1  SPECTRUM OF STORAGE DEVICE TECHNOLOGIES

| | Access Plus Transfer Time | Speed Reduction | Memory Size, Bits | Cents per bit[a] (System level) | Common Technology |
|---|---|---|---|---|---|
| Register | 2–20 ns | 1 | $10^3$–$10^4$ | 20–100 | Semiconductor flip-flops |
| Cache | 20–200 ns | 10 | $10^4$–$10^5$ | 1–10 | Semiconductor random-access memory (RAM) |
| Main memory | 200–2000 ns | 100 | $10^6$–$10^8$ | 0.1–0.5 | Semiconductor memory, ferrite core |
| Backing memory | 1–10 ms | $10^5$–$10^6$ | $10^7$–$10^9$ | 0.05–0.2 | Fixed head disc and drums, magnetic bubbles |
| Secondary memory | 20–100 ms | $10^6$–$10^7$ | $10^9$–$10^{11}$ | 0.01–0.0005 | Moving head disks |
| Mass memory | 10–100 sec | $10^8$–$10^9$ | $10^{11}$–$10^{12}$ | 2 to $8 \times 10^{-5}$ | Automated tape handlers, optical disks, microfilm handlers, strip handlers |

[a]The cost of memory cells diminishes typically 20% or 30% per year, so the values given are representative of the 1980–1983 time frame.

the availability of main memory resources, whereas the dynamic approach did not assume anything about program behavior and presumed that the main memory should grow and shrink according to program needs. The desire of developing programs with machine independence, program modularity, transferability, and efficient list structures made the static allocation concept less and less attractive and the dynamic approach more and more so.

Even under dynamic storage allocation, however, two different and divergent schools of thought existed; one advocated user dynamic storage allocation and the other opted for automatic storage allocation by the system. The proponents of dynamic storage allocation argued that, because the users were best informed about their algorithmic operation, they should be given the power to allocate and deallocate storage dynamically; others thought that, with increase in storage size, the users would not be able to perform these tasks efficiently and impartially, and the whole task should be relegated to the system. In 1961, a group at Manchester, England, proposed the concept of a *virtual* memory to address the problem of automatic dynamic storage allocation. The virtual memory, for the first time, gave the user the illusion of a single large, one-level storage space and relegated the complete responsibility for the efficient managing and moving information between the main memory store and the auxiliary store to the system. The problem of storage allocation thus disappeared from the users point of view. Since its inception in the Atlas system, the concept of virtual memory has been found to be very appealing and has been implemented in various systems: IMB 360/85 and 195, CDC 7600, Burroughs B6500 and larger series, GE 645, IBM 370/158 and 168, SYMBOL-2R, PDP 11/45 and 70, to name a few.

Concepts such as pipelining, look ahead, more sophistication in the handling of branches, multiprogramming, multiprocessing, and time sharing (the developments in the processor area), and deeper storage interleaving, memory hierarchies, and virtual memories (improvements in the memory area) have been excellent technological innovations for improving the general performance of the computer systems. However, all these attempts were only partially successful in bridging the gap between the speed of the processor and that of the main memory.

Ideally, what is desired to completely close the gap between the processor and the main memory is to build the main memory with the same technology as that of the processor registers. However, because it was not economically feasible to provide a large main storage with a cycle time commensurate with the processor, early designs resulted in a microsecond-to-millisecond multilevel hierarchical storage system, even though it was realized that to match the gap perfectly a nanosecond-to-microsecond hierarchy was necessary. Cache memories tend to provide this nanosecond-to-microsecond hierarchy.

In a cache-based system, a fast and small memory known as the buffer or the cache (with roughly the same speed as the processor registers) is interposed between the processor and the main memory. This cache serves as a transparent bridge between their speeds. It is transparent in the sense that it is invisible and inaccessible to the users, that is, completely hidden from them (to cache means to hide) and hence not directly addressable. However, by providing the processor with all the current information it requires at a faster speed, the cache creates the illusion of having a large main memory operating at the speed of the processor.

## 1.3 PAST AND PRESENT HIGH-SPEED HIERARCHIES

The concept of a nanosecond-to-microsecond hierarchy (a cache) was actually proposed more than a decade ago. Its implementation had not been feasible because of the lack of a suitable technology. In fact, as early as 1962, Bloom, Cohen, and Porter [B1] had proposed a technique known as a "look aside" memory and had found that, by using an associative memory of about 256 words of 100-ns cycle time, an effective cycle time of about 350 to 400 ns could be obtained in a memory system whose main memory cycle was 1 $\mu$s [L1]. The concept of a nanosecond-to-microsecond hierarchy was also implemented in embryonic form in other computers like the Ferranti Atlas [B8] and ETL-Mk-6 [T1]. In addition to the main store employing ferrite cores, the Atlas computer also had several thousand words of an entirely novel type of storage to which access was extremely fast (0.2 $\mu$s compared to that of 0.75 $\mu$s for the ferrite core). This core consisted of a wire mesh with small ferrite plugs inserted in the spaces, the contents of the store being determined by the presence or the absence of the plugs. However, this was essentially used as a read-only storage for storing subroutines and a large number of analytic functions only.

The ETL-Mk-6 also used a memory hierarchy of three levels, consisting of a drum, core, and a tunnel diode memory of 250-ns cycle time. The fastest memory was partitioned into a program stack, arithmetic stack, and index registers, of which only the latter two were accessible to the programmer. The idea of a program stack was essentially to contain spaces for short program loops. Wilkes [W1], in 1965, had proposed the use of a fast core memory acting as a slave to the slower core memory in such a way that, in all practical cases, the effective access time was nearer to that of the fast memory than that of the slow memory.

All these techniques had been proposed and implemented in embryonic form only in certain computers. They had not been implemented in any large-scale computer system because of a lack of suitable technology. With the availability of semiconductor monolithic memories, a nanosecond-to-microsecond hierarchy was implemented in 1968 for the first time in IBM 360 model 85, a large-scale computer system; it was termed a *cache system*.

A cache memory system has analogies with other systems employing memory hierarchies, such as a paged virtual memory system. A paged virtual memory system tends to achieve the speed of main memory at the cost of the auxiliary memory or backing store, whereas a cache memory system tends to achieve the speed of cache memory at the cost of main memory. A cache virtual memory system tends to give the illusion of a very large storage working at the speed of the cache or faster buffer. Even though in a virtual memory system, the innermost level of the virtual memory system or the main memory serves as a buffer to the next level, only the provision of a very high-speed, small-capacity memory between the processor(s) and the main memory has been termed a "cache virtual memory system" or a "buffered virtual memory system."

The design of a buffered virtual memory system is analogous to that of a paged virtual memory system. However, the major difference between the two is in the speed ratios between the innermost two memory levels. Table 1.2 summarizes the major differences between a cached virtual memory system and a paged virtual memory system.

**Table 1.2  DIFFERENCES BETWEEN A CACHED VIRTUAL MEMORY SYSTEM AND A PAGED VIRTUAL MEMORY SYSTEM**

| Cached Virtual Memory System | Paged Virtual Memory System |
|---|---|
| Data are moved in blocks of 4, 8, 16, or 32 words between the main memory and cache | Data are moved in pages, page size being 64 or 128 words, between the main memory and the backing store |
| Cache capacity is relatively small (4K to 16K bytes) | Main memory capacity is relatively large |
| Speed discrepancy between the cache and the main memory is relatively small (10 to 20) | Speed discrepancy between the main and the auxiliary memory is quite large (1000 to 10000) |
| No speed disparity between the processor and the cache | Large speed disparity between the processor and the main memory |
| Because of no speed disparity between the CPU and the cache, there is no need for any CPU task switching while data are being moved from the main memory to the buffer memory | Because of large speed disparity between the CPU and the main memory, CPU task switching is required for efficient CPU utilization while data are being transferred from the auxiliary store to the main memory, or vice versa |

## 1.3 Past and Present High-Speed Hierarchies

**Table 1.2 (*continued*)**

| Cached Virtual Memory System | Paged Virtual Memory System |
|---|---|
| Because of the lack of speed disparity the replacement algorithm for the cache memory is not that crucial | Because of speed disparity, the replacement algorithm for the main memory is extremely important, and very poor replacement strategy can very easily "thrash" the whole system |
| Also because of a lack of speed disparity, there is a wide choice of writing algorithms available, and the performance of the memory system is very sensitive to different writing algorithms | Because of speed disparity, the choice of different writing algorithms is limited |

(A cache or buffer tends to provide a required or localized subset of information at faster speed and cheaper price to the processor than a single, fast, large memory and provides an illusion of a large memory operating at the speed of the cache.) As long as the present memory speed–price conditions persist, the buffering approach will continue to be a cost-effective solution for matching speed between the processor and the main memory.

The IBM 360 model 85 was the first large-scale computer system to implement a large data cache. Since then various types of caches (e.g., address cache, instruction cache, name cache) have appeared in various large-scale computers. Table 1.3 illustrates the cache memories for some.

Once found only in large-scale computer systems, cache memories are now found in almost all higher minicomputer systems. The PDP 11/70 and 60 were the first to implement cache memories in minicomputer systems. Since then various types of cache memories have appeared in 32-bit minicomputer systems. Table 1.4 lists some of these.

Cache memories are becoming almost ubiquitous. It is very difficult to envision any computer system, at least for the next decade, without different types of caches. Cache memories are appearing now even in microcomputer systems and VLSI systems. VLSI microcomputer chips of the future will have various caches included in the chip itself.

The history of virtual memories and cache memories is described in more detail in Chapter 7.

Table 1.3  CACHE MEMORIES FOR LARGE-SCALE SYSTEMS

| System | Data Cache | Address Cache | Instruction Cache | Name Cache | Logical Add. Space | | |
|---|---|---|---|---|---|---|---|
| | *Amdahl 470V Series* | | | | | | |
| Model | 470V/5 | 470V/5-II | 470V/6 | 470V/6-II | 470V/7 | 470V/7A | 470V/B |
| Power vs. IBM | 3 × 158 | 3 × 3031 | 1.5 × 168 | 1.5 × 3032 | 1.2 × 3033 | 1 × 3033 | 1.5 × 3033 |
| Announced | 2/77 | 10/78 | 11/74 | 2/77 | 2/77 | 8/79 | 10/79 |
| CPU cycle time | 32.5 | 32.5 | 32.5 | 32.5 | 29 | 29 | 26 |
| MM capacity | 8M | 8M | 8M | 8M | 16M | 16M | 16M |
| MM cycle | 320 | 320 | 320 | 320 | 290 | 290 | 260 |
| Interleaved | 4-way | 4-way | 4-way | 4-way | 16-way | 16-way | 16-way |
| Cache capacity | 16K | 32K | 16K | 32K | 32K | 32K | 64K |
| Cycle time | 65 | 65 | 65 | 65 | 58 | — | 52 |

Table 1.3 (continued)

| System | Data Cache | Address Cache | Instruction Cache | Name Cache | Logical Add. Space | | | |
|---|---|---|---|---|---|---|---|---|
| | | | | | National Semiconductor | | | |
| Model | AS/6 | AS/6-2 | AS/7-7033 | AS/8-7034 | AS/3-3 | AS/3-4 | AS/3-5 | |
| Power vs. IBM | 1.2 × 3032 | 1.3 × 3032 | 1.1 × 3033 | — | 1.6 × 138 | 1 × 148 | 1.22 × | |
| Announced | 10/77 | 10/77 | 7/79 | 7/79 | 9/78 | 9/78 | 2/79 | |
| CPU time cycle | 72 | 72 | 72 | 42 | 115 | 115 | 115 | |
| MM capacity | 16M | 16M | 2M–16M | — | 2M | 4M | 8M | |
| MM cycle time | 360 | 360 | 150 | 100 | 1035 R | 1035 R | 920 R | |
| Interleaving | 4-way | 4-way | 8-way | No | No | No | | |
| Cache memory 64K | 64K | 64K | 64K | 64K | 4K | 4K | 4K | |
| Cache cycle | 72 | 72 | 72 | 21 | 115 | 115 | 115 | |

Table 1.3 (continued)

| System | Data Cache | Address Cache | Instruction Cache | Name Cache | Logical Add. Space | | |
|---|---|---|---|---|---|---|---|
| | | | | National Semiconductor | | | |
| Model | AS/5-1 | AS/5-3 | AS/6-2AP | AS/7031 | AS/3000N | AS/3000 | AS/7000N |
| Power vs. IBM | 1 × 158 | 1 × 158–3 | 2 × 3032 | 1 × 3031 | 1.22 × 4341 | 1 × 158–3 | 1.4 × 3031 |
| Announced | 10/76 | 10/76 | 3/79 | 12/78 | 1/80 | 1/80 | 1/80 |
| CPU cycle time | 115 | 115 | 72 | 92 | 115 | 115 | 72 |
| MM capacity | 8M | 8M | 16M | 8M | 2M–4M | 2M–8M | 2M–8M |
| MM cycle time | 1035 / 690 W | 920 R / 690 W | 360 | 460 | 920 R / 690 W | 920 R / 690 W | — |
| Interleaving | No | No | 4-way | No | No | No | 4-way |
| Cache memory | 8K | 16K | 64K | 32K | 16K | 8K | 16K |
| Cache cycle | 115 | 115 | 72 | 92 | 115 | 115 | 72 |

### Table 1.3 (continued)

| | National Semiconductor | |
|---|---|---|
| Model | AS/7000 | AS/7000DPC |
| Power vs. IBM | 1.0-1.1 × 3033N | not given |
| Announced | 1/80 | 1/80 |
| CPU cycle time | 72 | 72 |
| MM capacity | 4M–16M | 4M–16M |
| MM cycle time | not given | not given |
| Interleaving | 8 | 32 |
| Cache memory | 64K | 64K |
| Cache cycle | 72 | 21 |

| | Sperry UNIVAC 1100 Series | | |
|---|---|---|---|
| System models | 1100/60 H1, H2 | 1100/80 80, 81 | 1100/80 82, 83, 84 |
| CPU logic | ECL | ECL | ECL |
| Microprogrammed | Yes | Yes | Yes |
| CPUs | 1, 2 | 1 | 2, 3, 4 |
| Main memory capacity | 0.5M–1M | 0.5M–1M | 0.5M–4M |
| Word length | 36 bits | 36 bits | 36 bits |
| Cycle time | 575 | 650 | 650 |
| Technology | MOS | MOS | MOS |
| Cache capacity | 8K–16K | 4K–8K | 16K–32K |
| Cache cycle time | 116 | 125 | 125 |

| | Fujitsu FACOM M Series Mainframes | | |
|---|---|---|---|
| Model | FACOM M-180 (II, IIAD) | FACOM M-190 | FACOM M-200 |
| Power | 1 × 158–3 | 1 × 168–3 | 1 × 3031 |
| Announcement | 5/75 | 11/74 | 1/78 |
| CPUs | 1–2 | 1–2 | 1–4 |
| Main memory capacity | 0.5M–8M | 1M–16M | 2M–16M |
| Cycle time | 350 | 480 | — |
| Interleaving | 2– 4-way | 2– 4-way | 2– 4-way |
| Cache | 8K/16K | 16K | 64K |
| TLB | 256 | 32 IDs | — |
| Cycle time | 70 | 30 | — |

| | Hitachi's HITAC M Series Highlights | | | |
|---|---|---|---|---|
| Model | HITAC M-160H | HITAC M-170 | HITAC M-180 | HITAC M-200H |
| CPUs | 1 | 1 | 1–2 | 1–4 |
| Main memory capacity | 2M–6M | 0.5M–8M | 1M–16M | 4M–16M |
| Cycle time | — | — | — | — |
| Interleaving | No | 2-way | 4-way | 8-way |
| Cache | 8K | 32K | 64K | 64K |

**Table 1.4 CACHE MEMORIES FOR MINICOMPUTER SYSTEMS**

| System | Data Cache | Address Cache | Instruction Cache | Name Cache | Logical Add. Space |
|---|---|---|---|---|---|
| VAX 11/780 | 8 KB | | 8 KB | No | 4 GB |
| IBM 4331 | 8 KB | | ? | No | 16 MB |
| PRIME 750 | 16 KB | | 1 Cache Blk | No | 512 MB |
| PE 3240 | 8 KB | | 16 B | No | 16 MB |
| SEL 32/77 | 4 bytes | | 1 Inst. | No | 16 MB |
| MV/8000 | 16 KB | | 1 KB | No | 4 GB |

## PROBLEMS

1. Lack of availability of cheaper, faster, and larger memory chips has resulted in various processor–memory innovations. Discuss the impact of the availability of a very high-speed, larger and cheaper main memory system. What kind of impact would it have on the software organization? Would multiprogramming still be used? What would happen to the virtual memory scheme? What would happen to the cache concepts? Would future computer systems still have caches?

2. What are the factors one should consider in designing and building a hierarchical memory system?

# Chapter 2
# Basics of Buffered (Cache) Memories

## 2.1 INTRODUCTION

Even with the rapid improvements in memory technology, in many modern systems, memory costs are often a dominant hardware item. As indicated in Chapter 1, buffered (or cache) memory organizations are a cost-effective way of achieving high speed in memory systems at modest increases in cost per bit over slow memories, even for relatively small memories. The concept of a cache memory has been found practical for two simple reasons, programming and economics. The programming reason is that most conventional users programs tend to follow the "principle of locality"; that is, at any given instance of time the addressing pattern of a program tends to be localized to a subset of its total address space; the economic reason is that technology has not been able to provide a cheaper alternative to the use of a cache to achieve performance. A cache tends to provide a localized subset of information at a faster speed to the processor and provides an illusion of a larger main memory operating at the speed of the cache. Cache memories should continue to be cost effective as long as slow memory cells are significantly cheaper than fast ones.

In this chapter, the basic ingredients of a cache memory will be identified and a sample cache memory will be designed and evaluated to illustrate that, by using a small cache memory, performance can be dramatically improved at small increase in cost. For the present, a simple design will be used rather than a complex one. Various design parameters will be assumed to illustrate the concepts. In subsequent chapters, more complex design will be evaluated and various detailed aspects of buffered memories will be analyzed.

## 2.2 BASIC INGREDIENTS OF A CACHE MEMORY

The philosophy behind the concept of buffering or caching is to use a fast and relatively small memory between the processor and the main memory. The main function of the cache is to serve as a transparent bridge between the speed of the processor and the memory, that is, to provide all the data needed by the processor from the cache.

1. A buffered memory or cache memory basically consists of a small high-speed memory with main memory information. This information may be addresses, data, or instructions; thus, the cache may be an address cache, a data cache, or an instruction cache. The speed of the small memory typically is an order of magnitude faster than that of the main memory; its capacity typically is one or two orders of magnitude less than that of the main memory.
2. A cache memory system requires an *identifier* or *tag* store to indicate which entries of main memory have been copied into the cache store. These entires can associate with words, blocks, or pages depending on the organization. This special memory containing the associated entries or addresses is usually labeled the "*tag store*" or "*directory*" and constitutes a search memory.
3. A buffered memory requires a logical network that selects words or blocks to be removed when new entries need to be brought into cache. This particular logical network is labeled a *priority update list*.
4. A cache memory system requires control logic to generate all timing for synchronizing various activities, for example, searching the tag store, getting data out of cache, and replacing proper entries in the cache.

These requirements can be implemented in various ways depending upon desired cost-performance considerations. For purposes of illustration, however, let us consider the buffered memory arrangement indicated in Figure 2.1. Various factors affecting the size of buffer, its partitioning decisions, mapping considerations, and update list decisions will be discussed in later chapters.

## 2.3 Cost and Performance Effectiveness

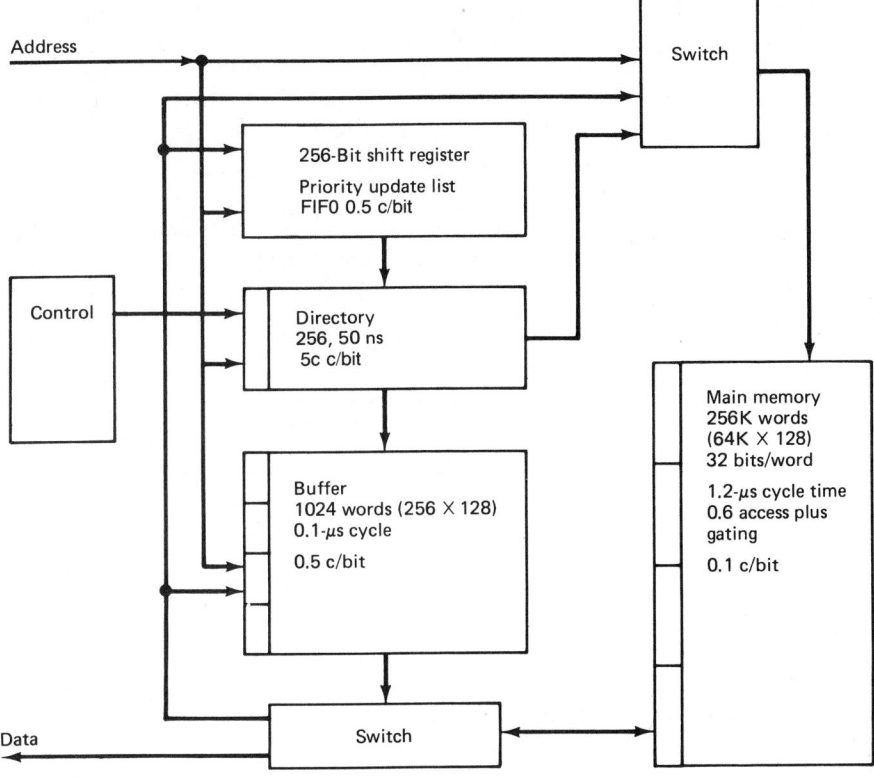

**Figure 2.1** Illustrative Buffered Memory.

## 2.3 COST AND PERFORMANCE EFFECTIVENESS

The intent of this example is to show why a buffer memory is cost effective. Therefore, representative OEM costs and sizes for 1981–1983 technology have been assumed for the main memory and also for the size and cost of a buffered memory that might be employed in such a system. Although memory costs can be expected to decrease with time, the ratio of costs can be expected to stay about the same. This example is that of a data cache memory; it is assumed that information is transferred to and from the cache from and to the main memory in 16-byte blocks, and the main memory and buffer are organized so that they have extra-long memory words of 16 bytes. In this way it is possible to transfer a multiple computer word to or from the main memory in one memory cycle. In this sample memory system, it is also assumed that the main memory size is

1 million bytes (1M bytes) and the main memory is addressed with a 20-bit address. Figure 2.2 illustrates the addressing of main memory. This is an example of a byte-addressable machine. The four lowest-order bits are used to address one of 16 bytes within the 64,000 blocks, where one block is defined to consist of 16 bytes. In this example it is assumed that the buffer contains space for 256 blocks, and each block entry is 16 bytes. The buffer is organized as a single, fully associative store. Since the buffer has space for 256 blocks, the tag store also has space for 256 entries, with each entry being assumed to be 16 bits wide. The priority update list is organized as a simple 256-bit shift register, one bit per each entry of the buffer.

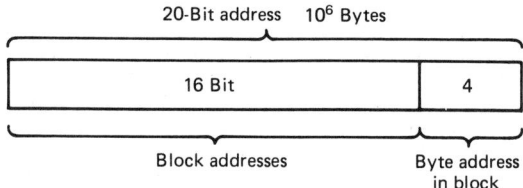

**Figure 2.2.** Address Assignment.

To compare the cost of the buffered memory system with that of an unbuffered memory system, the effective performance of the buffered memory system will be computed and then its cost developed. The cost-performance data will then be compared to a memory system consisting of single high-speed memory elements only. To evaluate the effective memory system performance and to make the analysis as simple as possible, the effective memory speed of the buffered memory will be computed assuming that a simple-swap algorithm is used to replace the contents of the buffer from the main memory when a new block must be loaded and an old block transferred out. Thus, when a new word or block must be brought from the main memory into the cache, the location in the cache to which it is to go is emptied first by transferring the old word or block into the main memory. It is further assumed that the memory system will not continue until the memory operation has completed its operation.

The effective cycle time of the buffered memory system can be computed in terms of system parameters and the probability of finding the desired word in the buffer. The probability or the fraction of times that a word is found in the buffer is defined as the hit ratio (HR). System performance can then be computed in terms of the following parameters:

Time to search the directory
Hit ratio

## 2.3 Cost and Performance Effectiveness

Buffer or cache memory cycle times
Slow memory cycle times

These terms are defined in Table 2.1.

In terms of the circuit speeds indicated in Table 2.1 and assuming a hit ratio of 0.95, the effective cycle time of the buffered memory system is computed as indicated in equations of Table 2.1. One of the most critical parameters in the system is the hit ratio. Although a typical value has been picked in this case, a more detailed experimental justification will be given later. Substituting in the appropriate values, one obtains an effective cycle time for the given memory system of 275 ns.

Table 2.2 itemizes the cost for the effective system in terms of the cost per bit indicated in Figure 2.1 and also includes an allowance for the controlled switching functions. As indicated in Table 2.2, the cost of providing the buffer for this relatively large memory is only 9.3% more than the slow memory alone. The speed enhancement, however, is greater than a factor of 4 (275 ns/1200 ns).

As a rough rule of thumb, the cost of a large memory is proportional to the square root of the speed. Alternatively, if the memory with a 275-ns effective cycle time were built without the buffer and simply were built with higher-speed memory cells, the cost would be about twice as high for main memory. Part B of Table 2.2 illustrates the cost of such a high-speed memory.

One notes that by using a small high-speed buffer (roughly 1/250 the capacity of main memory and about 12 times the speed of main memory)

**Table 2.1**

| | |
|---|---|
| TEFF | effective cycle time for system |
| TFRC | buffer read cycle |
| TFWC | buffer write cycle |
| TSRH | directory search time |
| TSRC | main memory read cycle |
| TSWC | main memory write cycle |
| HR | hit ratio = fraction of memory request found in buffer |
| MR | 1 − HR = miss ratio = fraction not found in buffer |

$$TEFF = \underbrace{TSRH + HR\ TFC}_{\text{working out of buffer}} + \underbrace{(1 - HR)\ (TSRH + TFC + TSRC + TSWC)}_{\text{must go to backing store}}$$

Sample parameters

$HR = 0.95$           $TFC = TFRC = TFWC = 100$ ns
$TSRH = 50$ ns         $TSRC = TSWC = 1200$ ns
$TEFF = 50 + 0.95 \times 100 + 0.05\ (50 + 100 + 1200 + 1200) = 275$ ns

**Table 2.2**

| | |
|---|---|
| A. Buffered systems | |
| Control | $ 100.00 |
| Switches | 100.00 |
| Buffer: 32,768 × 0.01 | 327.70 |
| Directory: 4096 × 0.05 | 204.80 |
| Update list: 256 × 0.5 | 128.00 |
| Main: 8,388,608 × 0.001 | 8,388.60 |
| | $9,249.10 |
| Cost increase | 860.50 (9.3%) |
| Speed enhancement | $\frac{1200}{275} = 4.36$ |
| B. Unbuffered system with fast main | |
| 8,388,608 × $\sqrt{4.36}$ × 0.001 = $17,516 | |

and because there is a high probability of finding the desired word in the buffer, it is possible to make a buffered memory system with high performance at a much lower cost than with a single high-speed memory.

In the course of succeeding chapters, various design parameters for cache memory systems will be investigated in detail. The impacts of various strategies and algorithms will also be discussed.

## PROBLEMS

1. Using the memory system of the example given in the chapter, compute the effective memory cycle time for hit ratios varying from 0 to 1.0 at 0.1 increments. Draw a graph of effective cycle time versus hit ratios. Discuss the significance of the hit ratio being 0 and being 1.
2. What must be the hit ratio for the buffered memory system to have exactly the same effective cycle time as the slow main memory? For this hit ratio, what would be the cost? Discuss the advantages and disadvantages of such an organization.
3. Assuming the buffer costs and other associated electronic costs remained the same, how small would the main memory have to be for the average cost per bit for the system to equal that of a single high-speed memory (4.36 × 0.1c/bit, HR = 0.95)?
4. Determine how much slower the system would be if the main memory required four read cycles to transfer a block rather than just one.
5. What would be the effective speed for the memory system for a hit ratio of 0.9 for a simple write-through algorithm (i.e., if no data need to be transferred back from the buffer to the main memory)? Assume the fraction of the read-to-write ratio to be 4 : 1. Assume the same hit ratio for both cases. Discuss the significance of this system.

# Chapter 3
# Design of Cache Memory Systems

## 3.1 INTRODUCTION

In this chapter the design considerations for cache virtual memory systems are examined. The various factors affecting the effective cycle time of a cache memory system are identified, and then the effective cycle times are computed for large and small memory systems. First, they are examined for small computing systems in which the main memory sizes are not large and may involve only one or two modules. For such systems, an optimum buffer arrangement is different than for a system with many main modules, as in the case of large computing systems. Basic design considerations are, however, the same for all systems. Second, larger systems are examined. Emphasis will be on two-level hierarchies.

The efficient design of a buffered virtual memory system consists of the following:

Design of a suitable hierarchical memory system (in nanosecond-to-microsecond hierarchy level) with minimum cost and maximum performance.

Design of a cache memory system to provide logical or virtual space far greater than the physical address space. This requires the system to have automatic control to do the memory management, thus enabling the users to work in a memory-independent environment.

Design of efficient units of information transfer between different levels of memories and the design of an efficient address translation scheme. An efficient address translation scheme implies that the address mapping should be designed in such a way as to minimize the apparent access time.

The formulation of an efficient memory management strategy includes the following three important policies:

Mapping policies, which pertain to address translation policies and space allocation policies.
Fetching policies or swapping algorithms.
Replacement policies or strategies.

The cache should be small and fast, and yet should achieve a very high probability of containing desired words. Because the cache should be small (compared to the backing store), there has to be some mechanism for mapping the addresses for the backing store to the cache addresses. Since the cache should achieve very high speed, all this address translation should not impose any extra time penalty. So, ideally, the mapping policies of any kind of caching scheme should be simple and cheap.

Swapping algorithms or fetching policies for the main and the buffered memory should be designed to either fetch all the information upon demand (known as the *demand rule*) or they should be allocated beforehand (known as *anticipatory rule*). Fetching policies can be designed to be the same for all the levels or they can be different. Cache memories, in general, get information on demand.

The selection of an efficient replacement policy or strategy requires a choice that maximizes the success frequency and improves overall efficiency.

Buffered memory system design parameters can be classified into intrinsic and extrinsic parameters. Effective buffer speed and effective costs are the two intrinsic parameters. Other parameters selected as a result of experimental data and subjected to system design can be classified as extrinsic parameters and are as follows:

Hit ratio
Buffer location
Buffer capacity
Block size
Control algorithms
Address mapping

## 3.1 Introduction

Fraction of read to write ratio
Writing algorithms
Number of main memory modules and how they are started
Effective delay or wait time for a single module
Effective average delay or wait time for a number of modules

Effective buffer speed should be almost equal to that of the processor cycle speed. If the overall effective access time of the buffered memory system is larger than the basic processor speed (cycle time), it may be pipelined to enhance concurrency and improve performance. When the cache operates at the same speed as the processor, there is no need for any pipelining of the processor operations. A cache operating faster than the basic processor cycle speed is of no advantage because the processor(s) will be requesting memory service at best at its own cycle speed.

In addition, in trying to design an efficient cache, one should give some thought to the following questions:

Is the system a conventional system or an unconventional system?
Is it a large, medium, or very small system?
Should the buffer be allocated on a physical or functional basis?
Should the buffer be organized as a homogeneous unit or as heterogeneous units?

A buffered memory works because there is a *locality of reference;* that is, certain words in the memory are used much more often than others and, through a replacement strategy and swapping algorithm, these words tend to reside in the buffer. Locality of reference can be characterized by the hit-ratio parameter. In a later chapter, all factors influencing the hit ratio, such as buffer size, type of problem, swapping algorithm, replacement strategy, and block size, will be studied for their effect on hit ratios. However, in this chapter it is convenient to study the organization and performance of buffered memories in terms of basic parameters. The systems will be evaluated primarily then in terms of the hit ratio, the fraction of words written, the fraction of words flagged, the number of modules involved, the replacement strategy, and the type of swapping algorithm employed.

Depending upon the detailed nature of the system, a designer might find one of several swapping algorithms to be the most effective. In this chapter various buffer alternatives will be examined, and the resulting systems will be compared in terms of performance and other factors that are relevant. The most important criterion by which to compare a buffered memory system with another is the effective memory cycle time for a given hit ratio. Consequently, this will be used as the primary criterion.

One of the mechanisms often used to speed up memory performance is the overlapping of the operation of the main memory modules and the buffer. By continuing with CPU operations while a main memory is completing its cycle, it is possible to get higher performance out of a system; consequently, systems with and without overlap will be compared. Systems also will be studied to determine the effectiveness of using a write flag for buffer words.

## 3.2 BUFFER PARTITIONING

A buffered memory can be organized in numerous ways. One critical aspect is the way the contents of the directory or search memory tag the information contained in the buffer. The buffer can be organized so that any block or group of words in the buffer can come from any part of the main memory address space; this is labeled a *fully associative memory*. In addition, as discussed by Gibson [G1], the buffered memory can be partitioned into several smaller buffered memories with each of these pieces of a buffered memory serving part of the main memory. This is usually labeled a multiclass memory, and it has the advantage of simplifying the electronics.

Figure 3.1 depicts an arrangement in which the buffer is partitioned into several classes. In this example, a group of four words is transferred into or out of the buffer as a block; also, the buffer is partitioned into several classes with each class being serviced by segments of the buffer. The effectiveness of this type of arrangement depends upon the address assignment and the nature of the assembly procedure used to put words in the main memory. For systems organized in a conventional way, each successive block of words will be part of a new class. This is done so that in sequencing through a successive memory location, many classes in the buffer can be used, effectively allowing all the buffer to be operative on a particular problem.

More explicitly, a multiclassed buffered memory can be pictured in the following simple way. If the buffer is broken into two separate pieces each servicing half the main memory, it constitutes a system with two classes. If the buffer is broken into 32 distinct pieces, each piece servicing $1/32$nd of the main memory, it constitutes a buffer with 32 classes. Hit-ratio studies for conventionally organized systems have indicated that the number of classes can be made quite large without adversely affecting the hit ratio if proper address assignment is made. This reduces the electronic complexity of a buffer system. It is, therefore, very convenient to use a multiclass buffer, particularly for small memory systems.

## 3.3 Swapping Algorithms

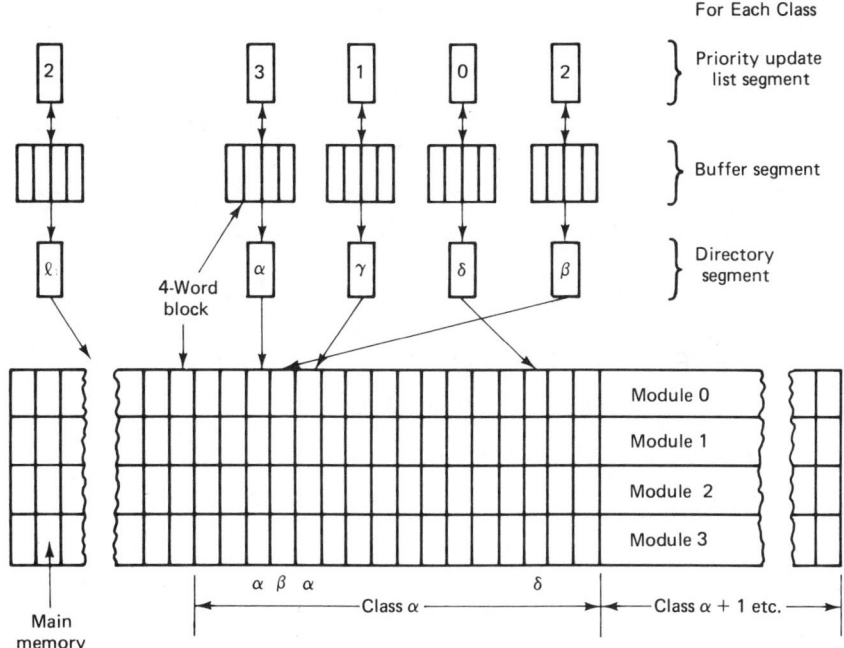

**Figure 3.1.** Directory Linking in a Multiclass Memory.

If the number of classes in the buffer is increased until each buffer block services a particular piece of the main memory, a *directly mapped* buffer memory is obtained. In this case, the miss ratio is increased over that of a fully associative buffer memory. Figure 3.2 depicts a directly mapped buffer.

Figure 3.3(a) illustrates the address assignment that would normally be made in a multiclass directory for a system with 16-byte blocks; one block per class, and 256 classes in the buffer. Words in a memory are normally assigned sequentially during assembly for program segments. To have nearly all the buffer operate on a problem, all classes should be involved. Figure 3.3(b) illustrates a less effective address assignment. Equivalent results would be obtained only if the program consists of extremely short single-block segments.

## 3.3 SWAPPING ALGORITHMS

A swapping algorithm specifies the order and manner in which words are transferred between a cache and main memory. It is the intent of part of this chapter to particularly highlight various swapping algorithms for small memory systems.

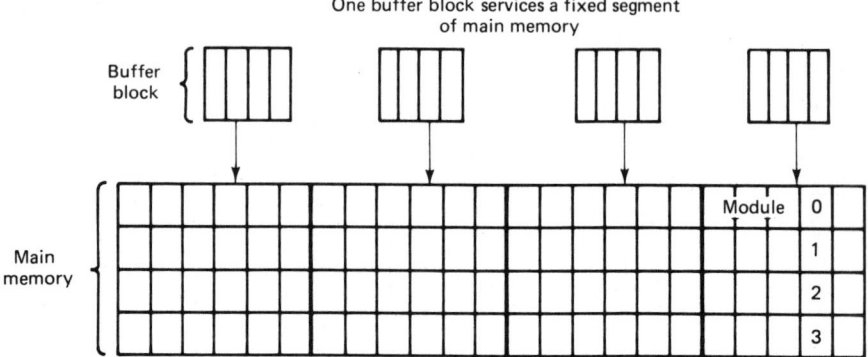

**Figure 3.2.** Directly Mapped Buffer.

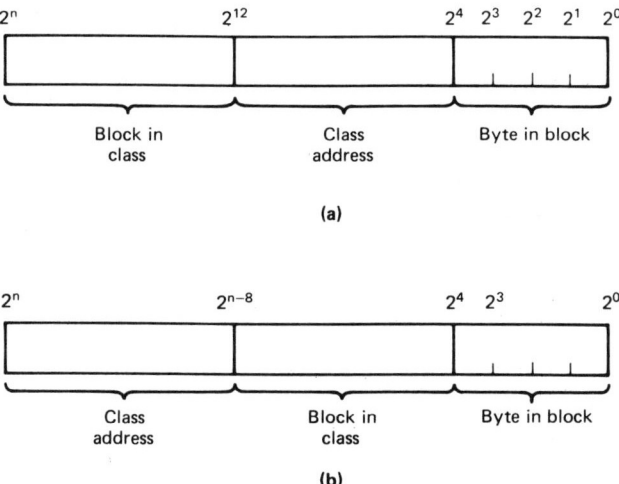

**Figure 3.3.** (a) "Normal" Buffer Address Assignment; (b) Address Assignment with Reduced Effectiveness.

For small memory systems, the main memory will be considered to consist of a single module, although multiple computer words might comprise a single memory word. A variety of swapping algorithms can be used. Four will be examined in our discussion. Some of the swapping algorithms will depend on parameters not used in the simple swap case. One is the fraction of buffer blocks written into after the blocks have been swapped into the buffer memory. If a block is not written into while in the buffer, there is no need to swap it back because a valid copy still resides in the main memory. In addition, because the CPU is allowed to proceed while the main memory is completing its cycle, a delay may

## 3.3 Swapping Algorithms

occur. This simply is the average time that the buffer has to wait until the main memory is available to transfer in the new block. Occasionally, there will be times in which the main memory will be busy and the buffer will have to wait almost a full main cycle before it can access for an operand.

In all the following computations, it is assumed that the probability of a block not being in the buffer is characterized by a single miss-ratio parameter, and the probability of a miss for any given block is statistically independent of that for any other block [E2]. In many situations this, of course, is not true; however, these simplifying assumptions lead to an effective working analytical tool.

If the CPU is started immediately upon receipt of the word from the backing store, some time can usually be saved because the CPU can be working out of the buffer, while the main memory module is completing its memory cycle. The average waiting time depends not only on the miss ratio, but also on the read-write ratio and fraction of blocks flagged (written into while in the buffer). Both of these quantities are assumed to be statistically independent.

### 3.3.1 Swapping Algorithms Details

A buffered memory system can employ several types of writing or swapping algorithms for exchanging the data between the buffer and the main memory. The way the information is written into the main memory system (particularly in the main memory) is an important factor for the computation of effective cycle time.

Various types of writing algorithms that have been investigated for various buffered memory systems are as follows:

> Write through (WT) or store through (ST) algorithm
> Simple Swap (SS) or conflicting usage writeback (CUW) algorithm
> Flagged swap (FS) or flagged conflicting writeback (CUX) algorithm
> Flagged register swap (FRS) algorithm

*Note:* The following discussion of swapping algorithms refers to the transfer of either words or blocks.

### 3.3.2 Write Through (WT) Algorithm

The simplest algorithm for writing policy in a buffered memory system is the write through algorithm. In the WT algorithm, whenever there is a write request for a given address, that particular address is updated in both the fast memory as well as the main memory, even if there is a copy of that address in the fast buffer. This constant updating of buffer as well as main memory at every write request keeps the information in the main memory up to date rather than stale. Hence, if there is a request for an address that does not exist in the fast buffer, the word (*block*) that is supposed to be transferred to the main memory is simply overwritten (without any need for transferring that particular word to the main memory), because a clean copy of it is already in the main memory. Besides the ease of implementation, it is conceptually simple and has been implemented in various cache-based systems.

This scheme can be a particularly valuable feature in systems with multiprocessors with dedicated cache and sharing a common memory. By employing a write through algorithm, along with some type of locking mechanism, the main memory is kept up to date, and the need for directory search for different processors for finding the latest copy or for replacing a particular word is avoided. Even though the WT algorithm is conceptually simple, it has one major drawback: it does not tend to minimize the fraction of successful references to main memory. The fraction of references to main memory approaches asympototically the fraction of writes (rather than zero) as the cache size increases [B3]. Hence, more sophisticated writing schemes have to be analyzed. Figure 3.4 is a flow chart description of the WT algorithm.

### 3.3.3 Simple Swap (SS) or Conflicting Usage Writeback (CUW) Algorithms

This scheme tends to minimize the number of main memory references by minimizing the number of main memory accesses per change in cache occupancy [B4]. Here the main memory is accessed if, and only if, the required word is not found in the fast buffer. By avoiding references to the main memory for every write request, unlike the WT algorithm, this scheme improves performance. However, since the main memory is not kept up to date, if the demanded word is not found to be in the fast buffer, an old word has to be replaced from the buffer to the main memory to make room for the new demanded word. Hence, a word is first transferred from the buffer to the main memory and swapped with the new demanded word. So now there is a two word transfer involved between the fast buffer and the main memory. In the WT algorithm, no data displacement was involved between the fast buffer and the main memory. However, the big advantage of the SS algorithm over the WT algorithm is that the fraction of memory references to main memory approach asymptotically the fraction of cache change occupancy rather than the number of writes. Also,

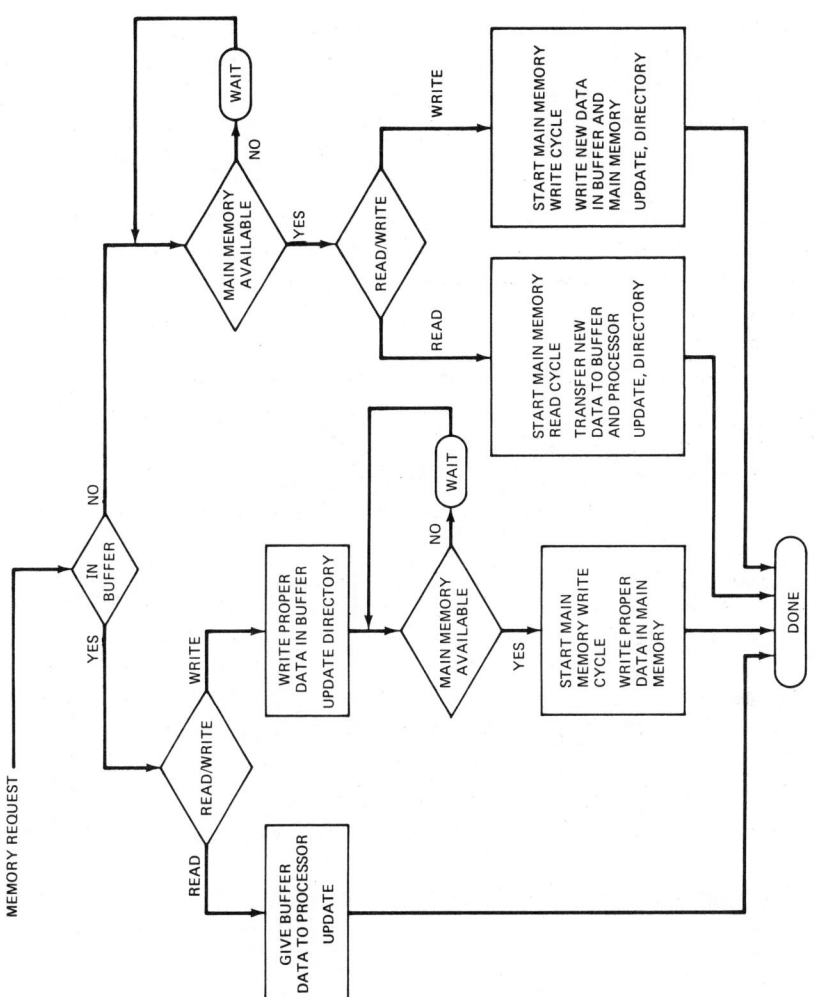

**Figure 3.4.** Write-Through (WT) Algorithm.

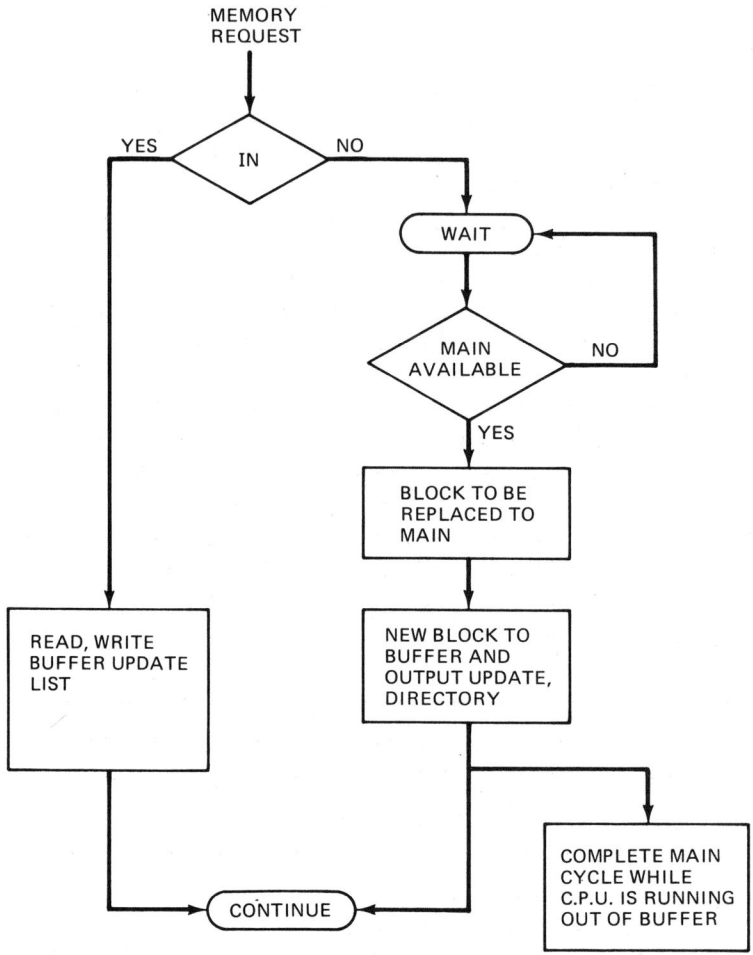

**Figure 3.5.** Simple Swap Algorithm with Overlap.

CPU operations may begin as soon as the new word is available if overlap is used. Figure 3.5 is a block diagram of the SS algorithm.

### 3.3.4 Flagged Swap (FS) or Flagged Conflicting Writeback (CUX) Algorithm

The SS algorithm tends to improve the effective cycle time over the WT algorithm, by reducing the number of main memory accesses. This factor can be further improved by keeping track of certain status information

## 3.4 Comparative Performance

associated with the words, such as whether the word to be transferred from the fast buffer to the main memory actually needs to be displaced or not. If a word since first brought in from the main memory has not been modified or written into (i.e., has been used as read-only), there is no need to transfer it back to the main memory, because the main memory already has a valid copy of this word; this saves some main memory accesses. However, if this word has been changed since it was brought back last, there is a need for displacing it. This modified status of the word can easily be kept track of by associating an extra flag bit with the word. By changing the flag bit, for a change in word, information about the status of the word can be derived; and words whose flag bits are on only need to be transferred to the main memory. The FS algorithm thus seems to combine the advantages of both the WT algorithm and the SS algorithm. Figure 3.6 is the control flow for the FS algorithm.

### 3.3.5 Flagged Register Swap (FRS) Algorithm

Another novel technique for improving the performance or the effective cycle time, over the FS algorithm, is by the provision of temporary register(s) between the fast buffer and the main memory. Now when data are to be transferred from the fast buffer to the main memory, they are first transferred to the temporary register(s); the new word is brought into the buffer immediately from the main memory, and subsequently the saved registered word is written into the main memory. Again CPU operation is started as soon as possible. The FRS algorithm has all the advantages of the FS algorithm; also it overlaps the main memory writing operations with the normal buffer operations, thus resulting in further improved performance. Figure 3.7 is the control flow of the FRS algorithm.

## 3.4 COMPARATIVE PERFORMANCE

The performances of buffered memory systems are evaluated next for the various algorithms, assuming random write requests, misses, and flagged words and that buffer operations are overlapped with main memory operations. The following terms as previously defined are used:

- FR  Fraction of reads (relative to total number of memory accesses)
- HR  Hit ratio
- MR  Miss ratio (1 - HR)

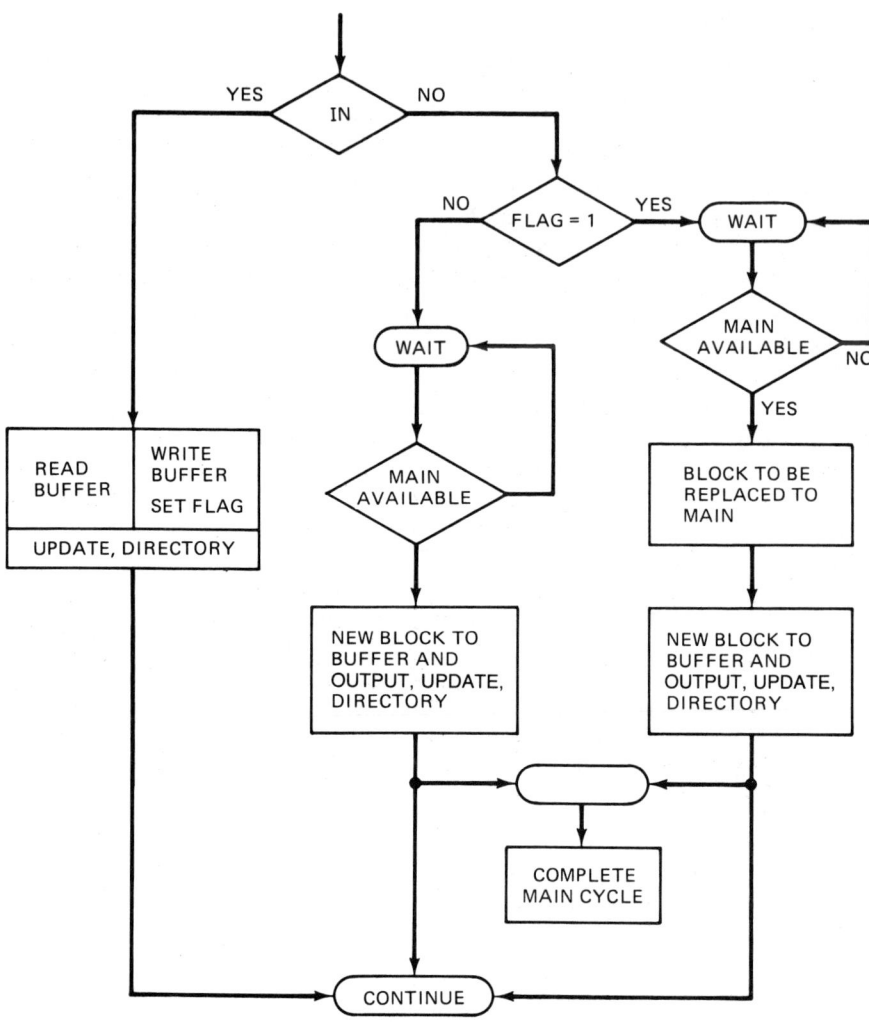

**Figure 3.6.** Flagged Swap with Overlap.

| | |
|---|---|
| TSRC | Main (slow) memory read cycle |
| TSRA | Main (slow) memory read access |
| TFRA | Buffer read access |
| TDFR | Data transfer time from main memory to buffer |
| TFRC | Buffer read cycle |
| TSRH | Directory search time |
| DF | Delay waiting for main memory to complete previous operation (single module) |

### 3.4 Comparative Performance

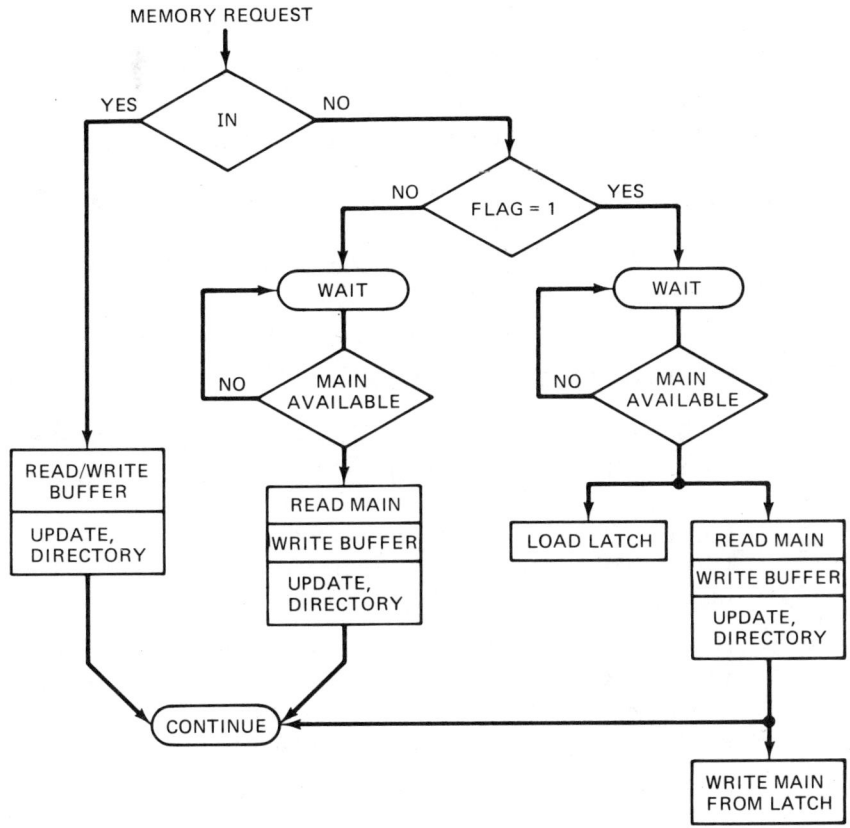

**Figure 3.7.** Flagged Registered Swap Algorithm with Overlap.

X     Fraction of buffer blocks flagged
TSWC  Main (slow) memory write cycle
TFWC  Buffer write cycle
TSC   Main memory cycle; read and write, the same
TFC   Buffer cycle; read and write, the same

#### 3.4.1 Single-Unit Memory Module Case

Specifically, memory system performance for the various algorithm implementations is computed as follows, including the delay in getting the main module (DF). It is also assumed that there is a single module.

A memory request for a buffered memory system can be classified into four categories:

Read requests with word (block) in: read hit (Rh).
Read requests with word out: read miss (Rm).
Write requests with word in: write hit (Wh).
Write requests with word out: write miss (Wm).

By appropriately averaging these events, an effective cycle time can be determined.

In the following expressions both conventional and computer notations are used for multiplication and powers.

## 3.4.2 Write Through Algorithm Timing

Twt =   FR $\star$ HR $\star$ TFRC + (1 − HR) $\star$ FR $\star$ (TSRH + TSRA + DFA + TDFR) + (1 − FR) $\star$ TFWC or (1 − FR) $\star$ (DFA + slow memory start, whichever is longer)
[DFA is the delay for the single module for WT case.
DFA can be thought of as consisting of two components: DFAr (delay due to read) and DFAw (delay due to write)]

DFAr =  (1 − HR) $\star$ FR $\star$ (TSRC − TSRA − TDFR) + (1 − HR) $\star$ FR $\star$ (TSRC − TSRA − TDFR − TFRC) $\star$ (FR $\star$ HR) + (1 − HR) $\star$ FR $\star$ (TSRC − TSRA − TDFR − 2 $\star$ TFRC) $\star$ (FR $\star$ HR) $\star\star$ 2 + $\cdots$ until delay terms vanish

DFAw =  (1 − FR) $\star$ (TSWC − TFWC) + (1 − FR) $\star$ (TSWC − TFWC − TFRC) $\star$ (FR $\star$ HR) + (1 − FR) $\star$ (TSWC − TFWC − 2 $\star$ TFRC) $\star$ (FR $\star$ HR) $\star\star$ 2 + $\cdots$ until delay terms vanish

DFAr is computed assuming previous use of main memory on read; and DFAw is computed assuming previous use of memory on write. The assumption is also made that each new written block is brought into the buffer. This may not be advantageous, particularly if direct memory access is used.

## 3.4.3 Simple Swap Algorithm Timing

Tss =   FR $\star$ HR $\star$ TFRC + (1 − HR) $\star$ FR $\star$ (TSRH + TSRA + TDFR + DFB + TSWC) + (1 − FR) $\star$ HR $\star$ TFWC + (1 − FR) $\star$ (1 − HR) $\star$ (TSRH + TSRA + TDFR + DFB + TSWC)

DFB is the delay for the SS case. Note that it is assumed that the timing for finding the proper word to be replaced is overlapped with the main memory access + data transfer time and hence not added separately.

## 3.4 Comparative Performance

$$DFB = (1 - HR) * (TSRC - TSRA - TDFR) + (1 - HR) * (TSRC - TSRA - TDFR - TFRC) * HR + (1 - HR) * (TSRC - TSRA - TDFR - 2 * TFRC) * (HR) ** 2 + \cdots$$ until delay term vanishes; for simplicity the fast read and write cycle times are assumed to be the same.

### 3.4.4 Flagged Swap and Flagged Registered Swap Algorithm Timing

$$Tfs = FR * HR * TFRC + (1 - HR) * FR * (TSRH + TSRA + TDFR + DFR + X * TSWC) + (1 - FR) * HR * TFWC + (1 - FR) * (1 - HR) * (TSRH + TSRA + TDFR + DFC + X * TSWC) + \cdots$$ until delay terms vanish

DFC is the same as the delay for the SS case. Note that it is assumed that the timing for finding the proper word to be replaced is overlapped with the main memory access + data transfer time and hence not added separately. Note that DFC would be the same as DFB.

$$Tfrs = FR * HR * TFRC + (1 - HR) * FR * (TSRH + TSRA + (1 - X) * DFD + X * DFE + TDFR) + (1 - FR) * HR * TFWC + (1 - FR) * (1 - HR) * (TSRH + TSRA + (1 - X) * DFD + X * DFE + 1DFR)$$

DFD is the delay for a single module case for the FRS algorithm for reading, and DFE is the delay for writing. DFD can be broken into two components, DFDr and DFDw, which are the same as DFEr and DFAw. DFE also can be broken into two components, DFEr and DFEw, respecitvely. DFEr and DFEw are computed as follows:

$$DFEr = (1 - HR) * FR * (TSRC - TSRA - TDFR + TSWC) + (1 - HR) * FR * (TSRC - TSRA - TDFR + TSWC - TFRC) * (HR * FR) + (1 - HR) * FR * (TSRC - TSRA - TDFR + TSWC - 2 * TFRC)(HR * FR) ** 2 + \cdots$$ until delay terms vanish $$+ (1 - HR) * FR * (TSRC - TSRA - TDFR + TSWC - TFWC) * [(1 - FR) * HR] + (1 - HR) * FR * (TSRC - TSRA - TDFR + TSWC - 2*TFRC) [(1 - FR) * HR] ** 2$$

$$DFEw = (1 - HR) * (1 - FR) * (TSRC - TSRA - TDFR + TSWC) + (1 - HR) * (1 - FR) * (TSRC - TSRA - TDFR + TSWC - TFWC) * (HR * FR) + (1 - HR) * (1 - FR) * (TSRC - TSRA - TDFR + TSWC - 2 * TFWC) * (HR * FR) ** 2$$

+ ··· until delay terms vanish + (1 − HR) ★ (1 − FR) ★ (TSRC − TSRA − TDFR + TSWC − TFWC ★ [(1 − FR) ★ HR] + (1 − HR) ★ (1 − FR) ★ (TSRC − TSRA − TDFR + TSWC − 2 ★ TFWC) ★ [(1 − FR) ★ HR] ★★2 + ··· until delay terms vanish

Combining these two formulas, and if we assume that TFRC = TFWC, then

DFE =  (1 − HR) ★ (TSRC − TSRA − TDFR + TSWC) + (1 − HR) ★ (TSRC − TSRA − TDFR + TSWC − TFRC) ★ HR + (1 − HR) ★ (TSRC − TSRA − TDFR + TSWC − 2 ★ TFRC) ★ (HR) ★★ 2 + ···.

In the preceding analysis, delay is computed only when a miss occurs by examining the probability of previous sequences of memory requests and figuring out the resulting delay these sequences might cause. Note that a previous successful use of the buffer in a sequence reduces the delay in gaining control of the main memory. For example, if three memory references back it was necessary to use the main memory (because of a miss) and if two succeeding references were made to the buffer (because of hits), the time required for the main memory to complete its operation is basically reduced by the two buffer cycle times.

Figure 3.8 depicts the delay that occurs if the last miss occurred three requests earlier. Average values are computed by assuming that the miss probability is constant and that the misses are statistically independent.

In these memory systems, it is implicitly assumed that a single job is involved.

Figure 3.9 illustrates the effect of various writing algorithms on the effective cycle time for memory systems as the hit ratio is varied with fixed fractions of the read-write ratio. The effective cycle time is defined as the average time to read or write the memory, assuming requests are always present. In a real processor this may not be the case because some instructions may be longer than the main memory cycle time. The results indicated in Figure 3.9 clearly demonstrate the superiority of the FRS algorithm for the system modeled employing single main memory modules or multiple modules in unison.

Figures 3.10 and 3.11 illustrate the effective cycle times versus hit ratios and fraction of reads (X = 0.25) for a 50-ns buffer with a 750-ns backing store and a 200-ns buffer with a 1500-ns backing store, respectively. The memory systems are seen to be insensitive to fraction of reads when the FRS algorithm is used. The figures also show that the hit ratio

## 3.5 Multimodule Main Memories

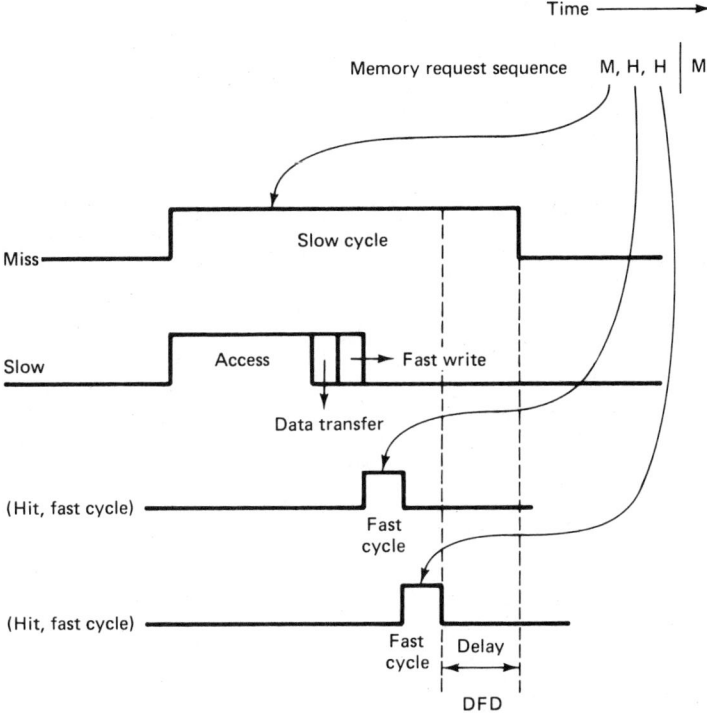

**Figure 3.8.** Computation of Delay.

can be as low as 0.80 to 0.82 to achieve a 4 to 1 increase in speed over the backing store. Even with the hit ratio as low as 0.7, an effective 2.5 to 3 increase in speed over the backing store can be achieved.

### 3.5 MULTIMODULE MAIN MEMORIES

If the main memory is made of several modules that can be operated independently, the write through algorithm in particular can be improved for a single buffer because more than one module can be busy writing at one time. Furthermore, such an arrangement is compatible with the time sharing of the bus transferring information from the main modules to the bus. Figure 3.12 depicts a buffered memory system employing a multiple-module main memory.

Computation of the effective cycle time for the various algorithms in the multimodule case must take into account the average delay in getting

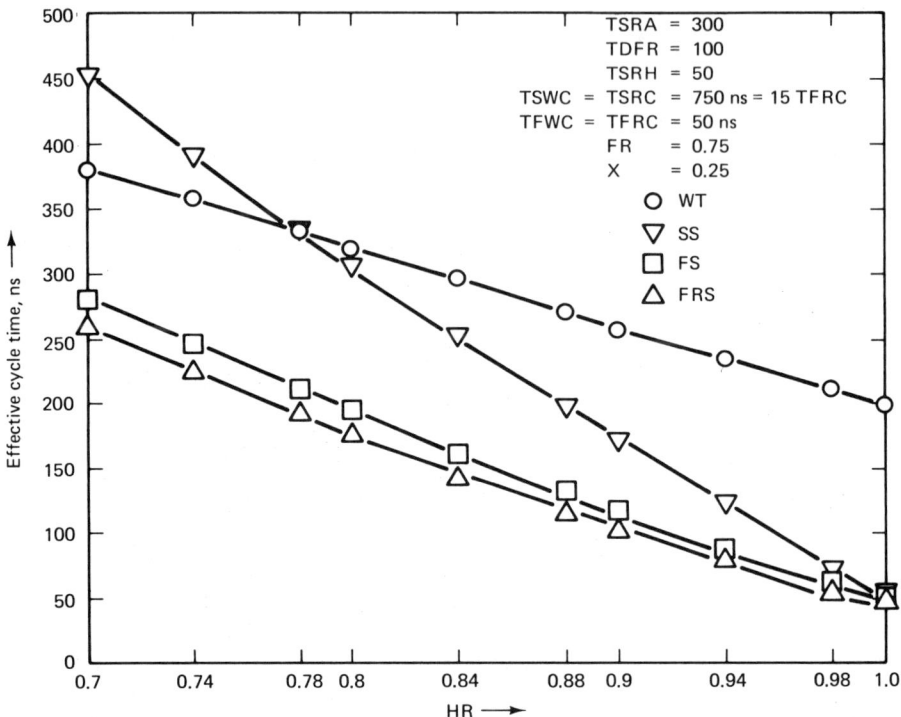

**Figure 3.9.** Effect of Replacement Algorithms on Performance of 50-ns Buffer Systems.

a new block transferred and, in the case of the write though algorithm, the delay in writing a single word of a block into the backing store. These delays will be labeled DS for single and DA for average module delay.

### 3.5.1 Single and Average Module Delay

An essential idea of multimodule memory interleaving is to distribute memory addresses sequentially among all the modules. Most programs tend to fetch instructions and data in some sequential manner. Hence, by distributing these addresses sequentially, all the modules can be in operation simultaneously and an increased memory bandwidth is achieved. The sequential distribution of addresses also tends to minimize memory conflicts. In practice, most programs do not follow *strictly* sequential behavior or random behavior in fetching their instructions and data. A sequence of consecutive memory requests to the same module will be made occasionally instead of sequentially to other modules.

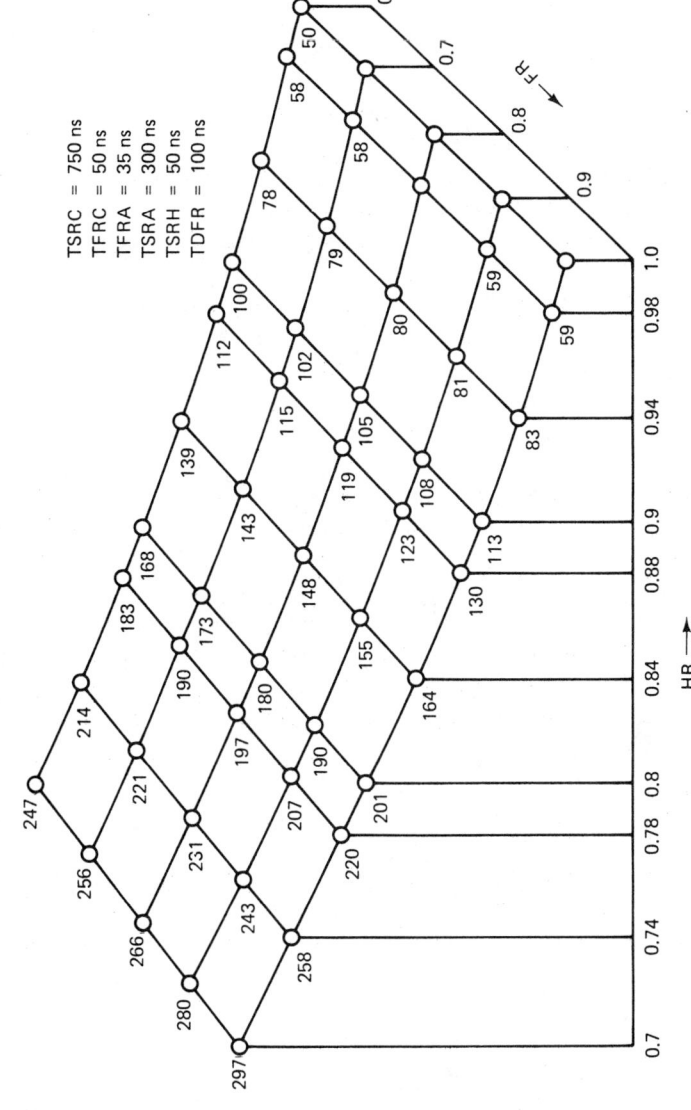

**Figure 3.10.** Effective Cycle Time Versus Hit Ratio and Fraction of Reads for a 50-ns Buffer.

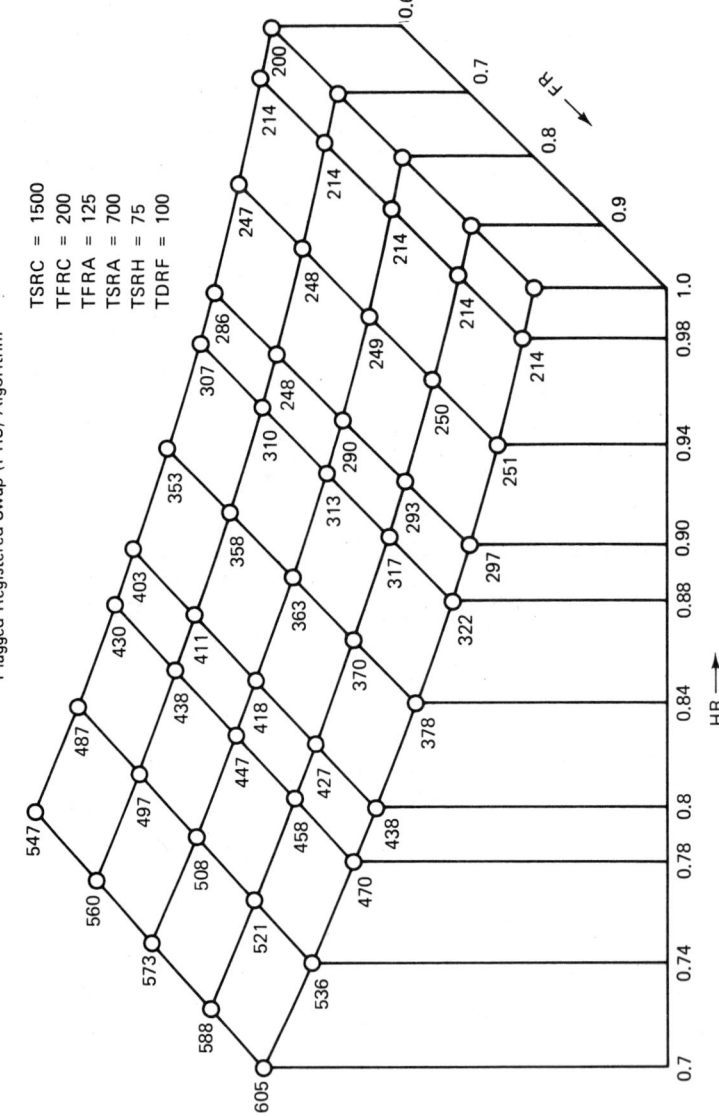

**Figure 3.11.** Effective Cycle Time Versus Hit Ratio and Fraction of Reads for a 200-ns Buffer System.

## 3.5 Multimodule Main Memories

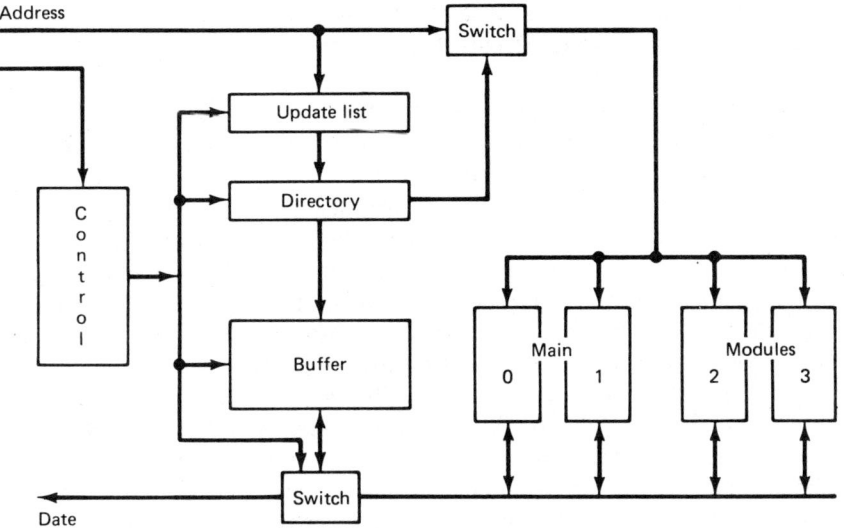

**Figure 3.12.** Buffer System with Multiple Main Modules.

For a buffered memory system, system status for read and write requests can each be further divided into two subcategories:

Read requests with word (block) in.
Read requests with word out.
Write requests with word in.
Write requests with word out.

Typically, all the memory requests as sent by a processor, or different processors, are resolved by a memory controller. After going through the directory search, the memory controller decides the memory module for which this is a particular request, decides the type of request (whether read or write), and also determines whether the requested word is in the fast buffer or not. Hence a particular memory request $P^j$ can belong to one of four possible categories: $P^j rbi$, $P^j rbo$, $P^j wbi$, or $P^j wbo$. Here $j$ indicates the module number (1 to $n$) and $rbi$, $rbo$, $wbi$, and $wbo$ indicate the memory request status: read with block in, read with block out, write with block in, and write with block out.

So for all four types of swapping algorithms, DS can be essentially divided into two portions: one portion contributed by previous read requests (DSR) and the other portion contributed by previous write requests (DSW).

## 3.5.2 Computation of Delay in Obtaining a Single Module (DS) for a Write Through Algorithm

If the desired memory request is a read request and if the required data are not in the buffer, then a particular main memory module has to be accessed to fetch the required data.

DSR is the delay caused by a previous read request in gaining use of a particular memory module. Since delay is caused by a sequence of consecutive memory requests to the same module, the delay can be computed by analyzing the sequence of possible past requests. The number of accesses to main memory depends upon the control algorithm; thus, DS also depends upon the type of control algorithm used.

Assume a block is transferred to the buffer by transferring, sequentially, a word from each backing module. The system can wait until all words in the block are transferred or can proceed as soon as the desired word is obtained. Although a slight improvement is obtained by proceeding as soon as the desired word is obtained, the resulting control algorithm is more complicated. The following computation is made for the more complicated case in order to indicate the procedures in calculating delays. The quantity $((N + 1)/2 \star TDFR)$ is the average data transfer time assuming a single word bus. Ideally, it would be desirable to be able to start another request immediately after this time. However, another request cannot be served until the memory cycle time is complete. Since additional time is obviously required to complete the block transfer, the delay time for a single module from a previous read block out request is equal to

$$TSRC - TSRA - ((N + 1)/2 \star TDFR)))$$

The $(N + 1)/2$ factor accounts for the fact that the desired module might be first, second, and so on, in the sequence of transfer.

The average single-module delay time depends on the fraction of writes, miss ratio, cycle time, access time, and transfer time, and a computation of delay will have to include these factors.

If a memory request sequence is read block out and then read block in, its probability of occurrence is given by

$$FR(1 - HR) \star FR\ HR$$

This sequence might be the memory read request sequence for a particular memory module that preceded another read request for the same particular module which encountered a miss.

The delay, or wait, due to this particular request sequence for the particular module is equal to

## 3.5 Multimodule Main Memories

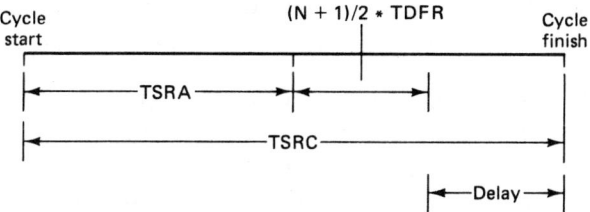

Request rbo

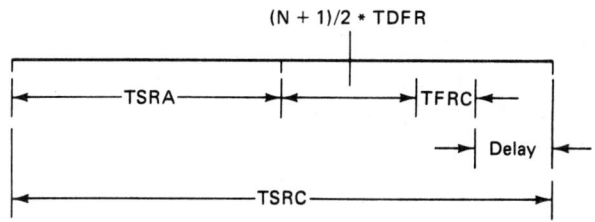

Request rbo, rbi

**Figure 3.13.** Computation of Delay.

$$\text{TSRC} - \text{TSRA} - (N + 1)/2 * \text{TDFR} - \text{TFRC})$$

The delay is depicted graphically in Figure 3.13. Note that a factor TFRC (fast buffer read cycle) is subtracted from the delay time because the buffer read cycle can be started before the end of the previous main memory cycle. The delay time for a particular module is decreased by this amount.

It follows that (TSRC − TSRA − (N + 1)/2 * TDFR) may overlay read requests found in the buffer. If the sequence of memory requests is

$$\underbrace{rbo, rbi, ----rbi}_{K}$$

and if $(T_{SRC} - T_{SRA} - (N + 1)/2 * \text{TDFR}) \leq K * \text{TFRC}$, all the above $K$ read block in requests can be overlapped.

### 3.5.3 DSR for WT, SS, FS, FRS Algorithms

The DSR depends upon the type of control algorithm, because the type of algorithm affects the number of accesses to the main memory.

For a WT algorithm with a *rbo* operation, the main memory has to be referenced only once (to bring in the demanded data) because the main memory is up to date and there is no need for displacing any information from buffer to main memory. However, for the SS algorithm, the main memory has to be referenced twice, once to transfer (read) a block of data to buffer and once to transfer (write) the required block of data from buffer to main memory. For FS and FRS algorithms, the number of main memory references for *rbo* operation depends upon the value of the flag bit. If the flag bit of the block of words to be replaced is on, this indicates that the block of words to be replaced has been changed since they were first brought from main memory. Therefore, a valid copy of this block no longer exists in the main memory and must be moved to the main memory before the new required block is brought into the buffer. This involves two references to main memory. If the flag bit of the block to be displaced is off, this indicates that the block is unchanged since it was brought into the buffer. The delay in obtaining a particular single module in the various cases can be computed in a straightforward manner as follows:

WT: DSR = FR(1 − HR)(TSC − TSRA − ((N + 1)/2)★TDFR) + FR(1 − HR) (TSC − TSRA − ((N + 1)/2) ★ TDFR − TFRC) ★ FR ★ HR + FR(1 − HR) (TSC − TSRA − ((N + 1)/2) ★ TDFR − 2TFRC)(FR ★ HR) ★★ 2 + ⋯

Proceeding the same way as with the WT alogirthm, DSR for SS, FS, and FRS algorithms can be written as follows:

SS DSR =   (1 − HR) ★ FR ★ (2 ★ TSC − TSRA − ((N + 1)/2) ★ TDFR) + (1 − HR)FR ★ (2 ★ TSC − TSRA − ((N + 1)/2) ★ TDFR − TFRC) ★ HR ★ FR + (1 − HR)FR ★ (2 ★ TSC − TSRA − ((N + 1)/2) ★ TDFR − 2 ★ TFRC) ★ (HR ★ FR) ★★ 2 + ⋯ until terms vanish

*FS and FRS DSR*

Note that DSR is not the same for both the FS and FRS algorithms because the FRS algorithm overlaps the write back operations in parallel with buffer operation. For *rbo,* the required block of data to be transferred from the buffer has to be first transferred to the main memory, and then the required data are read into the buffer.

FRS: DSR =   (1 − HR) ★ FR ★ X ★ (2TSRC − TSRA − ((N + 1)/2) ★ TDFR) + (1 − HR) ★ FR ★ X ★ (2 ★ TSRC − TSRA − ((N + 1)/2) ★ TDFR − TFRC) HR ★ FR + (1 − HR) ★ FR ★ X ★ (2 ★ TSRC − TSRA − ((N +

## 3.5 Multimodule Main Memories

$1)/2) \star \text{TDFR} - 2 \star \text{TFRC})(\text{HR} \star \text{FR}) \star\star 2 + \cdots +$
$(1 - \text{HR}) \star \text{FR}(1 - X) \star (\text{TSRC} - \text{TSRA} - ((N + 1)/2) \star \text{TDFR}) + (1 - \text{HR}) \star \text{FR}(1 - X)(\text{TSRC} - \text{TSRA} - ((N + 1)/2 \star \text{TDFR} - \text{TFRC}) \star \text{HR} \star \text{FR} + (1 - \text{HR}) \star \text{FR}(1 - X)(\text{TSRC} - \text{TSRA} - ((N + 1)/2) \star \text{TDFR} - 2 \text{TFRC})(\text{HR} \star \text{FR}) \star\star 2 + \cdots$

### DSR *For* FS

In the flagged swap algorithm, the writing, if necessary, is completed before the reading is performed. The delay is given by

$$\text{FS: DSR} = (1 - \text{HR}) \star \text{FR} \star (\text{TSRC} - \text{TSRA} - \frac{(N + 1)}{2} \text{TDFR})$$

$$+ (1 - \text{HR}) \star \text{FR} \star (\text{TSRC} - \text{TSRA} - \frac{(N + 1)}{2}\text{TDFR} - \text{TFRC}) \star \text{HR}$$

### 3.5.4 Maximum Average Module Delay (DA)

Maximum average delay for all modules (DA) can be computed in essentially the same way as for single-module delay. The DA can also be divided into DAR and DAW. DA depends upon the swapping algorithms and the writing algorithms. It can be derived as follows:

WT:DAR $= (1 - \text{HR}) \star \text{FR} \star (\text{TSC} - \text{TSRA} - \text{TDFR}) + (1 - \text{HR}) \star \text{FR} \star (\text{TSC} - \text{TSRA} - \text{TDFR} - \text{TFRC}) \star (\text{HR} \star \text{FR}) + (1 - \text{HR}) \star \text{FR} \star (\text{TSC} - \text{TSRA} - \text{TDFR} - 2.\text{TFRC}) \star (\text{HR} \star \text{FR}) \star\star 2 + \cdots$

SS:DAR $= (1 - \text{HR}) \star \text{FR}(\text{TSC} - \text{TSRA} - \text{TDFR}) + (1 - \text{HR}) \star \text{FR} (\text{TSC} - \text{TSRA} - \text{TDFR} - \text{TFRC}) \star (\text{HR} \star \text{FR}) + (1 - \text{HR}) \star \text{FR}(\text{TSC} - \text{TSRA} - \text{TDFR} - 2 \star \text{TFRC}) \star (\text{HR} \star \text{FR}) \star\star 2 + \cdots$

FS:DAR $= \text{FR} \star (1 - \text{HR}) \star X \star (\text{TSC} - \text{TSRA} - \text{TDFR}) + \text{FS} \star (1 - \text{HR}) \star X \star (\text{TSC} - \text{TSRA} - \text{TDFR} - \text{TFRC}) \star (\text{HR}) + \text{FR} \star (1 - \text{HR}) \star X \star (\text{TSC} - \text{TSRA} - \text{TDFR} - 2 \star \text{TFRC}) \star (\text{HR}) \star\star 2 + \cdots + \text{FR} \star (1 - \text{HR}) \star (1 - X) \star (\text{TSC} - \text{TSRA} - \text{TDFR}) + \text{FR} \star (1 - \text{HR}) \star (1 - X) \star (\text{TSC} - \text{TSRA} - \text{TDFR} - \text{TFRC}) \star \text{HR} + \text{FR} \star (1 - \text{HR}) \star (1 - X) \star (\text{TSC} - \text{TSRA} - \text{TDFR} - 2 \star \text{TFRC}) \star \text{HR} \star\star 2 + \text{FR} \star (1 - \text{HR}) \star (1 - X) \star (\text{TSC} - \text{TSRA} - \text{TDFR} - 2 \star \text{TFRC}) \star (\text{HR}) \star\star 2 + \cdots$

FRS:DAR =   FR $\star$ (1 $-$ HR) $\star$ X $\star$ (2TSC $-$ TSRA $-$ TDFR) + FR $\star$ (1 $-$ HR) $\star$ X $\star$ (2TSC $-$ TSRA $-$ TDFR $-$ TFRC) $\star$ (HR) + FR $\star$ (1 $-$ HR) $\star$ X $\star$ (2TSC $-$ TSRA $-$ TDFR $-$ 2.TFRC) $\star$ (HR) $\star\star$ 2 + FR $\star$ (1 $-$ HR) $\star$ (1 $-$ X) $\star$ (TSC $-$ TSRA $-$ TDFR) + FR $\star$ (1 $-$ HR) $\star$ (1 $-$ X) $\star$ (TSC $-$ TSRA $-$ TDFR $-$ TFRC) $\star$ HR + FR $\star$ (1 $-$ HR) $\star$ (1 $-$ X) $\star$ (TSC $-$ TSRA $-$ TDFR $-$ 2 $\star$ TFRC) $\star$ (HR) $\star\star$ 2 + $\cdots$

### Computation of DSW

Another factor in a multimodule system that affects the average single-module delay time is the delay from a miss on a previous write request. The DSW is also dependent upon the type of control algorithm.

### WT Algorithm

For the WT algorithm, any memory write operation involves a write into main memory, and it is immaterial whether the particular word (block) is in the buffer or not. Hence, for write through algorithms both *wbi* and *wbo* can be combined and be considered simply for writes. Since the buffer write cycle time is much shorter than the main memory write cycle time, the system must wait until the main memory operation is initiated.

Consider the memory request sequence of a write request followed by a read block in request immediately preceding the request of interest. The probability that the desired module is busy is given by

$$((1 - FR)/N) \star (HR \star FR)$$

The wait for the particular module is equal to

$$(TSWC - TSWS - TFRC)$$

TSWS is the write load time for writing in the main memory. This may be substantially less than a full write cycle.

The factor TFRC is subtracted here because the buffer read cycle can be started after the $T_{sws}$.

Hence, if the sequence of memory requests is

$$w, \underbrace{rbi - - - - rbi}_{K}$$

## 3.5 Multimodule Main Memories

and furthermore if (TSWS − TSWC) > $K$ TFRC, then $K$ of the preceding (read block in) requests can be overlapped with the previous memory operation and the effective delay for a particular module would decrease. Hence, for the write through algorithm,

DSW =   ((1 − FR)/N) ⋆ (TSWC − TSWS) + ((1 − FR)/N) ⋆ (TSWC − TSWS − TFRC) ⋆ HR ⋆ FR + ((1 − FR)/N ⋆ (TSWC − TSWS − 2 TFRC) ⋆ (HR ⋆ FR) ⋆⋆ 2 + ⋯ + ((1 − FR)/N) ⋆ ((1 − FR)(N − 1)/N) ⋆ (TSRC − TSWS − TFRC) + ((1 − FR)/N) ⋆ ((1 − FR)(N − 1)/N)² ⋆ (TSRC − TSWS − 2 TFRC)

### DSW for SS, FR, and FRS Algorithms

For SS, FS, and FRS algorithms, the main memory is referenced (for write) only if the required word (block) is not in the fast buffer. For SS the number of main memory references for *wbo* operation is equal to two, whereas for FS and FRS algorithms it depends on the probability of the block being flagged. The following expressions indicate values of the delays in obtaining use of the module as part of the whole block. For these algorithms the multimodules operate in unison, and there is little value in continuing operation until all modules have been transferred. Assume that TFWC = TFRC for the following modes considered.

SS:DSW = DAW =   ((1 − FR) ⋆ (1 − HR)(TSRC − TFWC − NTDFR) + ((1 − FR) ⋆ (1 − HR) ⋆ (TSWC − TFWC − TFWC − NTDFR)HR + ((1 − FR) ⋆ (1 − HR) ⋆ (TSWC − TFRC − 2TFWC − NTDFR)HR ⋆⋆ 2 + ⋯

FS:DSW = DAW =   ((1 − FR)(1 − HR) ⋆ X ⋆ (TSRC − TFWC − NTDFR) + ((1 − FR)(1 − HR) ⋆ X ⋆ (TSRC − TFRC − TFWC − NTDFR)HR + ((1 − FR) ⋆ (1 − HR) ⋆ X ⋆ (TSRC − TFRC − 2TFWC − NTDFR)HR ⋆⋆ 2 + ⋯ + ((1 − FR) ⋆ (1 − HR) ⋆ (1 − X)(TSRC − TFWC − NTDFR) + (1 − FR) ⋆ (1 − HR) ⋆ (1 − X)(TSRC − TFWC − NTDFR)HR + ((1 − FR(1 − HR) ⋆ (1 − X)(TSRC − TFRC − 2TFWC − NTDFR)HR ⋆⋆ 2 +′⋯

Proceeding in a similar way, DSW for the FRS algorithm can be computed as follows:

$$FRS:DSW = DAW = ((1 - FR) \star (1 - HR) \star X(TSRC - TFWC - NTDFR) + ((1 - FR) \star (1 - HR) \star X(TSRC - TFRC - TFWC - NTDFR)HR + ((1 - FR) \star (1 - HR) \star X(TSRC - TFRC - 2TFWC - NTDFR)HR^2 + \cdots + \cdots + ((1 - FR)/N) \star (1 - HR) \star (1 - X) \star (TSRC - TFWC - NTDFR) + ((1 - FR)/N) \star (1 - HR) \star (1 - X) \star (TSRC - TFRC - TFWC - NTDFR)HR + ((1 - FR)/N) \star (1 - HR) \star (1 - X) \star (TSRC - TFRC - 2TFWC - NTDFR)HR \star\star 2$$

## 3.6 EFFECTIVE CYCLE AND ACCESS TIMES

Once the single-module delay and average delay for all the modules have been computed, the effective cycle and access time of the memory system can be computed. Effective cycle time is the average time to read or write a word from the cache and can be computed as the average time for the following four buffer events:

Read with block out
Read with block in
Write with block out
Write with block in

Effective cycle times for the four swapping algorithms are as follows:

WT cycle = FR $\star$ HR $\star$ TFRC + (1 − HR) $\star$ FR $\star$ (TSRH + TSRA + DA + NTDFR) + (1 − FR)(DS + TSWS)

SS cycle = FR $\star$ HR $\star$ TFRC + (1 − HR) $\star$ FR $\star$ (TSRH + TSRA + NTDFR + TSWC + DA) + (1 − FR) $\star$ HR $\star$ TFWC + (1 − FR) $\star$ (1 − HR) $\star$ (TSRH + TSRA + NTDFR + TSWC + DA) + (1 − FR $\star$ (1 − HR) $\star$ (TSRH + TSRA + NTDFR + TSWC + DA)

FS cycle = FR $\star$ HR $\star$ TFRC + (1 − HR) $\star$ FR $\star$ (TSRH + TSRA + NTDFR + X TSWC + DA) + (1 − FR) $\star$ HR $\star$ TFWC + (1 − FR) $\star$ (1 − HR)(TSRH + XTSWC + TSRA + NTDFR + DA)

FRS cycle = FR $\star$ HR $\star$ TFRC + (1 − HR) $\star$ FR $\star$ (TSRH + TSRA + DA + NTDFR) + (1 − FR)HR $\star$ TFWC + (1 − FR)(1 − HR) $\star$ (TSRH + TSRA + DA + NTDFR)

## 3.6 Effective Cycle and Access Times

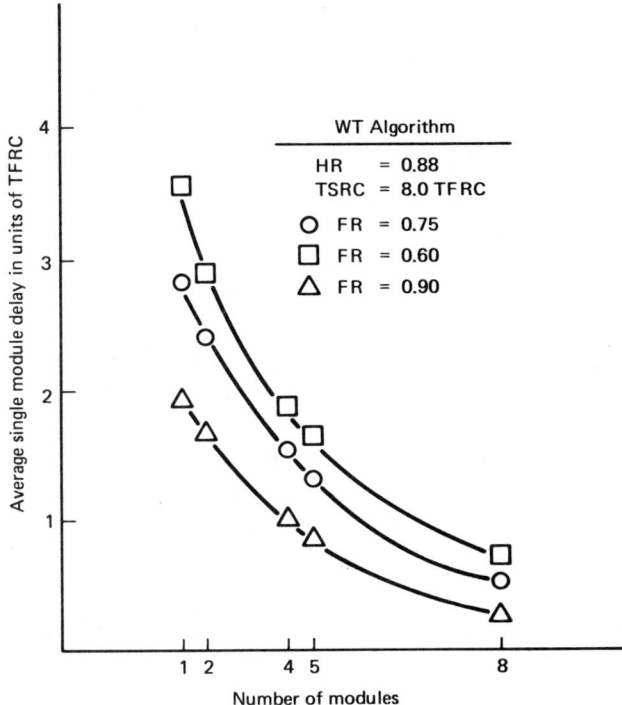

**Figure 3.14.** Effect of the Number of Modules on Delay with a Write Through.

Figure 3.14 illustrates for a write through algorithm the dependence of average single-module delay on the number of modules. The figure clearly demonstrates that the delay can be reduced by increasing the number of modules. Figure 3.15 shows the dependence of this delay on the hit ratio and fraction reads. Figures 3.16 through 3.18 show the effective cycle times for a write through algorithm as the ratio of the fast to slow memories speeds is changed from 4 to 8 to 16. The graphs also show the sensitivity of the write through algorithm to the fraction of reads.

Figures 3.19 through 3.21 show the effective cycle times for the FRS algorithm for speed ratios of 4, 8, and 16. Note that for this algorithm effective cycle time is nearly independent of the fraction of reads.

## PROBLEMS

1. Assume that a cache memory employs a flagged swap algorithm with HR = 0.95, X = 0.2, TFC = 0.1 $\mu$s, TSRC = TSWC = 1.0 $\mu$s, and

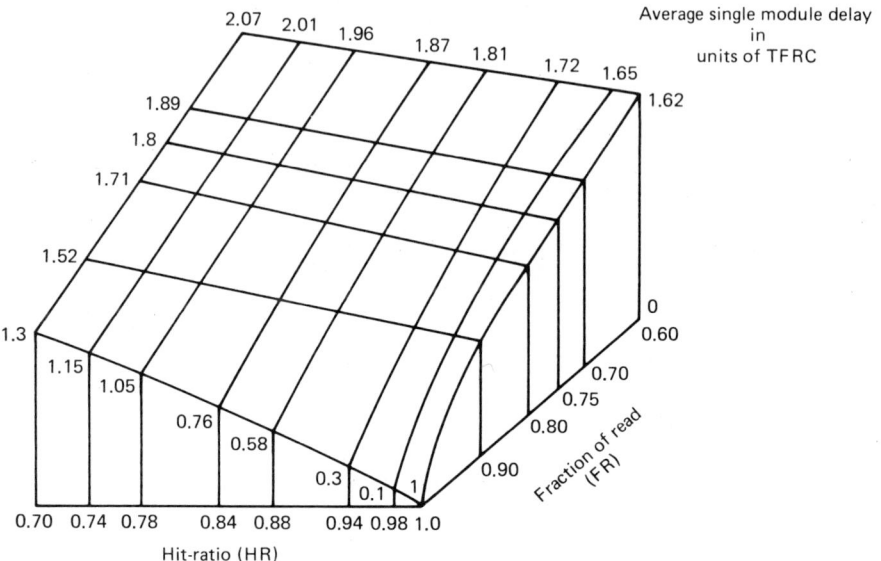

**Figure 3.15.** Delay for WT Algorithm Versus Hit Ratio and Fraction of Reads.

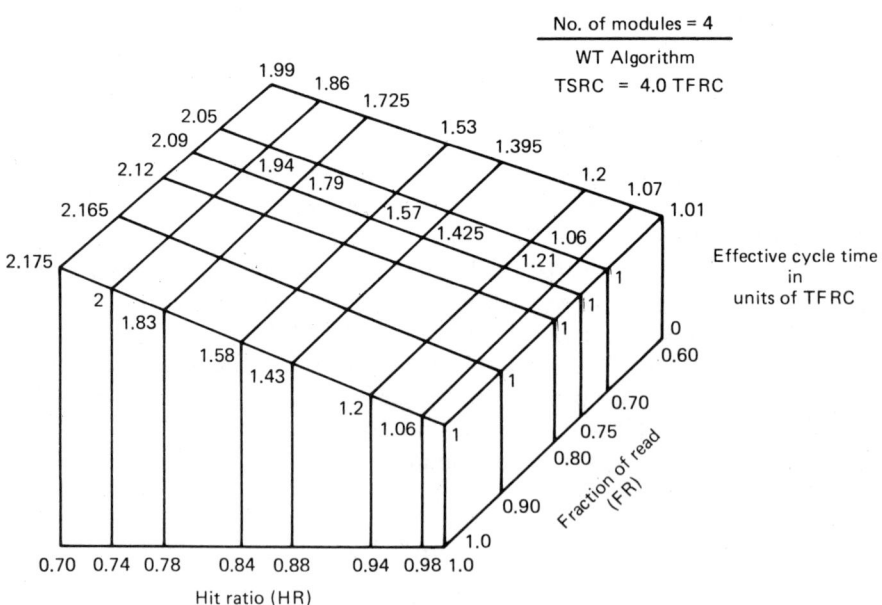

**Figure 3.16.** Effective Cycle Time for WT Algorithm.

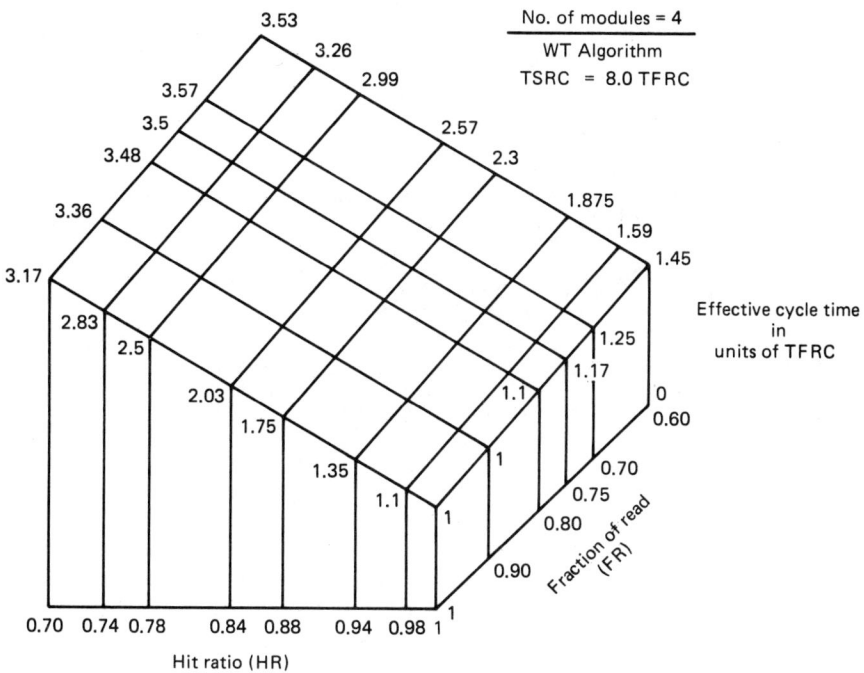

**Figure 3.17.** Effective Cycle Time for WT Algorithm Versus Hit Ratio and Fraction of Reads.

TSRA = 0.6 μs. Determine the effective cycle time for the memory with and without overlap of cache operations with the completion of the main memory cycle.

2. Assume that a cache memory employs a write through algorithm with FR = 0.8, HR = 0.95, TFC = 0.1 μs, and TSRC = TSWC = 1.0 μs. Determine which fraction of main memory requests originates from write operations and which fraction originates from misses during read operations.

3. Determine the difference in the effective memory speed for caches with the parameters specified in problem 2 if one brought in blocks in case of a write miss and the other did not.

4. Determine the effective cycle time for the cache of problem 1 if a simple swap algorithm without overlap were used instead of the flagged swap algorithm.

5. The computation of effective cycle time in problem 1 assumed the cache would begin a new operation immediately upon completion of the existing cycle. Suppose the cache was coupled with a processor that initiated a memory request every 0.3 μs. Determine the average delay in getting the main memory for overlapped operation.

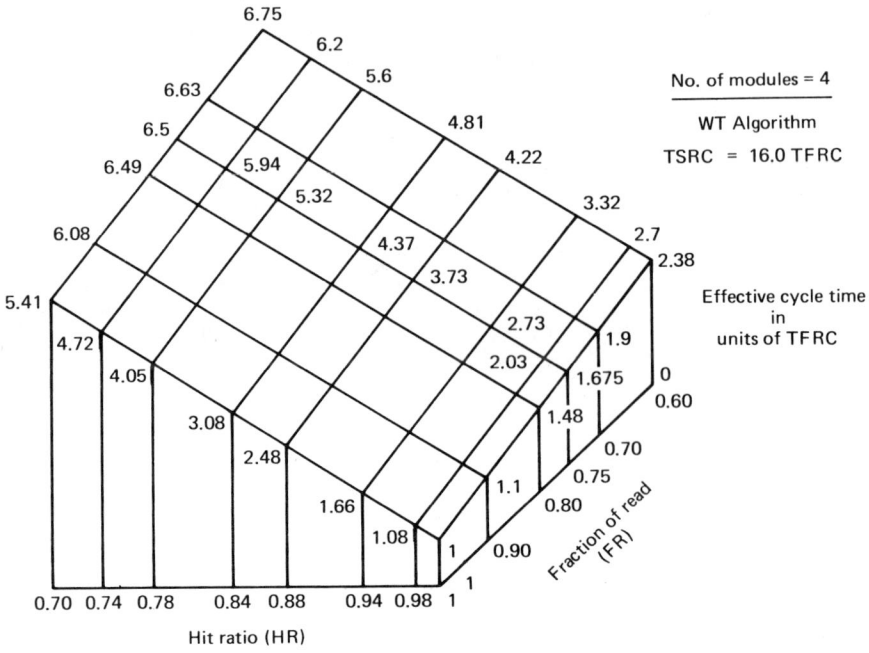

**Figure 3.18.** Effective Cycle Time for WT Algorithm Versus Hit Ratio and Fraction of Reads.

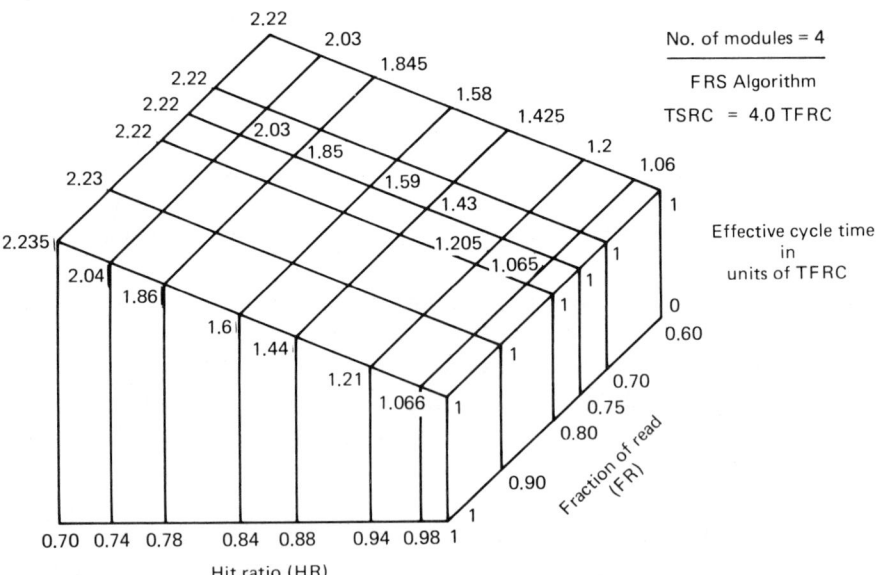

**Figure 3.19.** Effective Cycle Time for FRS Algorithm Versus Hit Ratio and Fraction of Reads.

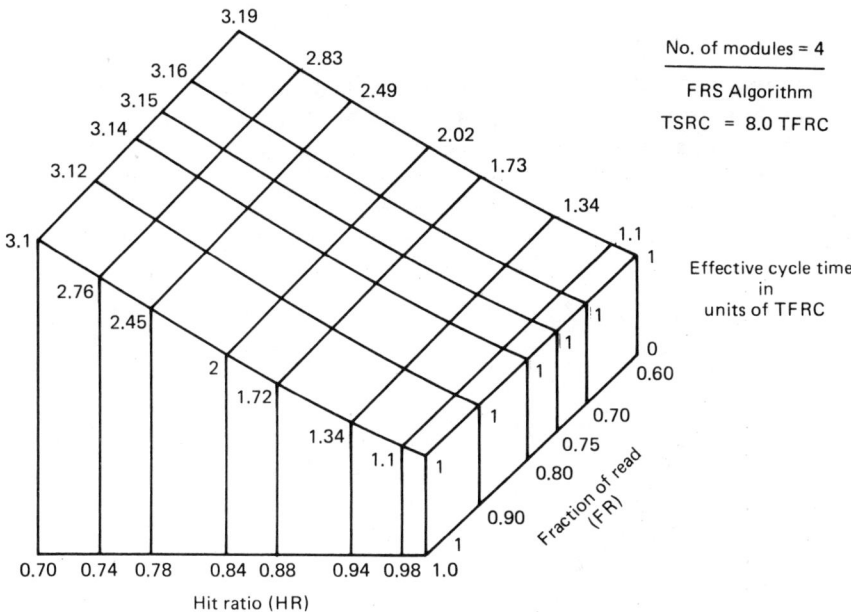

**Figure 3.20.** Effective Cycle Time for FRS Algorithm Versus Hit Ratio and Fraction of Reads.

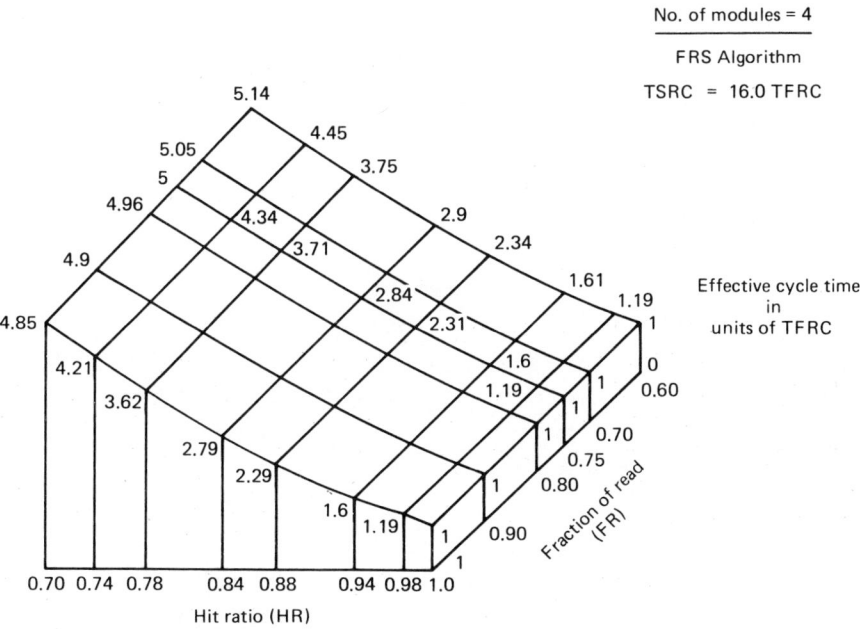

**Figure 3.21.** Effective Cycle Time for FRS Alogirthm Versus Hit Ratio and Fraction of Reads.

**6.** Suppose a cache memory employing a flagged swap algorithm without overlap (and with $x = 0.2$) had a main memory with a cycle time 100 times as long as the cache cycle. What must the hit ratio be to make the effective cycle time twice the cache cycle time?

# Chapter 4
# Hit Ratios and Factors That Affect Them

## 4.1 ANALYTICAL MODELS

The following analytical model is intended to give insights into hit ratios in buffered memories and to serve as an approximate tool for memory system analysis. For simplicity and convenience, discrete probabilities distributions will be approximated by continuous distribution functions when appropriate. More formal treatments are available in the literature [E2].

Because new job segments usually are executed and then dispatched, it is clear that the words in a computer main memory that are used most often within an interval change from time to time, and it is a simplifying assumption to consider the frequency of use of words or blocks as a time-stationary function. However, it is analytically convenient to assume that the frequency of use of a block is a time-stationary function once a buffer is filled; the time dependence can be introduced by assuming the subset of memory blocks used is switched on at the beginning of the job and remains fixed thereafter. The effect of job switching can then be included by considering buffer filling and by limiting the duration of the job. Executing new segments of the program would be analogous to job switching.

For the purpose of analysis, let us consider the frequency of use of blocks (one word or more words) in a memory and the equilibrium contents of a buffer to be characterized by a modified independent reference

(Markov chain) model as suggested by Easton [E2]. Specifically, define $P_{iJ}$ as the probability that the $J$th block will be selected next, having selected the $i$th block, and let it be given by

$$P_{ij} = (1 - r)\,\lambda_j$$

$$P_{ii} = r\,\lambda_i + (1 - r)\lambda_i$$

where $\lambda_i$ and $\lambda_j$ are the probabilities that the $i$th or $J$th blocks will be the next independent selections and $r$ is the probability that $i$th block will be immediately rereferenced in a Markov chain manner. The time average probability ($Zi$) of selecting the $i$th block simply is given by $Zi = \lambda_i$, even when rereferencing is included.

However, because there is a probability $r$ that a block just selected will be immediately rereferenced before an independent reference is made, the miss ratio in a buffer is reduced. Once referenced, a word is in the buffer, and immediate rereference (assuming LRU or FIFO replacement) neither causes a miss or changes the stack order. The miss ratio $M'_r$ for the modified independent reference model in equilibrium, in relation to the independent reference value $M_r$, is simply given by the following expression, because only $(1 - r)$ of the references can produce misses.

$$M'_r = (1 - r)\,M_r$$

If the value of $M_r$ is determined for the independent reference ($r = 0$) case, then the modified case can be determined simply by including the $(1 - r)$ term.

As shown by Sisson and Flynn [S6] and others [S10], there is a high probability that successive words in a memory of a conventional system will be used once having selected the first word. An average string length of 3 to 10 words is common. The parameter $r$ provides a parametric way of including this in the analytical model; the value of $r$ would be expected to increase as block size is increased.

To understand and analyze the operation of a buffer, it is convenient to treat the statistical quantities characterizing the frequency of use of the words or blocks ($\lambda i$) by the following, approximate discrete empirical expression when ordered in terms of diminishing frequency of use:

$$\lambda_i = \frac{\alpha_1}{(\alpha_o + iB)^{\alpha + 1}}$$

where $\alpha$, $\alpha_0$, and $\alpha_1$ are constants and $B$ is the number of words in a block.

Because the sum of probabilities must equal 1, one can write

## 4.1 Analytical Models

$$1 = \sum_{i=1}^{m} \lambda_i = \sum_{i=1}^{m} \frac{\alpha_1}{(\alpha_o + iB)^{\alpha + 1}}$$

where $m$ equals the number of blocks in the memory. To a reasonable approximation, the discrete distribution can be replaced by a continuous one with an unbounded upper limit of integration, provided the blocks are not too large and the frequency of use diminishes rapidly, as assumed here:

$$1 = \int_0^\infty \alpha \frac{a^\alpha}{(a + fW_B)^{\alpha + 1}} W_B df$$

The quantity $f$ is a dimensionless variable representing memory words in blocks equal to the number of words in the buffer. This approximation assumes that for reasonable values of parameters a negligible error is introduced by making the upper limit of integration unbounded:

$$0 = \int_{\frac{m}{W_B}}^\infty \alpha \frac{a^\alpha}{(a + fW_B)^{\alpha + 1}} W_B df$$

This requirement is equivalent to having a main memory much larger than the cache, with the tail of the distribution density function diminishing rapidly. If the distribution does not diminish rapidly with increasing $f$, the proper upper limit of integration should be used. (Experimentally, the exponent $\alpha$ is found to have a value of approximately 1 and increases slightly with block size.)

To analyze the performance of a buffer, again assume the words or blocks in a memory are ordered in terms of frequency of use, with the following simplified discrete density distribution and $a = a_0 = a_1$. (similar results would be obtained with other more precise distributions):

$$\lambda_i = \frac{a}{(a + iB)^2}$$

$$i = 1 \ldots M$$

Once brought into the buffer, the probability that a word will not be selected on the succeeding memory reference, assuming an independent reference stream, is given by the following, assuming $B = 1$ for simplicity:

$$P \text{ (not selected next)} = \left[1 - \frac{a}{(a + i)^2}\right]$$

Assuming a miss ratio $M_r$, $1/M_r$ memory requests are required for a miss on the average, and at most $W_B$ misses without selection must occur for the word to enter and then leave the buffer.

As it percolates through the LRU buffer stack, a block can be either pushed down by selection of a word lower in the stack or by a miss. For a block to leave on the average, less than $W_B/M_r$ references are required to account for this; let us introduce a parameter $k$ to adjust the average number of accesses required for a block to leave on the average.

One can then write the probability of a block leaving the buffer before being reselected as follows:

$$P\left\{\begin{array}{c}\text{a new block in the buffer not being}\\ \text{selected for } W_B/M_rk \text{ accesses}\end{array}\right\} = \left[1 - \frac{a}{(a+i)^2}\right]^{W_B/M_rk}$$

Recognizing for typical values of $a$ and $i$,

$$\frac{a}{(a+i)^2} \ll 1 \quad \text{and} \quad (1-\epsilon)^{1/\epsilon} \approx \frac{1}{e}$$

one can write ("exp" means exponent)

$$P\left\{\begin{array}{c}\text{block}\\ \text{leaving}\\ \text{in } W/M_rk \text{ accesses}\end{array}\right\} = \left(1 - \frac{a}{(a+i)^2}\right) \exp\left[\frac{(a+i)^2}{a} \cdot \frac{W_B}{M_rk} \cdot \frac{a}{(a+i)^2}\right]$$

$$(e) \exp\left[-\frac{W_B}{M_rk} \cdot \frac{a}{(a+i)^2}\right]$$

If the expression is written in terms of the continuous variable $f$ ($i = fW_B$), one obtains

$$P\left\{\begin{array}{c}\text{block}\\ \text{leaving}\end{array}\right\} = (e)\exp\left[-\frac{W_B}{M_rk} \cdot \frac{A}{(a+fW_B)^2}\right]$$

The probability of a block being in the buffer is then given by

$$P_1\left\{\begin{array}{c}\text{block}\\ \text{in buffer}\end{array}\right\} = P_1 = 1 - (e)\exp\left[-\frac{W_B}{M_rk} \cdot \frac{a}{(a+fW_B)^2}\right]$$

## 4.1 Analytical Models

This expression is obtained in the following way. Let $P_1$ be the probability that a block is in the buffer. Let $P_0$ be the probability it is out.

Consider the following queue diagram:

$$\left\{ \begin{array}{c} \text{chance block will exit} \\ \text{cache before being accessed again.} \end{array} \right\}$$

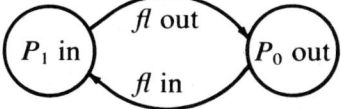

$$\left\{ \begin{array}{c} \text{rate at which blocks are} \\ \text{brought to top of stack} \end{array} \right\}$$

$$fl_{out} = \frac{a}{(a + fW_B)^2} \cdot R \text{ (e) exp}\left[ -\frac{W_B}{M_r k} \cdot \frac{a}{(a + fW_B)^2} \right] \quad \text{(for all blocks)}$$

$$fl_{in} = P_o \frac{a}{(a + fW_B)^2} \cdot R \quad \text{(for blocks not in cache)}$$

$P_1$ = probability block is in buffer

$P_o$ = probability block is out of buffer

where $R$ is the rate in accesses per second of selecting blocks. Noting that $(P_1 + P_0 = 1; fl_{in} = fl_{out})$, one obtains for equilibrium values of $P_1$

$$P_1 = 1 - P_0 = 1 - \text{(e) exp}\left[ -\frac{W_B}{M_r k} \cdot \frac{a}{(a + fW_B)^2} \right]$$

A plot of $P_1$ is shown in Figure 4.1 along with a frequency of use plot in Figure 4.2.

The miss ratio $M_r$ and the parameter $k$ can be evaluated by noting that, if the probability of a block being in the buffer is applied to all blocks, the number of resident blocks should equal the buffer size $W_B$; when the probability of being out of the buffer times the frequency of use is applied to all blocks, the miss ratio is obtained. With these two results, the parameter $k$ can be determined along with the miss ratio.

In terms of the probability that the block is in memory ($P_1$), the $M_r$ and buffer size expressions can be written as follows:

$$P_1(f) = 1 - \text{(e) exp}\left[ -\frac{W_B}{M_r k} \cdot \frac{a}{(a + fW_B)^2} \right]$$

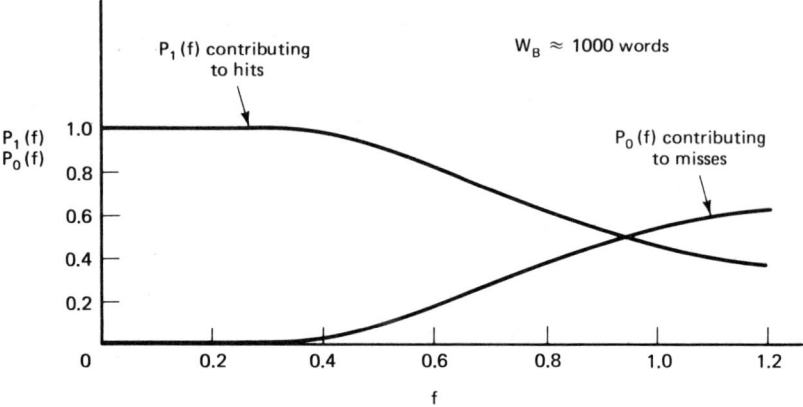

**Figure 4.1.** Chance of Blocks Being in or out of Buffer as a Function of Their Order in Frequency of Use: $\left[ \lambda(f) = \dfrac{a}{(a + fW_B)^2} \right]$

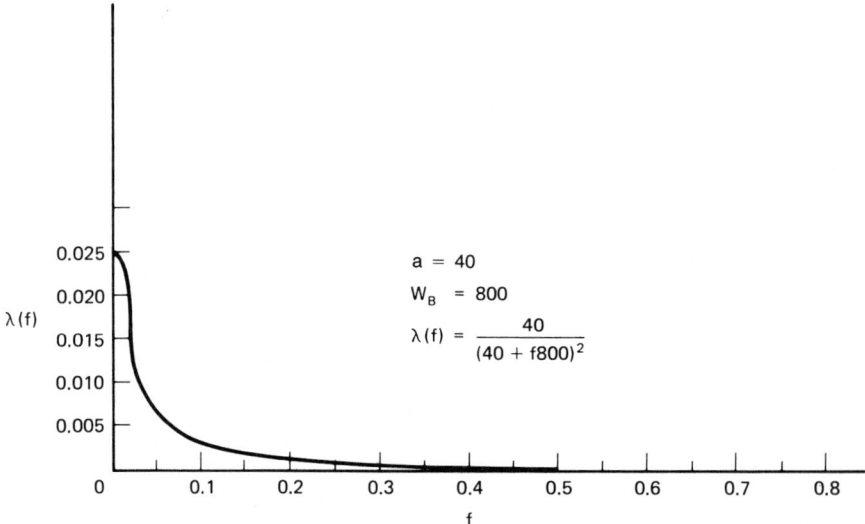

**Figure 4.2.** Assumed Frequency of Use Distribution.

Let

$$X = \sqrt{M_r k / W_B a}\, (a + fW_B); \text{ then}$$
$$P_1(X) = 1 - e^{-(1/x^2)}$$

## 4.1 Analytical Models

$$dx = \sqrt{\frac{M_r k}{W_B a}} W_B df$$

$$W_B = \sqrt{\frac{W_B a}{M_r k}} \int_{\infty}^{\infty} \frac{(1 - e^{-\frac{1}{x^2}})}{\sqrt{M_r ka/W_B}} dx$$

Noting that $\sqrt{\frac{M_r ka}{W_B}} \ll 1$ and numerically integrating, one obtains

$$W_B = \sqrt{\frac{W_B a}{M_r k}} \left[ 1.783 - \sqrt{\frac{M_r ka}{W_B}} \right]$$

$$W_B + a = \sqrt{\frac{W_B a}{M_r k}} \, 1.783$$

$$M_r = \frac{W_B}{(W_B + a)^2} \frac{a}{k} \, 1.783^2$$

The 1.783 value arises from the numerical integration.
The hit and miss ratios can be directly computed then as follows:

$$H_r = \int_0^{\infty} \left(1 - (e) \exp\left[ -\frac{W_B}{M_r k} \cdot \frac{a}{(a + fW_B)^2} \right]\right) \frac{aW_B df}{(a + fW_B)^2}$$

$$= 1 - \int_0^{\infty} \frac{M_r k}{M_r k} \cdot (e) \exp\left( -\frac{W_B}{M_r k} \frac{a}{(a + fW_B)^2} \right) \cdot \frac{aW_B}{(a + fW_B)^2} df$$

Noting that

$$H_r = 1 - M_r$$

and letting:

$$u = \frac{1}{\sqrt{M_r k/W_B a} \, (a + fW_B)}$$

one obtains

$$M_r = \sqrt{\frac{M_r ka}{W_B}} \int_{00}^{0} e^{-u^2} du$$

Again performing a numerical integration, and noting that $\sqrt{W_B/aM_r k} \gg 1$, we obtain

$$M_r = \frac{ka}{W_B} \frac{\pi}{4}$$

From the two expressions, $k$ can be evaluated:

$$M_r = \frac{ka}{W_B} \frac{\pi}{4}$$

$$M_r = \frac{W_B}{(a + W_B)^2} \frac{a}{k} (1.783)^2$$

$$k^2 = \frac{W_B^2}{(a + W_B)^2} \frac{(1.783)^2 \, 2^2}{\pi}$$

$$k^2 = \frac{W_B}{(a + W_B)} \frac{1.783 \times 2}{\sqrt{\pi}}$$

A simple expression for the miss ratio is then obtained.

$$M_r = \frac{ka}{W_B} \frac{\pi}{4} = \frac{a}{W_B} \frac{\pi}{4} \frac{W_B}{(a + W_B)} \frac{1.783 \times 2}{\sqrt{\pi}}$$

$$= \frac{a(1.58)}{(a + W_B)}$$

Note from the above equation that the first $W_B$ most frequently used words have a high probability of residing in the buffer. In terms of a very simple stack model in which the first $W_B$ stack locations reside in the buffer [M8], one can write:

$$H_{r_1} = \int_0^1 \frac{a_1 \, W_B \, df_1}{(a + f_1 \, W_B)^2}$$

and

$$M_{r1} = \int_1^\infty \frac{a_1 \, W_B \, df_1}{(a + f_1 W_B)^2}$$

$$= \frac{a_1}{(a + W_B)} = \frac{a \times 1.58}{(a + W_B)}$$

where $\dfrac{a_1}{(a + f_1 \, W_B)^2}$ is the probability of selecting the word at a distance $f_1 W_B$ into the stack.

Because a few of the less frequently used words are always cycling through the buffer, the miss ratio is increased by 1.58 over a perfect ordering of words. If the frequency of use were known beforehand, the most frequently used words would always be kept in the buffer, and the miss ratio would be reduced in the ratio of 1 to 1.58 over the LRU stack case. Our analysis shows that the stack location frequency of use can be derived from the frequency of use distribution of the blocks. Because blocks with low frequency of use are occasionally brought into the buffer, the stack distribution is more "spread out" than the distribution characterizing frequency of use. In terms of reaccessing the same word, the miss ratio is reduced by $(1 - r)$.

As a working model in further calculations, it will be assumed that the miss ratio for a buffer is of the form

$$M_r = \frac{a_1}{(a_0 + W_B)^\alpha}$$

and the frequency of use of words or blocks by position in the stack is given by

$$Z(f) = \frac{\alpha a_1}{(a_0 + fW_B)^{\alpha + 1}}$$

Furthermore, as shown later, a buffer filled with $fW_B$ words has an approximate incremental hit ratio given by the following expression, assuming the initial time stationary frequency of use distribution given previously:

$$M_r(f) = \frac{a_1}{(a_0 + fW_B)^\alpha}$$

If a different frequency of use expression were assumed, similar results would be obtained but with slightly different constants.

## 4.2 HIT RATIO DEPENDENCE ON BLOCK SIZE

With the introduction of rereferencing into the blocks of words in the buffer, many qualitative features of the dependence of hit ratios on block size can be predicted.

Consider that the instruction and data streams have a high probability of using the next word in sequence. Assuming initial requests into a new block are randomly distributed and most requests involve sequences in only increasing or decreasing address, one can approximate the truncated string length $l$ in a block by the following expression:

$$l = \frac{1}{B} \sum_{J=1}^{B} \left\{ \sum_{n=l}^{J} \frac{n(L-1)^{n-1}}{L^n} + \frac{J(L-1)^J}{L^J} \right\}$$

where $B$ is the number of words in a block and $L$ is the average string length in an unblocked memory. The expression assumes uniform probability of entry at each word in a block and a Markov process.

Figure 4.3 shows a comparison of the probability of the next word being selected from the same block as predicted by this simple model and the experimental results of Scherr [S10]. The fit is reasonable for an appropriate choice of parameters.

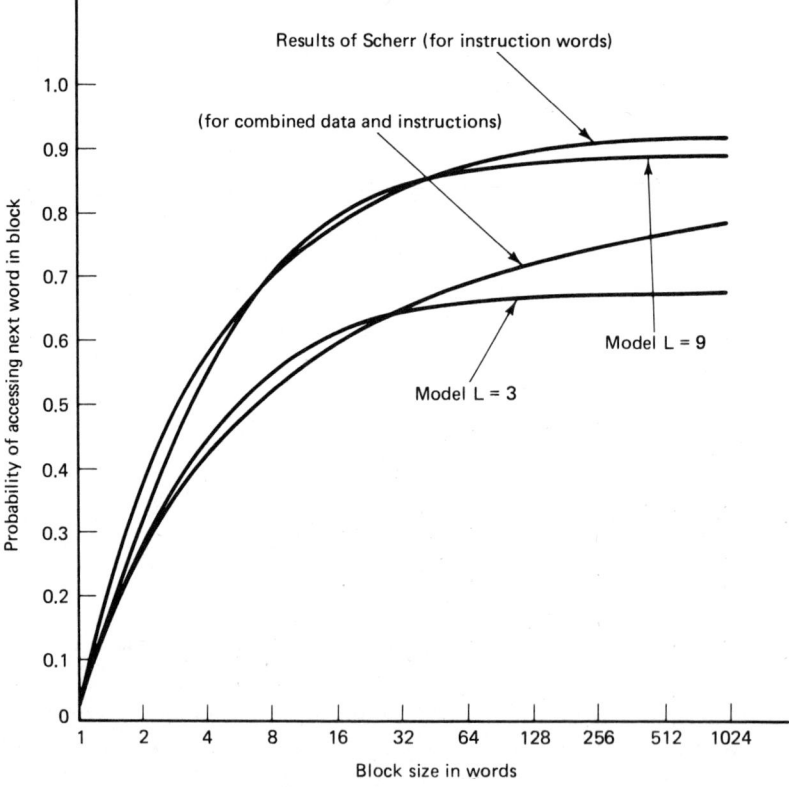

**Figure 4.3.** Probability of Accessing Sucessively into the Same Block.

## 4.2 Hit Ratio Dependence on Block Size

A single program typically involves up to four address fields: instruction, two operands, and a result. When the data fields are combined with the instruction field, it is not surprising that the probability of the next word being in the same block is diminished. However, as far as buffer operation is concerned, a low miss ratio can be maintained as long as the next word of each field is in the same block. The effective string length for the buffer is determined by an appropriate average of the string lengths for each field.

In terms of previously defined parameters for the modified independent reference model, one obtains

$$1 - r = \frac{1}{l}$$

If single words are moved in and out of the buffer, block string length obviously will be very nearly 1. Only such unusual instructions as a jump to the same location would continuously rereference a word.

In a usual program, hit ratios diminish rapidly as the number of blocks is reduced to four or less. Four blocks at most are currently active: program, two operands, and a result block for a single program. If the dependence of the miss ratio on the number of blocks and block size is introduced with a first-order approximation in terms of block size $B$ and the empirical parameter $\delta$, the following miss ratio expression results:

$$M_r = \frac{a^\alpha \cdot (1.58}{l[a + W_B \left[1 - \frac{\delta(B - l)}{W_B}\right]]^\alpha}$$

$$= \frac{a^\alpha \cdot (1.58)}{l[a + W_B - (B - l)\delta]^\alpha}$$

The $B - l$ term vanishes in the case $B = l = 1$ in which single words are moved in one at a time. Note that if $\delta = 4$ and there were four blocks in the memory the effective buffer size is reduced by the amount $B$ exceeds $l$ in each block.

Figure 4.4 compares the analytic model results with the experimental data of Mattson [M10] as the block size is increased. The fit, considering the simplicity of the model, is surprisingly good. The value of the four parameters are $a = 23$, $L = 5$, $\delta = 3$, and $\alpha = 0.75$.

Figure 4.5 shows the model prediction in comparison to the experimental results of Strecker [S7] for small block sizes. Again, for a judicious choice of parameters, the fit is good.

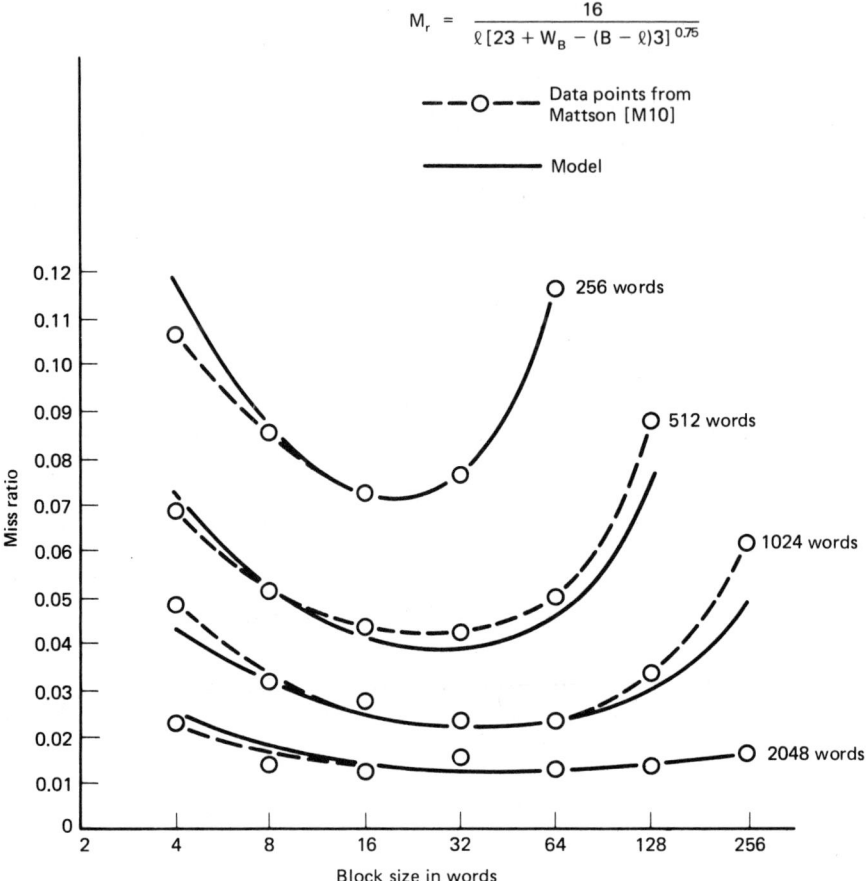

**Figure 4.4.** Miss Ratios as a Function of Cache and Block Sizes.

## 4.3 BUFFER FILLING AND COLD-START MISS RATIOS

For purposes of analysis, let us assume a new job starts with an empty buffer. Kaplan and Winder [K2] indicated that typically only 20% of the words associated with an old job are retained when the processor switches to a new job. These words are likely to be associated with the operating system. Again let $f$ be the fraction of the buffer filled with new job words and again let the miss ratio be given by

### 4.3 Buffer Filling and Cold-Start Miss Ratios

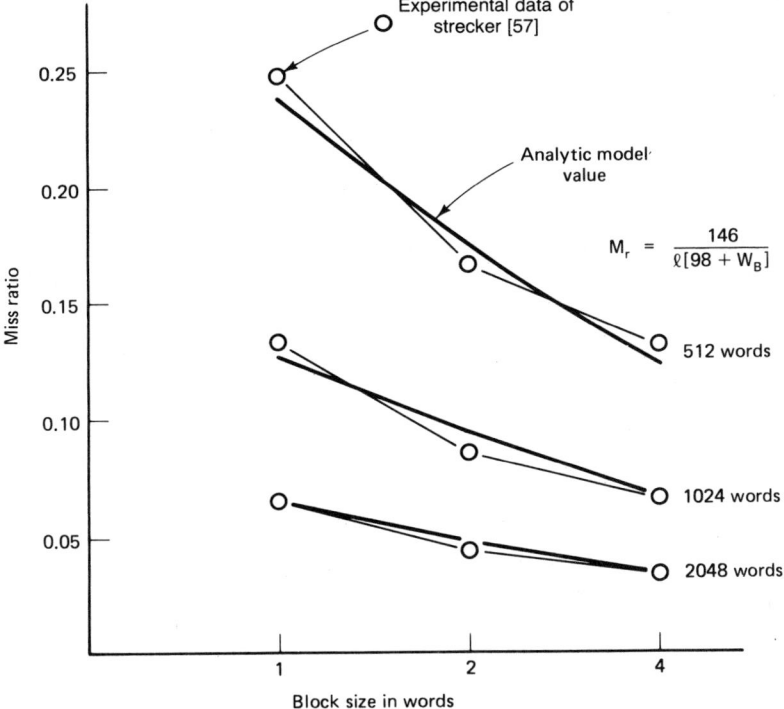

**Figure 4.5.** Miss Ratio as a Function of Cache and Block Sizes.

$$M_r = \frac{a_1}{(a_0 + fW_B)^\alpha}$$

Let $R$ be the memory request rate (requests per second) and $t$ be the time in seconds from the beginning of a new job. Also let $B$ equal the number of words per block. The filling of the buffer can then be expressed in terms of the following differential equation, for LRU or first in first out filling:

$$df' = \frac{1}{W_B} \frac{a_1}{(a_0 + W_B f')^\alpha} B \cdot R \, dt'$$

The expression assumes that all old words are flushed before any words from a new job are swapped. Separating variables and integrating by parts, one obtains

$$\int_0^{f(t)} W_B(a_0 + W_B f')^\alpha df' = \int_0^t a_1 BR \, dt'$$

$$(a_0 + W_B f(t))^{\alpha + 1} - a_0^{\alpha + 1} = (\alpha + 1) BRt a_1$$

$$f(t) = \frac{1}{W_B}\left[(\alpha + 1)a_1 BRt + a_0^{\alpha + 1}\right] \frac{a_0}{W_B}$$

The total number of memory requests to fill the buffer can be simply found by setting $f = 1$:

$$RT_{fl} = \frac{(a_0 + W_B)^{\alpha + 1} - a_0^{\alpha + 1}}{(\alpha + 1)a_1 B}$$

and the time to fill $T_{fL}$ by

$$T_{fL} = \frac{(a_0 + W_B)^{\alpha + 1} - a_0^{(\alpha + 1)}}{(\alpha + 1)a_1 BR}$$

The average hit ($M_{rf}$) ratio during filling can be computed in a straightforward manner:

$$\frac{a_1}{(a_0 + f(t)W_B)^\alpha} = \frac{a_1}{\left[(1/W_B)(a_0^{\alpha + 1}) + (\alpha + 1) a_1 BRt)^{\alpha/\alpha + 1} \dfrac{a_0}{W_B}\right]^\alpha}$$

neglecting $a_0 W_B$.

$$M_{rf} \approx \frac{1}{BRT} \int_0^T \frac{a_1 BR \, dt}{(a_0^{\alpha + 1}) + (\alpha + 1) a_1 BRt)^{\alpha/\alpha + 1}} \quad \text{for } T \leq T_{fL}$$

Integrating, one obtains

$$M_{rf} = \frac{a_0}{BRT}\left[\left(1 + (\alpha + 1)\frac{a_1}{a_0^\alpha}\frac{BRT}{a_0}\right)^{1/\alpha + 1} - 1\right]$$

Let $u = \dfrac{BRT}{a_0}$; then

$$M_{rf} = \frac{1}{u}\left[\left(1 + \frac{(\alpha + 1) a_1}{a_0^\alpha} u\right)^{1/\alpha + 1} - 1\right]$$

Once full, the incremental hit ratio assumes its normal value. Averaging over time for $T > T_{fL}$ one obtains

## 4.3 Buffer Filling and Cold-Start Miss Ratios

$$M_{re} = \frac{1}{T}\left[ T_{fL}\, M_{rf}(T_{fL}) + (T - T_{fL})\frac{a_1}{(a_0 + W_B)^\alpha}\right]$$

Figure 4.6 ($a_e = a_1 = 40$) shows a plot of the incremental and average hit ratio as the buffer fills for a 2000-word buffer.

If a random replacement strategy is used, before filling completely, new words continuously are replaced, and the differential expression is given by

$$df' = \frac{1}{W_B}\left[\frac{a_1}{(a_0 + f'W_B)^\alpha} - \frac{a_1}{(a_0 + W_B)^\alpha}\right]BR\,dt'$$

Separating variables and integrating in a straightforward manner, one obtains, for $\alpha = 1$

$$f(t) = 1 - (e)\exp\left\{-\frac{W_B}{a + W_B}f(t)\right\}(e)\exp\left[-\frac{a_1 BRt}{(a_0 + W_B)^2}\right]$$

Filling in this case takes place more slowly.

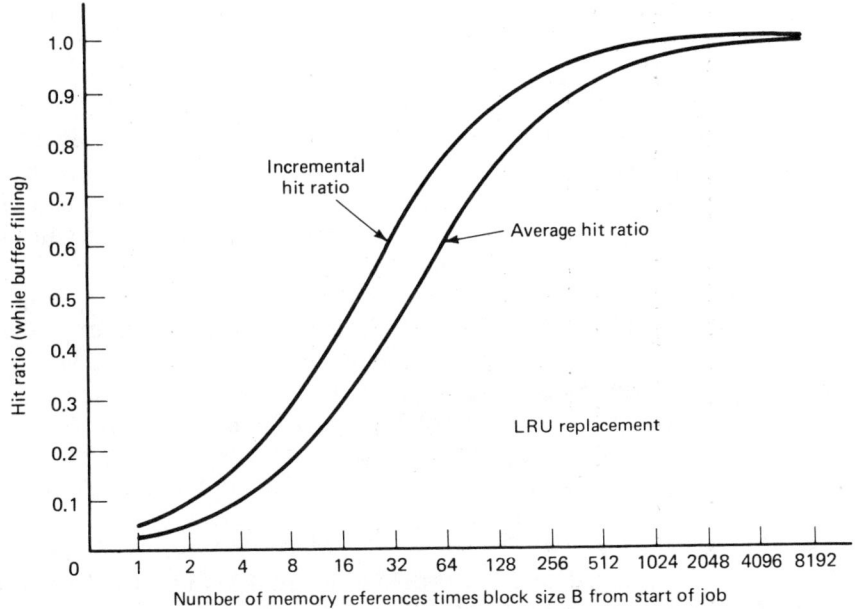

**Figure 4.6.** Hit Ratio as a Function of Filling.

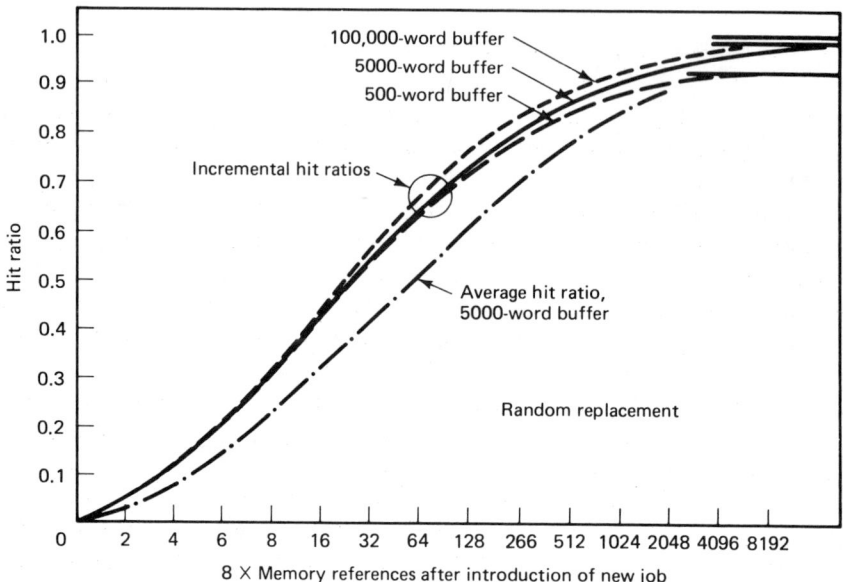

**Figure 4.7.** Hit Ratio as the Buffer Fills.

For $a_0 = a_1 = 40$, Figure 4.7 shows a plot of the hit ratio as the buffer fills for various sized buffers for random replacement. The average hit ratio also is shown versus times all references since the beginning of the job.

The results clearly show for all cases that with single word blocks more than a thousand memory references are necessary before average hit ratios greater than 0.9 can be achieved. For interactive jobs where a few thousand instructions are performed before a new job is switched in, it is evident that large blocks should be used so that the buffer can fill with fewer misses and achieve higher average hit ratios.

Figure 4.8 shows a comparison of miss ratio predicted by the simple theory and that measured by Strecker [S7] for small blocks. The exponent $\alpha$ was assumed to equal 1. The fit is again found to be quite good. Approximately 4900 references are required to fill the buffer. Figure 4.9 compares the experimental results of Easton [E2] and the simple theory for $\alpha$ assumed to equal 1. Again the fit is adequate. A more precise choice of $\alpha$ would improve the fit. Approximately 800 memory requests would fill the buffer in this case. Fewer requests are required because of the larger 8-word block size and larger constants $a_0$ and $a_1$. Little performance enhancement is achieved because of the increased delay in getting a block if blocks are made too large. It is also apparent that, if blocks are made

## 4.3 Buffer Filling and Cold-Start Miss Ratios

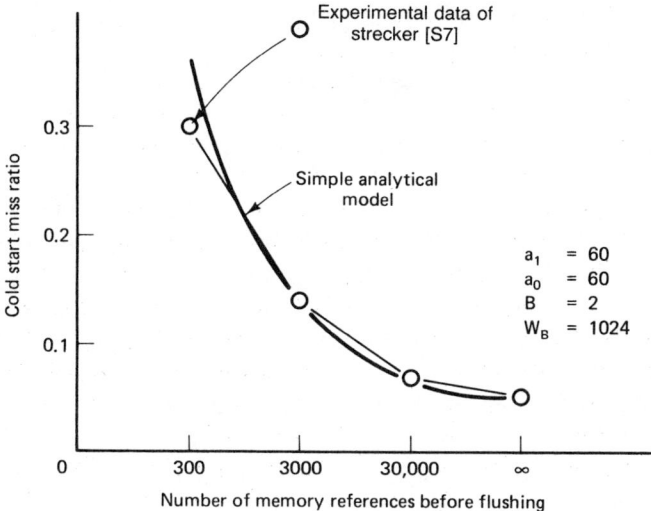

**Figure 4.8.** Effect of Job Switching or Flushing on Hit Ratios.

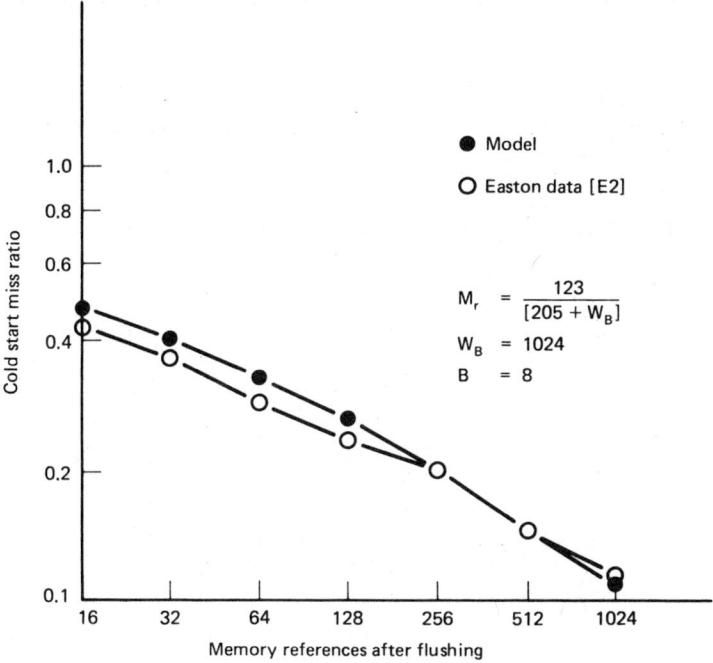

**Figure 4.9.** Memory References after Flushing.

too large, many words not belonging to the set of frequently used words are brought into the buffer.

## PROBLEMS

1. Assume that $\lambda(f) = \nu W_B e^{-fW_B}$; if $\nu = 10^{-2}$ and $W_B = 1000$, determine the probability that a word as a function of $f$ is in the cache.
2. The analysis relating frequency of use for blocks to hit ratios assumed a LRU stack in which the least recently used block was replaced. Determine the effect on the hit ratio if a FIFO strategy is used.
3. Assuming the exponential frequency of use form of problem 1, determine the expression for the miss ratio and hit ratio as a function of $W_B$.
4. For a block size of 16 words ($B = 16$) and a string length of 10 ($L = 10$), determine the effective string length $l$.
5. The miss ratio expression for a full buffer is given by $50/(50 + 1024)$, where the block size is 4. Determine the number of memory requests to fill the buffer.
6. Suppose the miss ratio given in problem 5 characterizes that for an interactive job that is processed for 5000 memory requests and then switched out. Determine the average miss ratio.
7. An LRU replacement strategy produces a lower cold-start miss ratio than one with random replacement. Compare the incremental miss ratios for the two cases for the buffer parameters indicated in problem 5 at the end of 1024 references.
8. Repeat problem 7 with the block size increased to 32 words ($B = 32$).

# Chapter 5
# Memory Hierarchy Organizations

## 5.1 INTRODUCTION

Although in small systems it is customary to have a single cache serve for both data and instruction words, it is evident that multiple cache memories can be used to enhance system performance. This can include a variety of techniques in which caches are dedicated to functions, to modules, or to processors. It is also evident that cache arrangements can be used not only for two-level hierarchies, but for three or more levels as well. In the following material, several of these types of organizations are examined.

## 5.2 MULTIPLE BUFFERED MODULES

It has been traditional to enhance the bandwidth of memory systems on large computers by interleaving memory modules. A similar technique can be applied to buffered memory systems by buffering individual interleaved modules. This technique becomes appropriate either when the buffer speed is not high enough or short program duration prevents the obtaining of high hit ratios by use of a large buffer.

To demonstrate the effectiveness of this technique, consider two possible memory system organizations: one employs a single large buffer,

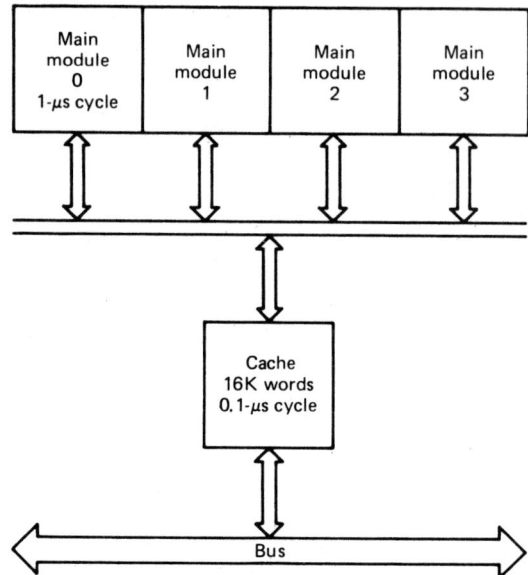

**Figure 5.1.** Single-Buffer Serving Several Modules.

and the other employs a smaller buffer attached to each interleaved module. These organizations are illustrated in Figures 5.1 and 5.2.

To make the most effective use of the four modules in the single-buffer case, it would be appropriate to have blocks consisting of four words. In the case of the buffered, single modules, blocks consisting of single words would typically occur for the most pessimistic case. However, because of the small blocks, more misses would be required to fill a buffer of equal size. To account for this, assume the following miss ratio approximations, consistent with the data of Strecker [S7]:

For a single large buffer,

$$M_{rs} = \frac{20}{20 + W_B}$$

and for a multiple buffer

$$M_{rm} = \frac{40}{40 + W_B}$$

where $W_B$ is the number of words in the buffer.

## 5.2 Multiple Buffered Modules

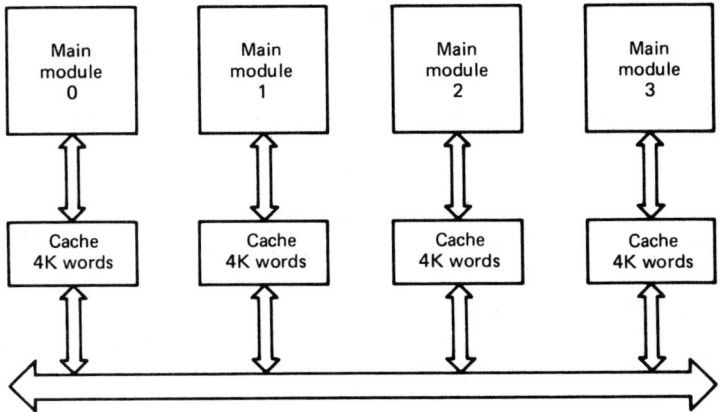

**Figure 5.2.** A Buffer Serving Each Module.

For the sake of simple computation, assume both systems employ a flagged swap algorithm with the fraction flagged equal to 0.2 and with no overlap. Algorithms with overlap would make the performance enhancement of the multiple-module system even more pronounced. It also will be assumed that the numbers of modules out of $N$ that can be simultaneously kept busy is $N^{0.56}$ [H3], corresponding to statistically independent memory request. In most real program streams, this is a pessimistic assumption.

The effective cycle time for the single- and multimodule cases can then be simply computed assuming single, long jobs in each system.

For the single-buffer case,

$$M_{rs} = \frac{20}{20 + 16{,}384} = 0.00122$$

$$T_{ceff} = (1 - 0.00122)0.1 \ \mu s + 0.00122(0.1 + 1.2 \times 1.0)$$

$$= 0.1015 \ \mu s$$

For the multiple buffer case,

$$M_{rm} = \frac{40}{40 + 4096} = 0.00967$$

$$T_{ceff} = (1 - 0.00967) \times 0.1 + 0.00967(0.1 + 1.2 \times 1.0)$$

$$= 0.1116 \ \mu s$$

Interleaving the modules to keep $(4)^{0.56}$ busy, the effective speed is $T_{ceff}/(4)^{0.56} = 0.0513$ μs.

In a large system, multiprogramming is employed so that the buffer space for each job is reduced. Consider such a case in which eight jobs are resident and one-eighth of each buffer is arbitrarily allocated to each job for the buffer size assumed previously. The effective cycle times are increased because of an increased miss ratio, as noted below, but the performance enhancement of the multimodule case is still pronounced. For further improvement in the multimodule case, the buffer size can be increased, although for the single-module case, enlarging the buffer provides little improvement.

For the single-buffer-case,

$$M_{rs} = \frac{20}{20 + 2048} = 0.00967$$

$$T_{ceff} = (1 - 0.00967) \times 0.1 + 0.000967 (0.1 + 1.2 \times 1.0)$$
$$= 0.1115 \text{ μs}$$

For the multiple buffer case,

$$M_{rm} = \frac{40}{40 + 512} = 0.0725$$

$$T_{ceff} = \frac{1}{(4)^{0.56}} [(1 - 0.0725)0.1 + 0.0725(0.1 + 1.2 \times 1.0)]$$
$$= 0.086 \text{ μs}$$

In general, a buffer memory system can be designed to have a very high effective bandwidth by combining buffering and interleaving techniques; this becomes particularly important when the performance of a single buffer becomes limiting.

If cache memories are located close to the main modules rather than close to the processor, the delays associated with a bus can pose a serious limit on throughput. Figure 5.3 illustrates the case where the cache memories are located close to a cross bar switch serving multiprocessors. In this case, the processors of necessity would be located physically close to the switch to reduce bus delays and would form a tightly coupled system. Because less bus bandwidth is required, the main modules could be coupled to their respective caches by longer buses.

To optimize such a system, it is desirable to have many caches operating concurrently. The manner in which blocks are organized in each cache would depend on the types of processing being carried on. If the

## 5.3 Coherence of Cache Information

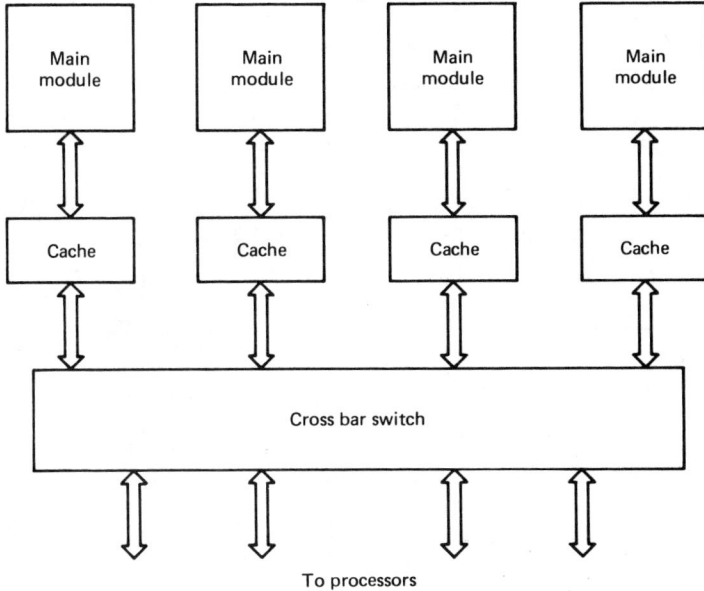

**Figure 5.3.** Multiprocessor, Multicache System.

multiple processors were involved in independent problems, cache blocks would be organized in the normal manner. If, on the other hand, the multiprocessors were intended to pipeline vector data, cache blocks optimally would not contain contiguous words, but every $n$th word, where $n$ is the number of caches. Successive words then would come from successive caches. Each cache in such a system services disjoint memory space from every other cache.

## 5.3 COHERENCE OF CACHE INFORMATION

Figure 5.4 illustrates an organization in which a cache is dedicated to each processor in a multiprocessor system. In such a system a problem occurs in regard to coherence of the information. A memory scheme is labeled *coherent* if the value returned on a read operation is always the value given on the last write operation. If multiple copies are kept and some means is not provided to simultaneously update all copies on a write, the memory system obviously is not coherent.

In the classical solution, each cache employs a write through algorithm. In addition, every cache is connected to an auxiliary data path over which all other active units send the addresses of blocks to be modified. Each cache monitors this path to check for matches with its directory

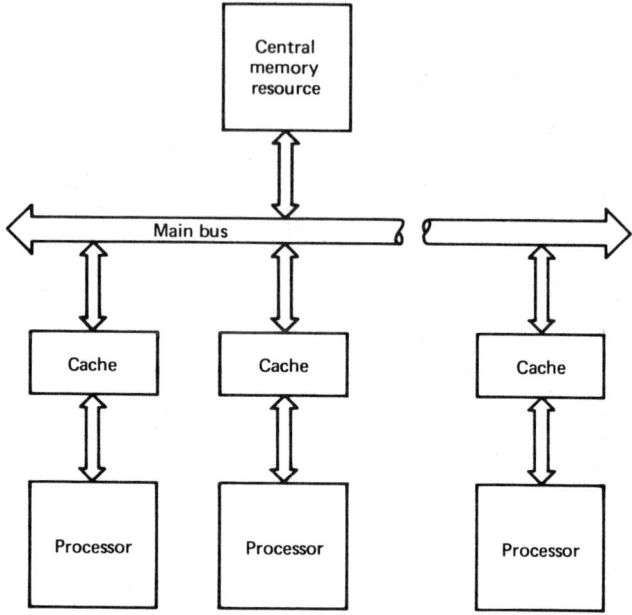

**Figure 5.4.** Multiprocessor System with a Cache for Each Processor.

contents. In case of a match, the block must be updated or declared invalid. Obviously, this search traffic reduces the effective speed of the cache.

Tang [T3] proposed a technique to resolve the coherence problem by maintaining directory copies of each cache directory in the main memory. Censier and Feautrier [C6] proposed a technique in which three types of flags to maintain coherence and more efficient swapping algorithms are used. In their technique a private flag is maintained for each block. When this flag is set in a cache, the cache is the only one to have a valid copy of the block and can employ a swap algorithm. The second type of flag consists of cache presence flags associated with each block in main memory, indicating in which caches a valid block copy resides. The copies may or may not be identical to the main memory copy. When a cache interrogates main memory, invalidation and update requests need be sent only to those caches for which the presence flags have been set. The last flag consists of a modified flag for each block in main memory. This flag is zero if the main memory block agrees with all cache copies but is set to 1 if it differs. The three flag types provide sufficient information to maintain coherence. The presence flags reflect the physical makeup of the system because there is one for each cache.

## 5.4 ORGANIZATION OF A MULTIPLE CACHE-PROCESSOR SYSTEM

In a variety of systems environments, it is desirable to have not only multiprocessors, but also the ability to add processors (or remove them) without hardware modification of the central memory facility. In addition, it is often advantageous to optimize the use of the central memory and the bus, rather than the individual processor. A cache memory technique will be presented that adds relatively little hardware to the caches, substantially reduces bus traffic in comparison to a simple write through technique [B4], and provides a system that can be conveniently enlarged or reduced. The system provides an effective compromise between bus traffic reduction and system complexity. In such systems, particularly as processor speeds are increased, a cache memory attached to each processor can significantly enhance the system's performance. The bus traffic or the traffic in and out of the shared memory can be the limiting factors on system throughput in such systems.

Local buses such as the Unibus* have traffic rates of about $2.5 \times 10^6$ words per second. Many current minicomputers require instructions and operand words at this rate, and, without a cache, a single processor is fully capable of using the total bus capacity. Attachment of a cache greatly reduces the required bus traffic of a processor and allows the use of multiple processors. The throughput of the system then can be increased by adding processors until the bus limit again is reached. If the local bus or communication network is longer than the Unibus and has a lower word rate, the use of a cache may become necessary to keep even a single processor busy.

An analysis of many programs shows that on the average 0.1 to 0.3 of a processor's memory requests involve writes [C6]. As a consequence, the bus traffic generated by a processor is, at the very minimum, 0.1 to 0.3 fraction of its memory requests when its cache employs a write through algorithm. On the other hand, if a flagged swap algorithm [P3] is employed in the cache, bus traffic can be further reduced, but problems of coherence may arise.

Figure 5.5 depicts a system with a single bus where part of the system memory, along with a centralized memory, is distributed to various processors. For the sake of simplicity, the bus arbitration scheme shown involves a bus request and bus grant arrangement for allocating use of the bus. The system assumes that the caches handle both data and instructions.

The system assumes an interrupt technique for updating caches in the case of writable multiple copies as evidenced by the search interrupt

*Registered trademark of Digital Equipment Corp.

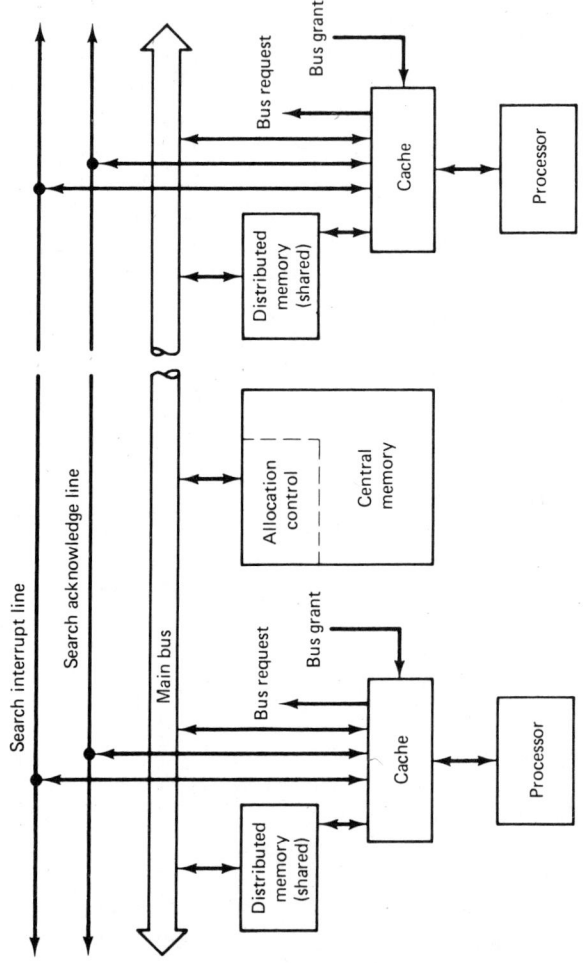

**Figure 5.5** Assumed Multiprocessor Organization.

## 5.4 Organization of a Multiple Cache-Processor System

and search acknowledge lines of Figure 5.5. Figure 5.6 depicts the timing sequence for the interrupt and acknowledge signals. In this system, bus-initiated cache searches only occur for selected write operations signaled by the search interrupt. (These write operations will be discussed more fully later.) As noted by the timing indicated in Figure 5.6, cache operations are much faster than main memory operations and can overlap the writing to main memory. In this way, cache search operations do not lengthen the period of time the bus is in use for a write operation. An individual cache will delay one cache cycle at most before responding to the interrupt.

In the example shown in Figure 5.6, a single large multicomputer word transfer is implied. In most instances the memory blocks would consist of multiple words. Appropriate clocking can be provided to implement sequential writing of the words in a block, or the bus width can be enlarged to accommodate the block size (if not too large) so that it can be written in a single clock period.

If dynamic reallocation of memory space is employed, the bus requires additional control signals and a certain overhead bus time to make the reallocations. This bus traffic should be small in comparison to the normal traffic and will not be considered in the following computations. For dynamic memory reallocation, bus assignment control resides at the central memory resource.

In terms of memory usage, the memory used by any processor in the system at any instant in time can be partitioned into the following categories:

1. Memory local with a processor and used exclusively by that processor (*local*). Not accessible by other processors and not having an image in the central memory.
2. Part of the central memory dedicated to a single processor (*private*). A fixed part of a central memory that can be written or read only by one processor. This part of central memory is permanently locked by one processor.
3. Shared central or processor memory which is read-only (*read only*).
4. Central or processor memory that is temporarily locked for single-processor use (*locked*). Only one processor has access to the memory until it is released (*unlocked*).
5. Shared, read-write memory (*shared*).

The essence of the technique is the assigning of two bits (three, if local is considered) to form an extension to the memory protect field for a block. This information is loaded into the cache directory to identify the category of use for each block resident in the cache. The cache uses

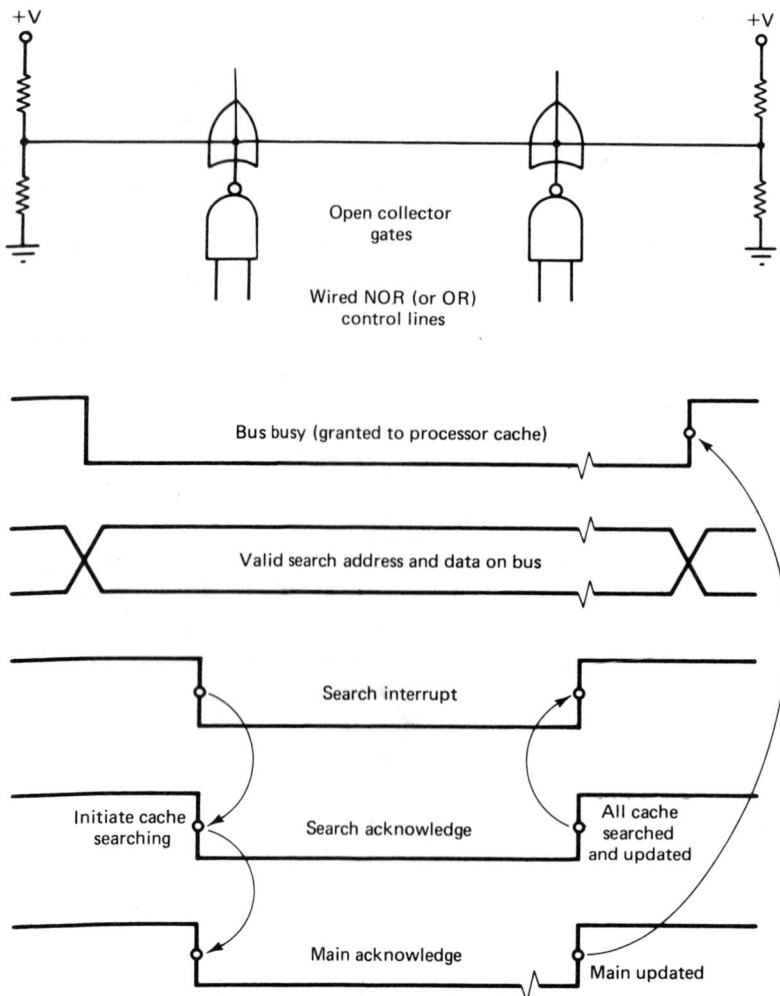

**Figure 5.6.** Signal Timing for Multiple Copies in Caches and Main Memory.

a write-through algorithm for just shared read-write blocks and uses a flagged swap algorithm for all other categories of memory usage not involving multiple cache copies.

Figure 5.7 illustrates the two (or three) additional bits that must be added to the normal directory word to implement the method. These bits, relating to the category of use, are assigned by the central controller when a block is assigned. In the local case, the local memory would provide the bits. Figure 5.8(a) through (c) illustrate the control flow for the in-

## 5.4 Organization of a Multiple Cache-Processor System

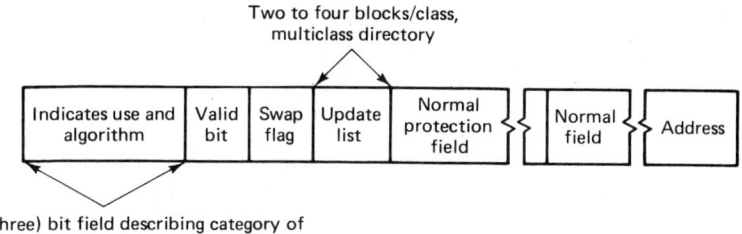

**Figure 5.7.** Cache Directory Fields.

dividual cache memories. The central facility responsible for memory allocation can have a software image of the processors using the bus, or the processors can provide unique identification to the central facility at the time allocations are requested. In either case, assuming an adequate protection field, the central memory hardware organization is not directly dependent on the number of processors.

The performance of the illustrated technique can be simply evaluated by comparing the bus traffic generated by a processor using the technique to that generated by a processor employing a simple write-through algorithm. For convenience, memory references to strictly local memory are not considered in this analysis. These references would not contribute to bus activity, regardless of the swapping algorithm.

Consider the following "average" parameters for the processor with cache memories:

$M_r$ = miss ratio for the caches

$f_r$ = fraction of memory references that are reads

$x$ = fraction of blocks modified in the cache

$S_f$ = fraction of memory references relating to shared read-write memory involving central memory blocks

$B_T$ = bus traffic rate

For a cache memory using a simple write-through swapping algorithm, the bus traffic generated by a processor ($B_{TW}$) in terms of its memory request rate to the cache ($R_m$) is given by

$$B_{TW} = \{[M_r (f_r + (1 - f_r)2) + (1 - M_r)(1 - f_r)]\}R_m$$
$$= (1 - f_r + M_r)R_m$$

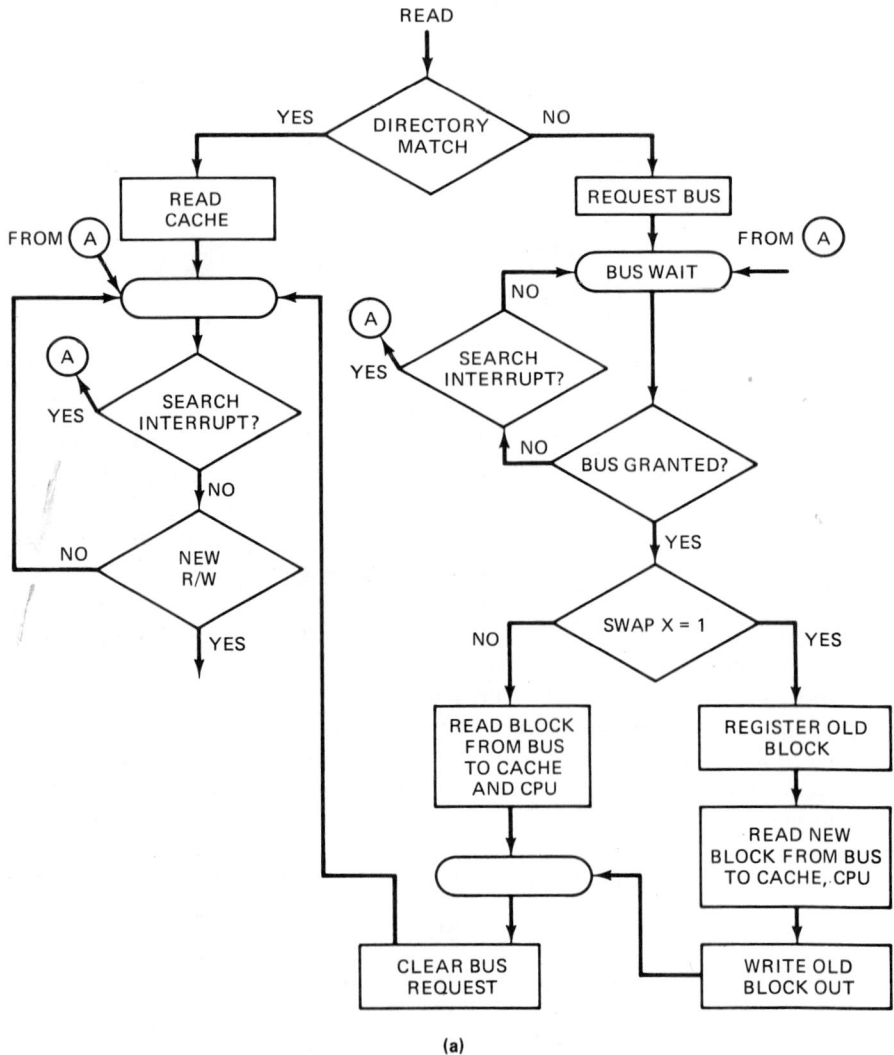

**Figure 5.8.** (a) Cache Read Control.

The expression assumes that normal writes involve less than one block and that the required block is brought in when writing occurs if it is not present. (A choice can be made not to bring in the block.) For the proposed case of the switched algorithm in terms of the shared fraction ($S_f$), the bus traffic is given by

## 5.4 Organization of a Multiple Cache-Processor System

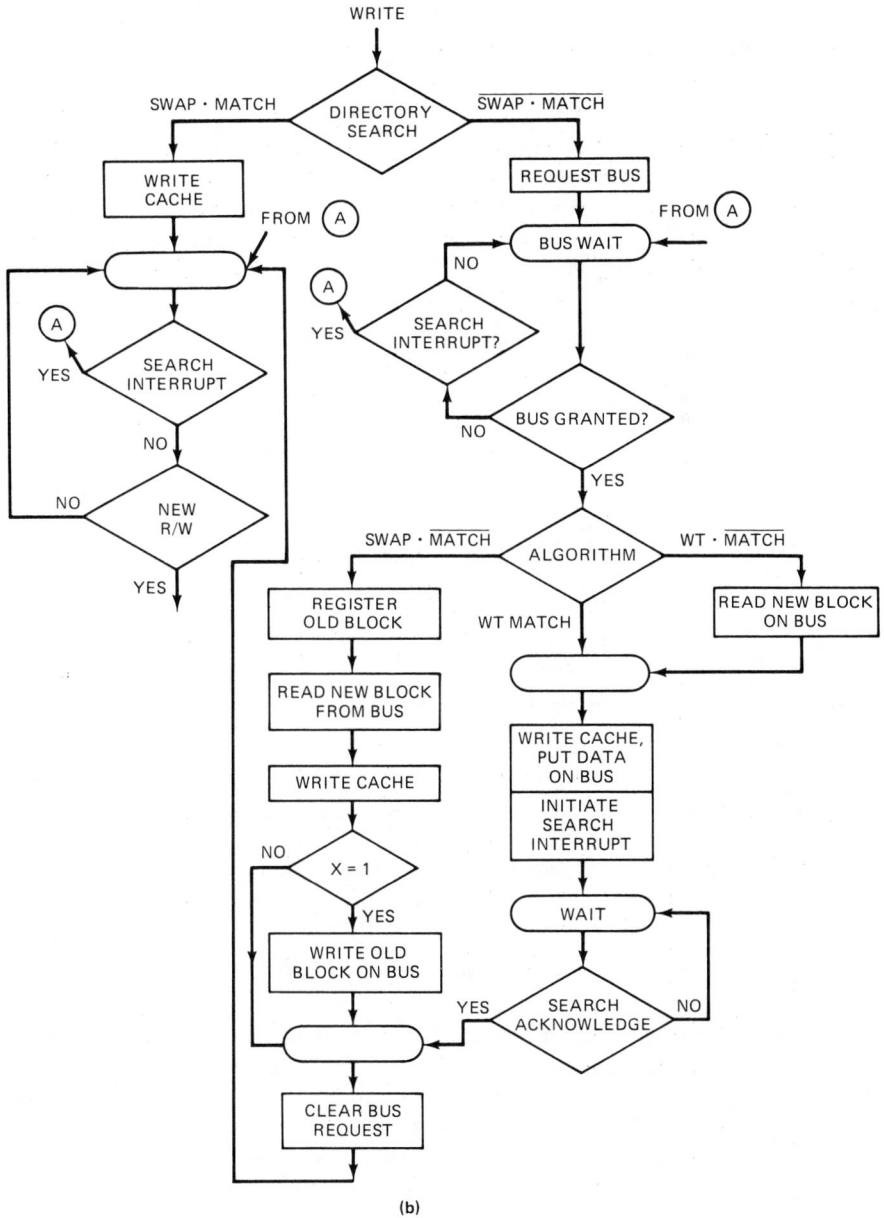

**Figure 5.8b** (*continued*) Cache Write Control.

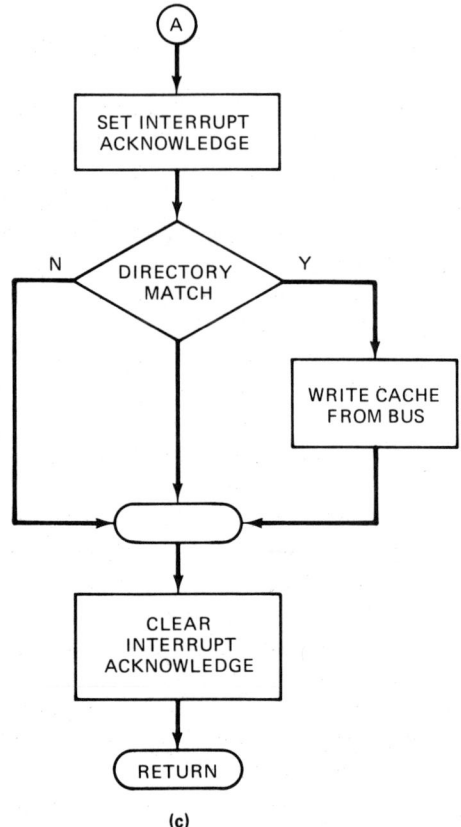

**Figure 5.8c** *(continued)* Cache Multicopy Update Control.

$$B_{TS} = S_f (1 - f_r + M_r)R_m + (1 - S_f)M_r (1 + x)R_m$$

Neglecting control traffic and strictly local memory references, these two expressions give the generated bus traffic for a processor in terms of the defined parameters. The traffic reduction ratio ($B_{TW}/B_{TS}$) for the nominal parameters is illustrated in Figure 5.9 for various values of the fraction of read-write memory references ($S_f$). It is important to note that, if the amount of shared memory usage is small, an order of magnitude or more reduction in bus traffic can be achieved. As a result, the number of processors can be increased by an order of magnitude before bus saturation occurs.

The results of Figure 5.9 show that, as the miss ratio is reduced by increasing the buffer size, additional gains can be made. For a miss ratio

## 5.4 Organization of a Multiple Cache-Processor System

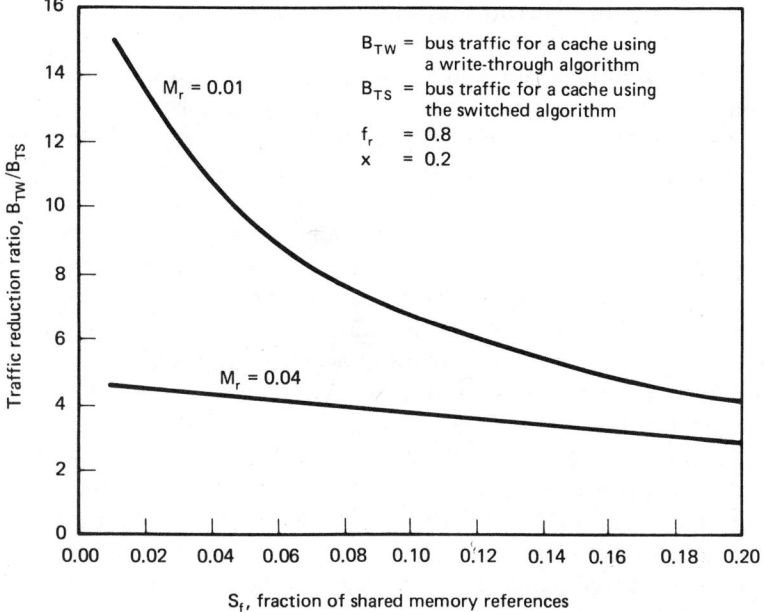

**Figure 5.9.** Traffic Reduction Ratio Versus Fraction of Shared Memory References ($S_f$).

of 0.01 and a shared fraction of 0.04, the bus traffic for the technique is reduced by a factor of 50 from that generated by a processor without a cache.

If cache bus requests were characterized by Poisson arrivals and enough processors were attached to the bus that their traffic would equal the bus capacity if all were busy, the system would operate at 80% to 90% of capacity, depending on the number of processors attached. With the addition of a few additional processors, bus saturation can be approached at the expense of increased wait time for the individual processors.

As a specific example, if 20 fully busy processors generated traffic equal to the bus capacity, the bus and each of the processors would be busy 81% of the time. If the number of processors were increased to 25, the bus would be busy 93.5% of the time and each processor would be busy 75% of the time. These results can be verified with the simple queuing model discussed in the next section.

In the illustrated system, a processor in control of the bus interrupts all other processor caches for a directory search only when writes to shared blocks are involved. Consequently, most bus transactions do not produce interrupts. Because cache memories have shorter memory cycle times than the central memory, the directory search and updates can occur concurrent to bus transfer writes when shared blocks are involved. Access to the bus, which is granted to a single processor at a time, ensures that only one processor at a time can update shared information.

The switched algorithm cache techniques offer several attractive features. The expected reduction in processor bus traffic is large, processors can be added or deleted without alteration of the hardware, and modest additional cache and central memory hardware is required. In addition, bus control information is reduced in comparison to more sophisticated methods [C3]. The fraction of memory references involving write operations is typically 10% to 30%; the fraction of references to shared read-write memory can be expected to be small. The memory regions that do involve shared read-write memory typically apply to communication buffers, shared files, and the like, with substantial probabilities of multiple active buffer copies. More complicated schemes with replicated directories or presence flags would reduce bus traffic only in those cases where a shared read-write block is resident in a single cache for a write operation. In many applications this would occur infrequently.

The illustrated scheme emphasizes the bus and central memory as the limiting resources and minimizes bus traffic at a slight loss of processor utilization, in comparison to the techniques of Tang, and Censier and Feautrier.

## 5.5 BUS PERFORMANCE IN SERVICING MULTIPROCESSORS

The performance of a bus in servicing processor needs can be analyzed by approximating the processors and bus as exponential servers. Figure 5.10 illustrates five processing units, each with a bus request rate $\lambda p$ when in operation. The bus is assumed to have a service rate $\lambda B$. Figure 5.11 illustrates a queuing diagram for the system. Note that if all processors are busy they are generating requests at five times the rate one processor would. Furthermore, in this simple example, it is assumed that each processor involves disjoint memory space, so global directory searching is not required.

The time average equilibrium conditions for the probabilities $P_0$, $P_1$, $P_2$, $P_3$, $P_4$, and $P_5$ can be expressed as follows, neglecting the transient parts of the solution:

$$P_0 + P_1 + P_2 + P_3 + P_4 + P_5 = 1$$

$$0 = \frac{dP_0}{dt} = -5\lambda p \, P_0 + P_1 \lambda \beta$$

## 5.5 Bus Performance in Servicing Multiprocessors

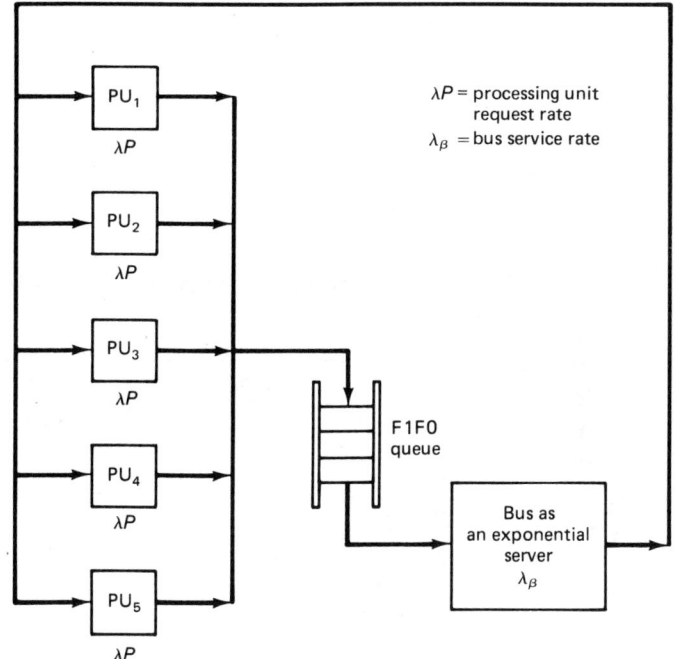

**Figure 5.10.** Bus and Processing Unit Queuing Arrangement.

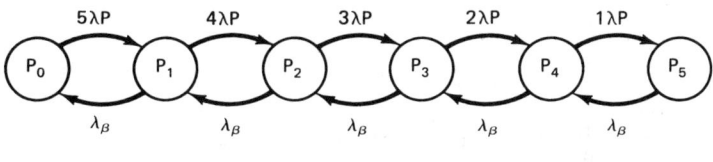

Probability, $P_0$ = no bus requests
$P_1$ = one bus request
$P_2$ = two bus requests
$P_3$ = three bus requests
$P_4$ = four bus requests
$P_5$ = five bus requests

**Figure 5.11.** Queuing Diagram for Processor Arrangement.

$$0 = \frac{dP_1}{dt} = -P_1\lambda\beta - 4\lambda p P_1 + 5\lambda p P_0 + P_2\lambda\beta$$

$$0 = \frac{dP_2}{dt} = -P_2\lambda\beta - 3\lambda p P_2 + 4\lambda p P_1 + P_3\lambda\beta$$

$$0 = \frac{dP_3}{dt} = -P_3\lambda\beta - 2\lambda\rho P_3 + 3\lambda\rho P_2 + P_4\lambda\beta$$

$$0 = \frac{dP_4}{dt} = -P_4\lambda\beta - \lambda\rho P_4 + 2\lambda\rho P_3 + P_5\lambda\beta$$

$$0 = \frac{dP_5}{dt} = -P_5\lambda\beta + P_4\lambda\rho$$

Solving the simultaneous equations for the value of the probabilities, one obtains

$$P_0 = \cfrac{1}{\cfrac{1}{1} + \cfrac{5\lambda\rho}{\lambda\beta} + \cfrac{5 \times 4\,\lambda\rho^2}{\lambda\beta^2} + \cfrac{5 \times 4 \times 3\lambda\rho^3}{\lambda\beta^3} + \cfrac{5 \times 4 \times 3 \times 2\lambda\rho^4}{\lambda\beta^4} + \cfrac{5 \times 4 \times 3 \times 2 \times \lambda\rho^5}{\lambda\beta^5}} = \frac{1}{D}$$

$$P_1 = \frac{5\lambda\rho/\lambda\beta}{D}, \quad P_2 = \frac{5 \times 4\lambda\rho^2/\lambda\beta^2}{D}$$

$$P_3 = \frac{(5 \times 4 \times 3\lambda\rho^3)/\lambda\beta^3}{D}, \quad P_4 = \frac{(5 \times 4 \times 3 \times 2\lambda\rho^4)/\lambda\beta^4}{D}$$

$$P_5 = \frac{(5 \times 4 \times 3 \times 2\lambda\rho^5/\lambda\beta^5)}{D}$$

If, as an example, the bus service rate were $\lambda\beta = 5\lambda\rho$, the bus would be idle ($P_0$) only 28.5% of the time and each processor would be busy 71.5% of the time. If the bus service rate were $\lambda\beta = 4\lambda\rho$, the bus idle time would be only 19.9% and each processor would be busy 64.1% of the time.

As is evident from the expression for bus idle time ($P_0$), more or faster processors can be added to minimize bus idle time; however, this results in each processor being idle more of the time.

## 5.6 OPTIMIZING THREE-LEVEL HIERARCHIES

Up to this point, only two-level hierarchies have been considered. However, with appropriate technology, three or more levels may comprise an optimum system. In the following material, an analysis is made for the optimum allocation of resources.

Figure 5.12 illustrates a three-level hierarchy for which it is assumed

## 5.6 Optimizing Three-Level Hierarchies

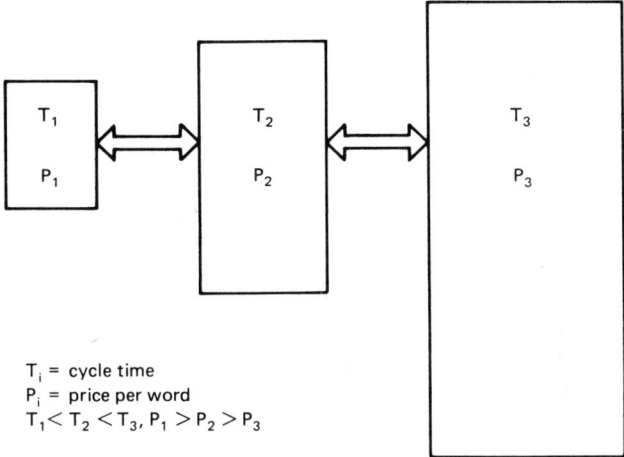

**Figure 5.12.** Three-Level Hierarchy.

that a flagged swap algorithm is used for the first two levels. Furthermore, it is assumed that the hierarchy operates on a simple demand basis for obtaining new blocks. In addition, the following definitions and assumptions are made:

$T_i$ = cycle time for the $i$th level
$P_i$ = price per word for $i$th level
$W_i$ = number of words in $i$th memory
$D_i$ = dollars allocated to the $i$th level memory
$S$ = fixed total dollars available for first two levels
$M_{ri} = \dfrac{a^\alpha}{(a + \dfrac{D_i}{P_i})^\alpha}$, the assumed approximation for the miss ratio as a function of level words $\dfrac{D_i}{P_i}$
$x$ = fraction of blocks flagged, assumed the same in the first two levels

To optimize the system, the fixed amount of dollars ($S$) will be divided so as to minimize the effective cycle time ($T_{eff}$). Implicit in the effective cycle time expression given next, is the assumption that a higher-level memory contains all words of lower-level memories.

$$T_{eff} = (1 - M_{r1})T_1 + (H_{r2} - H_{r1})[T_1 + (1 + x)T_2]$$
$$+ (1 - H_{r2})[T_1 + T_2 + (1 + x)T_3]$$
$$= T_1 + M_{r1}(1 + x)T_2 + M_{r2}[T_3(1 + x) - xT_2]$$
$$= T_1 + M_{r1}(1 + x)T_2 + M_{r2}[(1 + x)T'_3]$$

where

$$T'_3 = T_3 - \frac{x}{(1 + x)}T_2.$$

Noting that for fixed resources

$$S = W_1 P_1 + W_2 P_2 = D_1 + D_2$$

and substituting for $M_{r1}$ and $M_{r2}$, one obtains

$$T_{eff} = T_1 + \frac{a^\alpha (1 + x)T_2}{\left(a + \dfrac{D_1}{P_1}\right)^\alpha} + \frac{a^\alpha (1 + x)T'_3}{\left(a + \dfrac{S - D_1}{P_2}\right)^\alpha}$$

Differentiating $T_{eff}$ with respect to $D_1$ and equating the results to zero to obtain a minimum (and checking and derivative for positive value), one obtains

$$0 = \frac{dT_{eff}}{dD_1} = -\frac{\alpha a^\alpha (1 + x)T_2}{P_1\left(a + \dfrac{D_1}{P_1}\right)^{\alpha + 1}} + \frac{\alpha a^\alpha (1 + x)T'_3}{P_2\left(a + \dfrac{S - D_1}{P_2}\right)^{\alpha + 1}}$$

Solving for $D_1$, one obtains

$$D_1 = \frac{S - a\left[\left(\dfrac{P_1 T_3}{P_2 T_2}\right)^{\frac{1}{\alpha+1}} - 1\right]P_2}{1 + \left[\left(\dfrac{P_2}{P_1}\right)^\alpha \dfrac{T_3}{T_2}\right]^{\frac{1}{\alpha+1}}}$$

In general, the second term in the numerator is much smaller than $S$ for cases of interest; one then obtains the following approximate expression for the optimum division of resources:

## 5.6 Optimizing Three-Level Hierarchies

$$D_1 = \frac{S}{1 + \left[\left(\frac{P_2}{P_1}\right)^{\alpha}\frac{T_3}{T_2}\right]^{\frac{1}{\alpha+1}}}$$

The price of memory on an empirical basis is found to increase approximately as the square root of the speed. If this relation is used to establish the cost of the second-level memory in relation to the first level, one obtains

$$P_2 = \sqrt{\frac{T_1}{T_2}} P_1$$

Assuming this relationship, one then can also determine an optimum cycle time for the second-level memory. When a substitution is made for the value of $P_2$ in the expression for $T_{eff}$, one obtains

$$T_{eff} = T_1 + \frac{a^{\alpha}(1+x)T_2}{\left(a + \frac{D_1}{P_1}\right)^{\alpha}} + \frac{a^{\alpha}(1+x)T'_3}{\left(a + \frac{(S-D_1)}{P_1}\frac{T_2^{1/2}}{T_1^{1/2}}\right)^{\alpha}}$$

This expression can be minimized by setting the partial derivatives with respect to $D_1$ and $T_2$ equal to zero. The partial differentiation with respect to $D_1$ yields the previous result. The partial differentiation with respect to $T_2$ yields

$$0 = \frac{dT_{eff}}{dT_2} = \frac{a^{\alpha}(1+x)}{\left(a + \frac{D_1}{P_1}\right)^{\alpha}} - \frac{\alpha a^{\alpha}T'_3(1+x)(S-D_1)}{2T_1^{1/2}T_2^{1/2}P_1\left[a + \frac{S-D_1}{P_1}\frac{T_2^{1/2}}{T_1^{1/2}}\right]^{\alpha+1}}$$

If one assumes that $a \ll \frac{D_1}{P_1}$ or $\frac{S-D_1}{P_1}$ and rearranges the terms, one obtains

$$T_2^{\alpha+2/2} = \frac{\alpha}{2}\left(\frac{D_1}{S-D_1}\right)\alpha T_1^{\alpha/2}T'_3$$

Noting that

$$\frac{D_1}{S - D_1} = \frac{T_2 (2 + \alpha)/2(\alpha + 1)}{T^{\alpha/z \,(\alpha+1)} \, T_3^{1/(\alpha+1)}}$$

one obtains

$$T_2 = \left(\frac{\alpha}{2}\right)^{[2(\alpha+1)/(\alpha+2)]} T_1^{1/(\alpha+2)} \, T_3'^{[2/(\alpha+2)]}$$

As a more concrete example, let one consider a supercomputer with a 10-ns cycle time first-level memory, a second-level memory with a selectable speed, and a third-level memory with 2560-ns cycle time. If one assumes that $\alpha = 1$, one obtains that the optimum value of $T_2$ is given by

$$T_2 = \left(\frac{1}{2}\right)^{4/3} \times 10^{\,1/3} \times 2560^{\,2/3}$$

$$= 160 \text{ ns}$$

Figure 5.13 illustrates the effective cycle time for this system in units of $T_1$ as both the value of $S$ is varied and the value of $T_2$ is varied. The

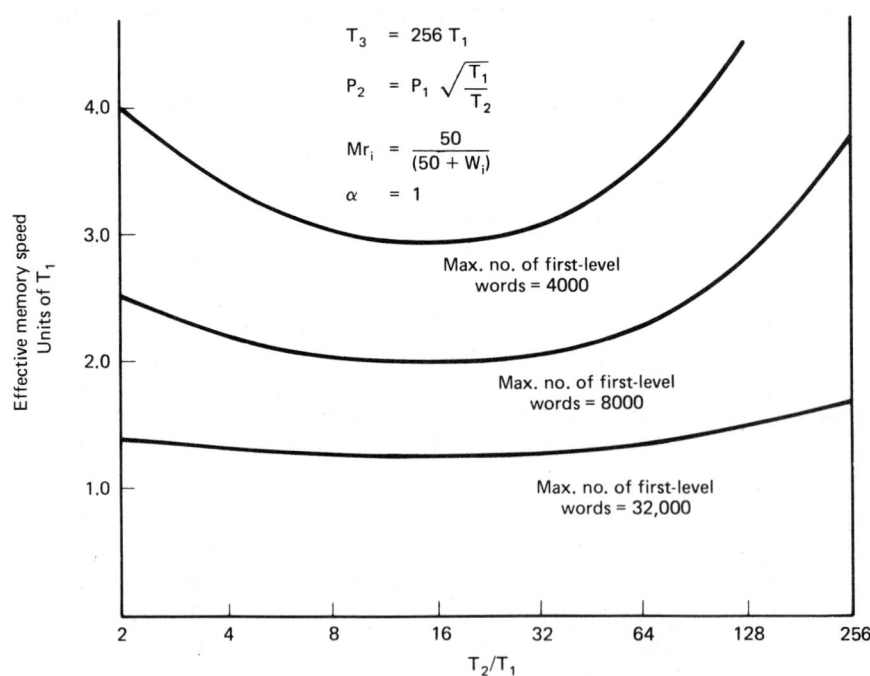

**Figure 5.13.** Speed Ratio between First and Second Memory: $T_2/T_1$.

figure clearly indicates the broad minimum in effective cycle time occurring when $T_2 = 160$ ns.

In a practical case, memory speeds and prices are not precisely related by a smooth function. In many cases there even may be gaps in the price performance curve for memories. The broad minimum in the effective cycle time curves of Figure 5.13 indicates that the speed of the second level is not critical for good performance, however.

## 5.7 SAMPLE CACHE DESIGN FOR A MULTIPROCESSOR SYSTEM

As an example, the following material outlines the design of a simple cache memory for a multiprocessor system operating off a single bus. The design employs a multiclass arrangement with two blocks per class, with each block containing one word, with a LRU replacement strategy, and with a switched replacement algorithm. For those memory blocks not involving write through, a flagged registered swapped algorithm is employed. For simplicity's sake, the block size is limited to one word and the address range is limited to 22 bits. Figure 5.14 is a block diagram for the memory. Figure 5.15 (a) and (b) indicates the address bit assignment and the directory bit assignment.

In the arrangement, both word and byte writes are provided. As a consequence, in the case of a miss on a write, the current valid word is brought in from main memory for those blocks involving the swapping algorithm. For the case of write-through in the case of a miss, the word is not brought into the cache.

It is assumed that the type of usage to which a block is applied is maintained with the block. In the case of a write to a missing block, this information must be obtained from the bus resident memory before the cache processing can proceed. A signal from the cache (block status unknow) signals the bus resident memory to provide the block usage bits and other appropriate signals. For example, the scenario for bus activity in the case of a write to a missing block would be for the central memory to read the block and send the block status bits to the cache with control of the bus. The cache, upon finding that the block has a write-through status, would initiate a global search interrupt and write on the bus.

Figures 5.16 through 5.18 are flow charts for the control during read, write, and external cache search operations. In the design shown, the cache is locally clocked by the processor clock. If the bus is of several tens of feet in length, bus signals obviously must be considered as asynchronous with respect to local clocks. Provisions also must be made to allocate bus use to the various caches. An arbitration scheme is not shown here, however.

The initialization routine simply sets all the filled flags (F) in the

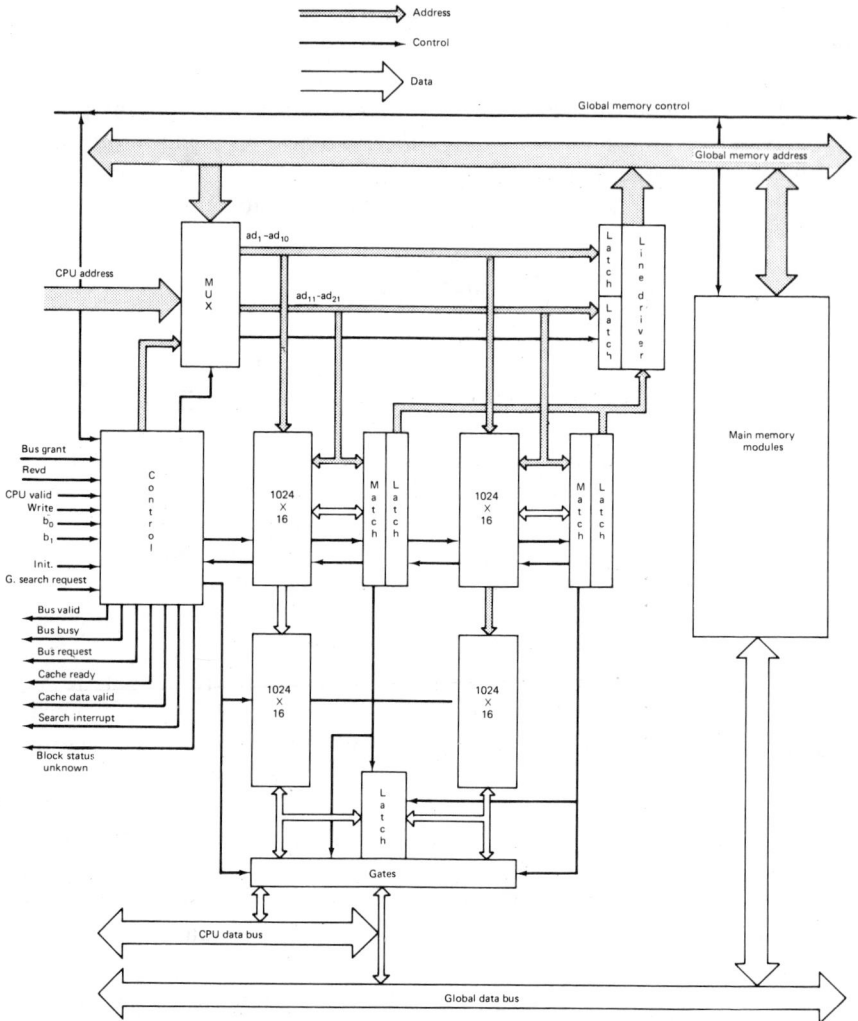

**Figure 5.14.** Block Diagram of Cache.

directory file to zero to indicate that the cache is empty. As operation is started, the available cache space is filled before swapping occurs.

The implementation assumes logic delays appropriate for advanced Schottky devices and cycle time appropriate for advanced static memory devices. In general, devices similar to those commercially available have been assumed, although not necessarily matched to, an individual manufacturer's specifications. Only some of the electronic details are shown; many are not included because some electronic details are specific to particular implementations and others are routine.

## 5.7 Sample Cache Design for a Multiprocessor System

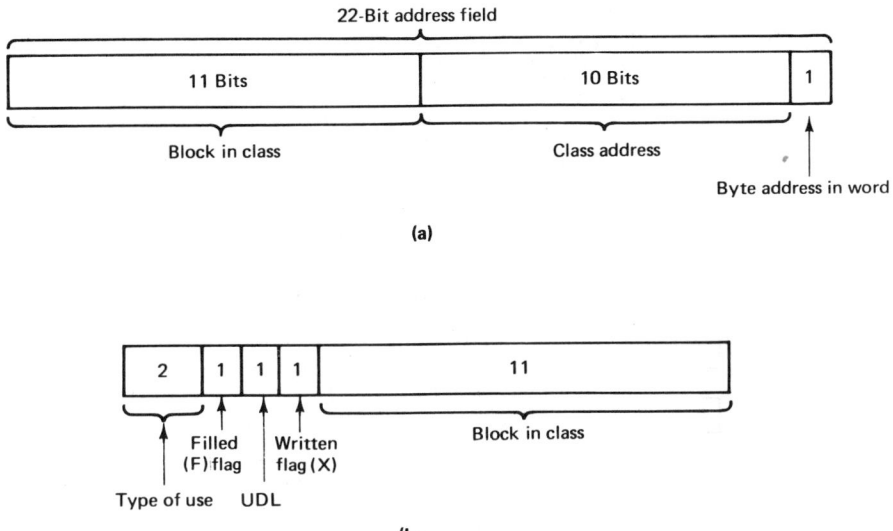

**Figure 5.15** (a) Address Bit Assignment; (b) Directory Bit Assignment.

Features such as parity checking or error correction have not been included in the design. Commercial designs would most likely include these features. Figure 5.19 illustrates an appropriate set of memory integrated circuits and gate circuits to form the data portion of the cache. Memory cells with a 45-ns cycle time and a 20-ns chip select time are shown along with a 16-bit latch and tridirectional gates. The global data bus is assumed to be tristate. The data memory cells have common I/O pins and, as a consequence, both performance and cost are diminished slightly.

Figure 5.20 illustrates an appropriate set of integrated circuits to implement the directory, update lists, flags, latches, and match circuits. Because individual bits in a word need to be selectively written, a 1K by 1 memory cell with a 25-ns cycle time was selected. These directory memory cells with access times shorter than those for the data portion are sufficiently fast to overlap the directory match operation with the data access operations. Figure 5.21 illustrates an appropriate set of integrated circuits to provide the input address multiplexing, the address latching, and bus driving.

Figure 5.22(a) and (b) illustrates the timing for the two memory integrated circuits selected. Figure 5.23 illustrates appropriate timing for the proposed design during a read operation with a hit. Similar timing diagrams would characterize write operations. The hypothetical design indicated would have a 67-ns access time and 100-ns cycle time for a read operation with the desired data resident in the cache.

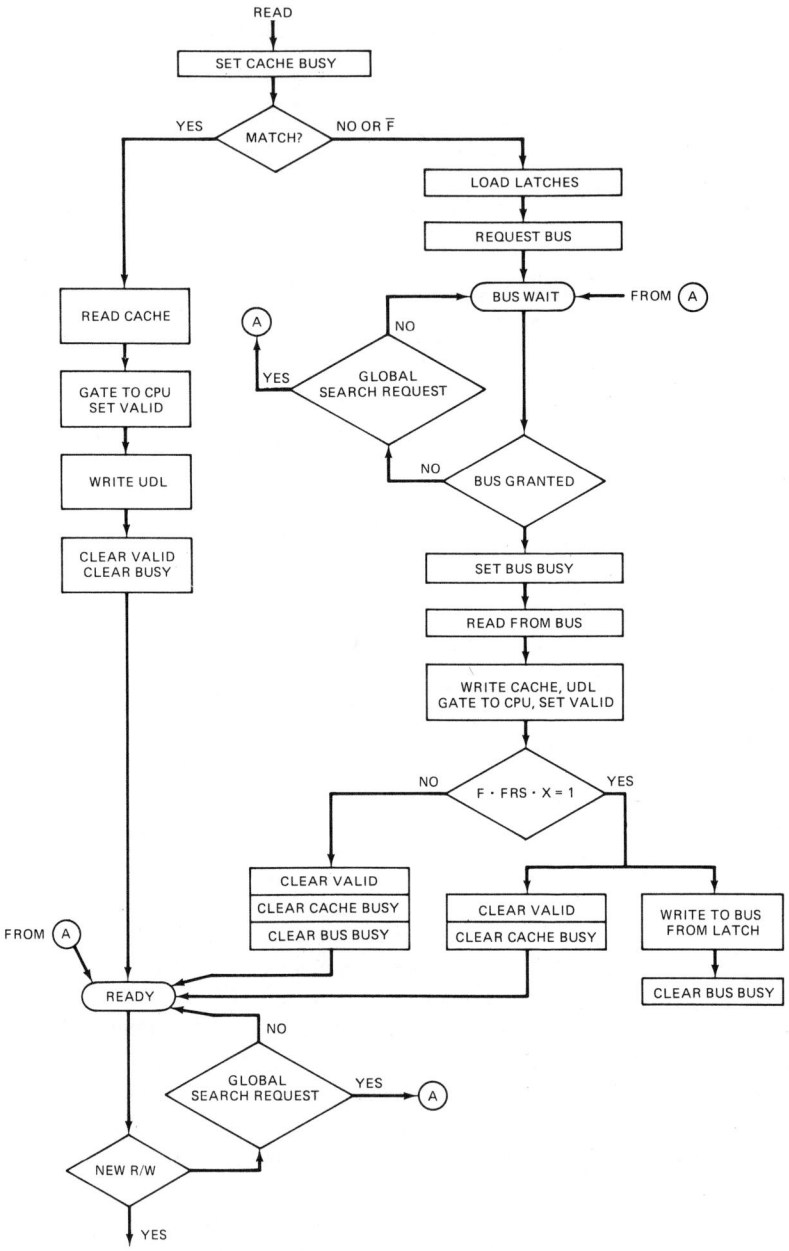

**Figure 5.16.** Cache Read Control Flow Chart.

## 5.7 Sample Cache Design for a Multiprocessor System

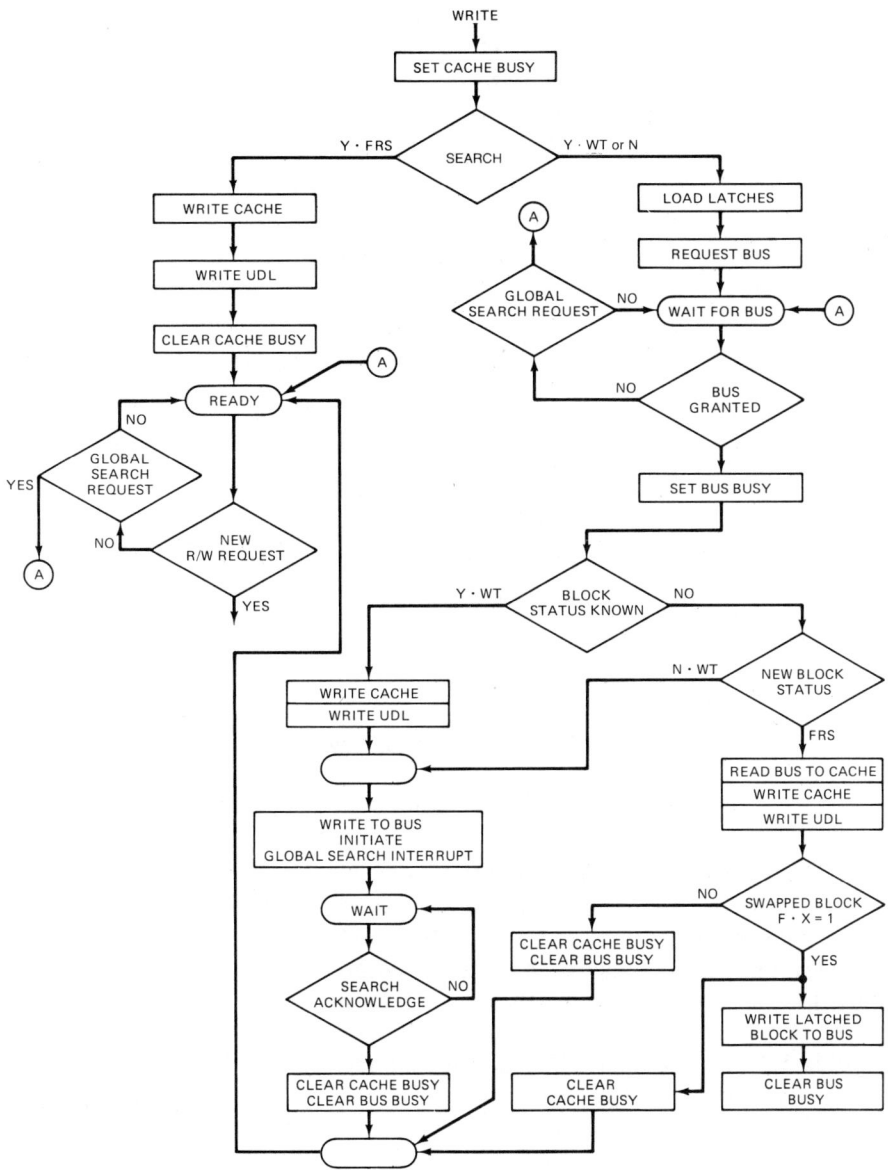

**Figure 5.17.** Cache Write Flow Chart.

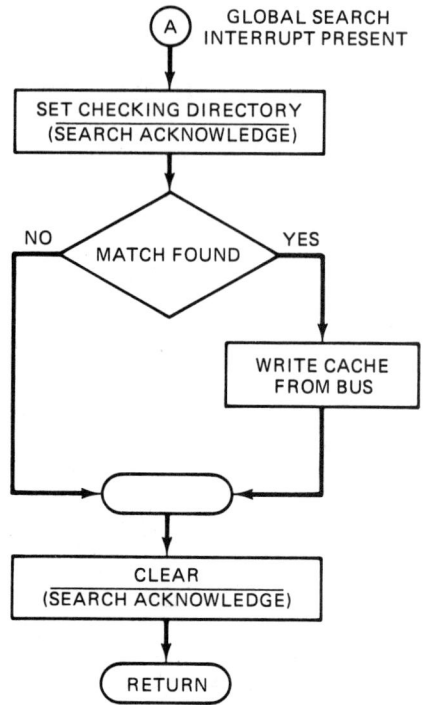

**Figure 5.18.** Servicing Global Search Interrupt.

Figure 5.24 is a more detailed block diagram for the control logic. A functional block is shown to handle power-up and initialization. This would involve an address sequencer to set all "filled" flags to zero and initialize circuits to ensure the system entered an appropriate state on start-up. The read, write, and search interrupt logic provides the appropriate state control and timing to execute the control flow indicated in Figures 5.16 through 5.18. The status and gate control logic provides the necessary control and gating signals to latches, multiplexers, gates, and so on. The control logic can be conveniently implemented by using a flip-flop per state to map directly onto the states indicated in the flow charts.

The incomplete sample design indicates that, at the current state of technology, the required number of integrated circuits to implement a cache memory is modest. A majority of the devices used consist of high-speed memory integrated circuits. The illustrative design also shows that it is possible to achieve adequate performance with standard devices for many applications.

## 5.8 Virtual Memory Systems

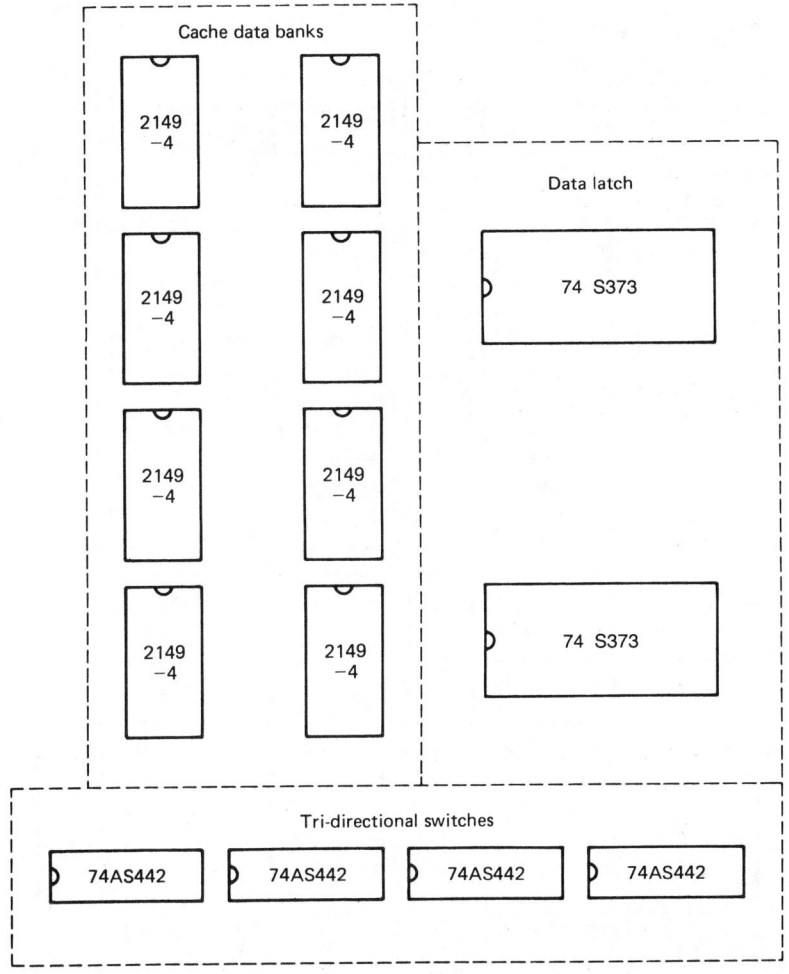

**Figure 5.19.** Data and Gate Portion of Cache.

## 5.8 VIRTUAL MEMORY SYSTEMS

### 5.8.1 Organization and Mapping

In a large multiprogrammed, multiprocessor system, such as illustrated in Figure 5.25, on-line secondary storage might comprise $2^{32}$ bytes ($Ns$ = 32), the address range of each processor might be $2^{24}$ bytes ($Npa$ = 24), and each processor might have $2^{20}$ ($Np$ = 20) bytes of populated

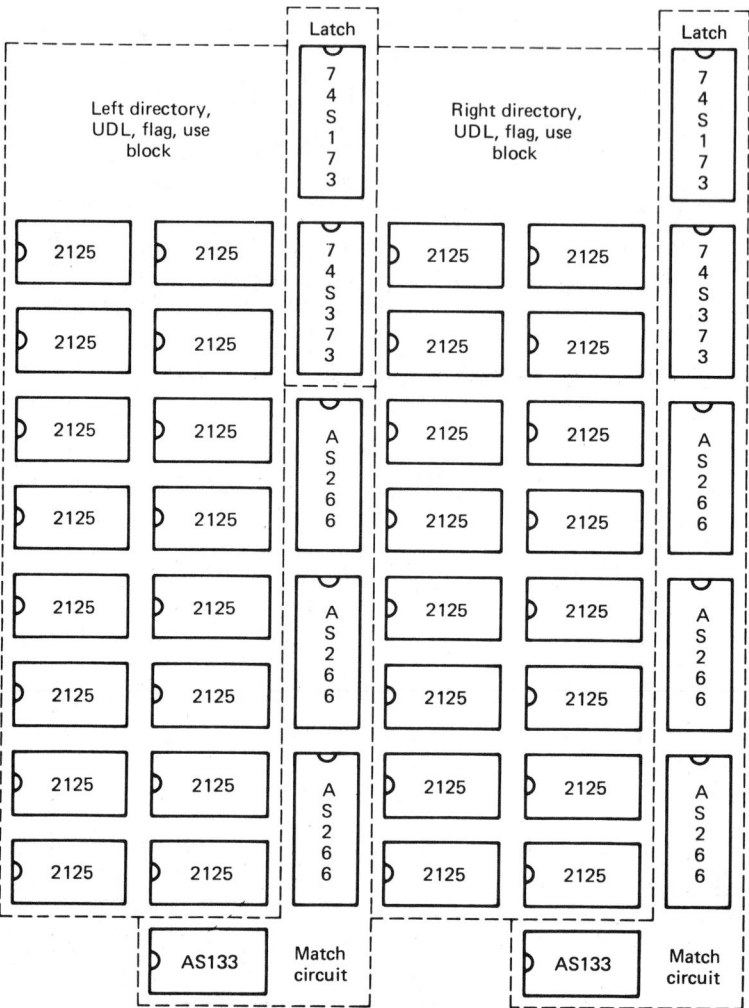

**Figure 5.20.** Directory, Update List, and Control Bit Portion of Cache.

main storage. In operation the virtual memory system for each processor must provide operands and instructions for the variety of jobs in each processor at a rate that will keep the processor busy, assuming input and output is not a limiting factor. The available memory in each processor must be allocated among the various jobs and the most frequently used words kept in the main memory for each job in a way that is transparent to the programmer. In addition, some blocks of information must be

## 5.8 Virtual Memory Systems

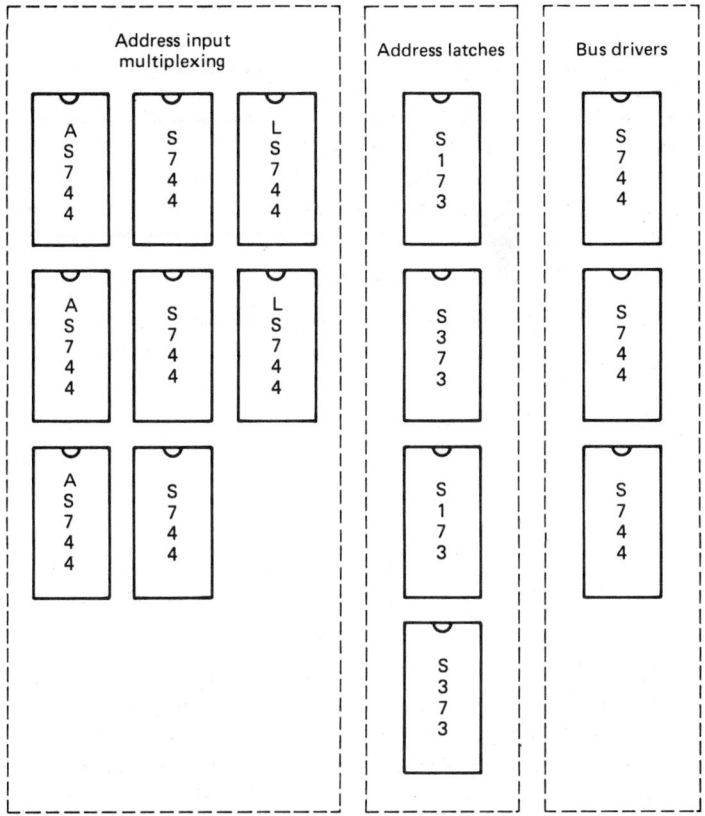

**Figure 5.21.** Address Gating.

shared and other blocks of information must be protected so that they are available only to the owning user. This rather complicated system obviously should be implemented in a cost-effective way. As noted by Matick [M11], operation of a virtual memory system and secondary storage system involves three mappings, as shown in Figure 5.26. The secondary storage typically is blocked into pages of 512 to 4096 bytes to optimize the transfer characteristics of the disk or drum storage device (4096 will be assumed in our example). Secondary storage is allocated to users (mapped into logical storage) a page at a time so that byte level addressing need not occur at the first mapping levels. Also, since the physical main memory of a processor usually represents only a fraction of the potentially addressable main memory, the need for an enlarged virtual main memory is often met by a hierarchy using a much slower and cheaper paging disk or drum to give the effect of a fully populated

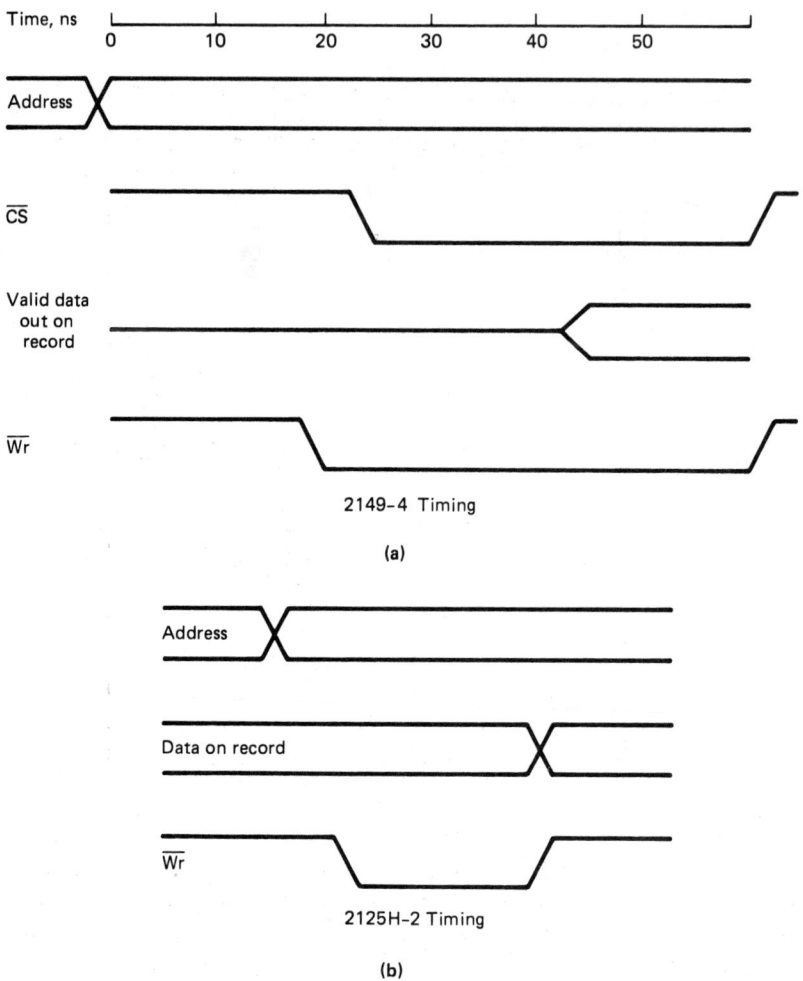

**Figure 5.22.** Cache Memory Device Timing.

main memory. The addressing formats for such an arrangement are shown in Figure 5.27.

A single-user program, in principle, could use nearly all the addressable memory space to hold the pages of the job on which the user is working. However, the usual case is to share the main memory among several active jobs.

From a design point of view, the main memory is serving as a buffer for the paging disk, and the paging disk is serving as working storage for processing secondary storage resident user problems. The fundamental

## 5.8 Virtual Memory Systems

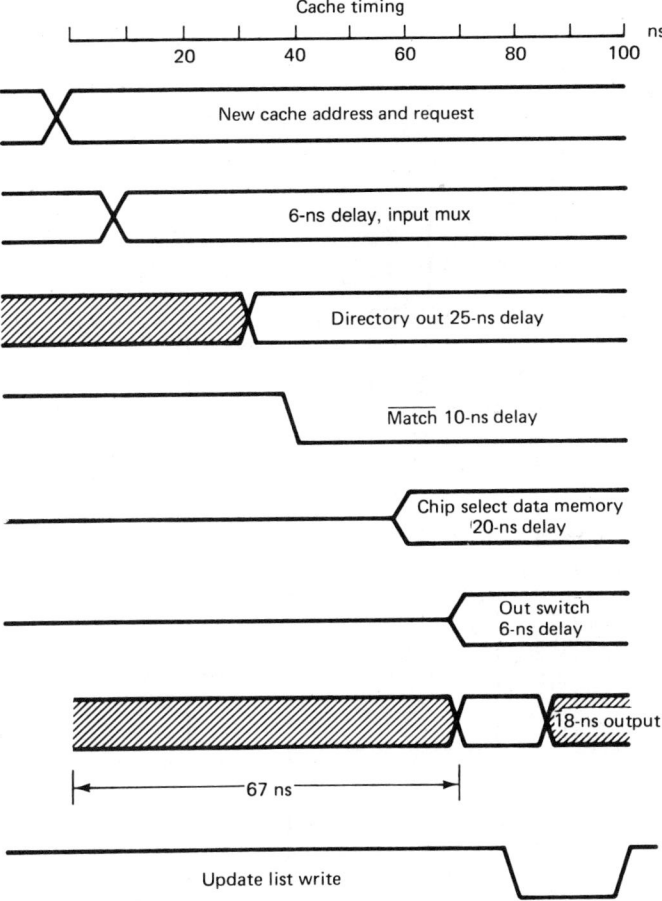

**Figure 5.23.** Cache Timing on a Read with Directory Match.

design goal, then, is to keep information streaming in and out, so that no serious bottlenecks occur. The pages mapped from the secondary logical memory of a user to the addressable logical memory of the processor comprise the subset that is being directly processed.

Because of the relatively low speed of existing secondary memory devices, most of the operations involved in maps 1 and 2 of Figure 5.26 can be performed by software routines. However, many of the operations involved with map 3 must be supported by hardware. For example, base and offset registers may be used to provide linkage information, and other registers associated with memory blocks may provide protect or lock functions.

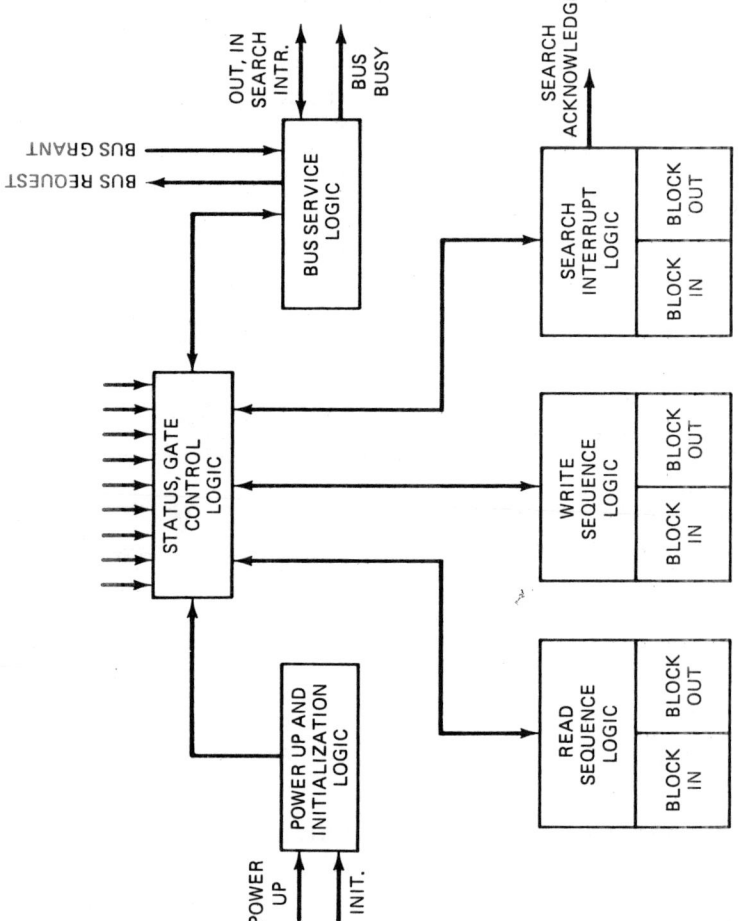

**Figure 5.24.** Cache Control Block Diagram.

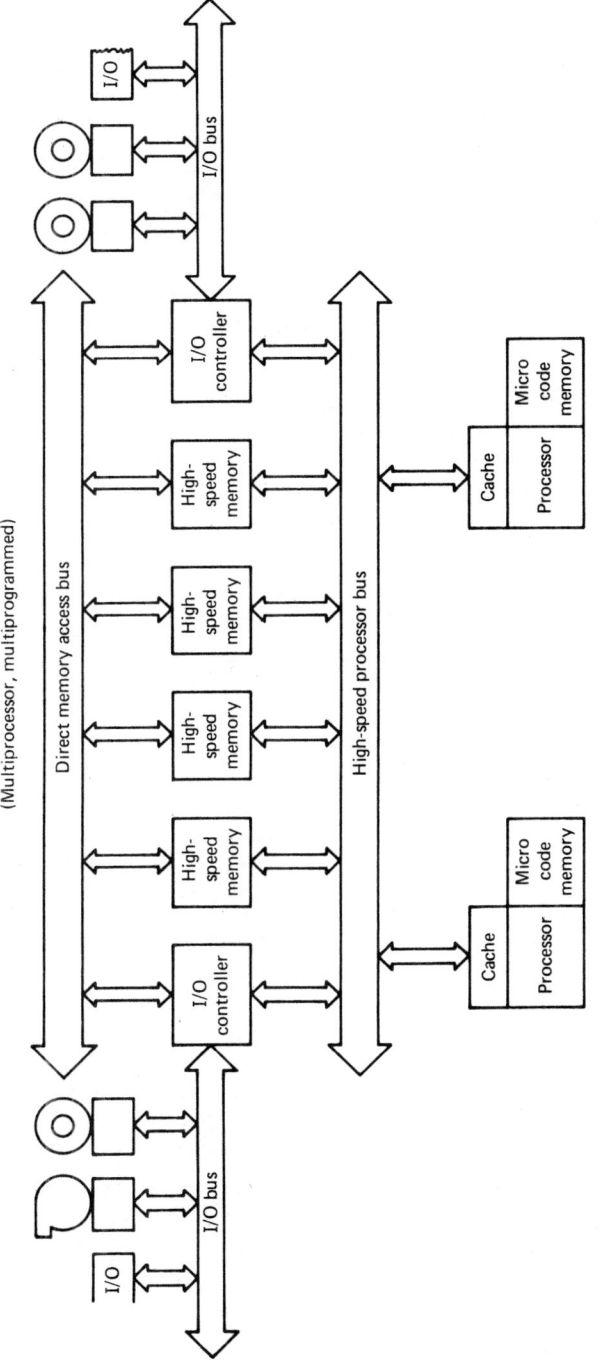

**Figure 5.25.** Large Multiprogrammed Multiprocessor System.

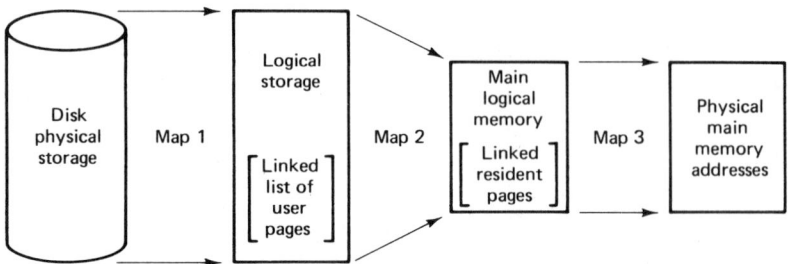

**Figure 5.26.** Storage Mappings.

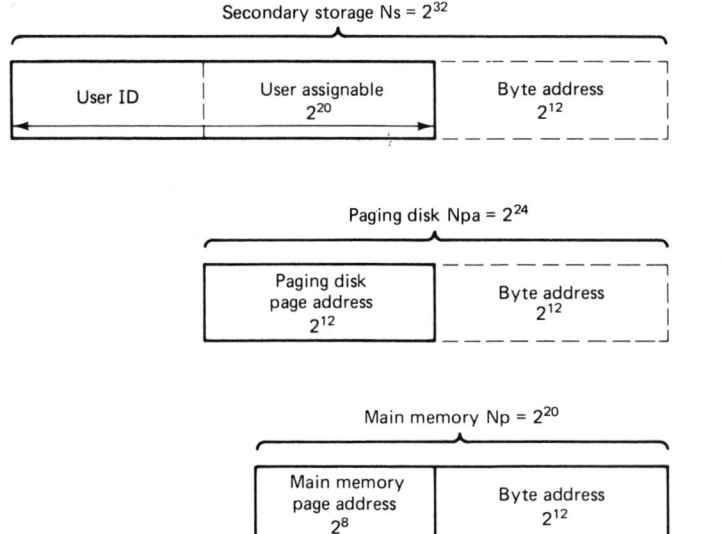

**Figure 5.27.** Addressing Formats.

A key problem in the design of virtual memory systems employing paging disks, drums, or similar devices is to overcome the great disparity between the page access time of a paging disk and that of the main high-speed memory. A main memory typically has an access time ranging from 0.2 to 1.0 $\mu$s, and a paging disk has an effective access time of 5 to 10 ms, representing a speed ratio of $10^4$. For many problems, multiprogramming provides an effective technique for keeping a processor busy. In a multiprogramming environment the processor may start working on another job, if possible, while the memory system is fetching a needed page. In this way the access and page transfer time are overlapped with the processor execution time on another job. For the multiprocessor, multiprogrammed example assumed, the problem can be further complicated if both processors sometimes contend for the same resource (*contention*). As a result, a system with two processors typically achieves only 1.75 times the throughput of a single system.

For other job environments (e.g., an interactive environment), paging disks are at best marginal in performance. This need for a paging memory with shorter access times has been a motivating factor for the development of gap-filling memories, such as bubbles.

### 5.8.2 Page Fault Ratio

As in the case of cache memory systems, a critical parameter is the fraction of memory requests for which a desired page is not found in the main memory. This ratio, by custom, is called the *page fault ratio* rather than the miss ratio, although the similarity is obvious. As with the smaller blocks used in a cache memory, the page fault ratio depends on the page size; the primary dependence, however, is on the size of the main memory segment allocated to each job. Figure 5.28 illustrates typical page fault

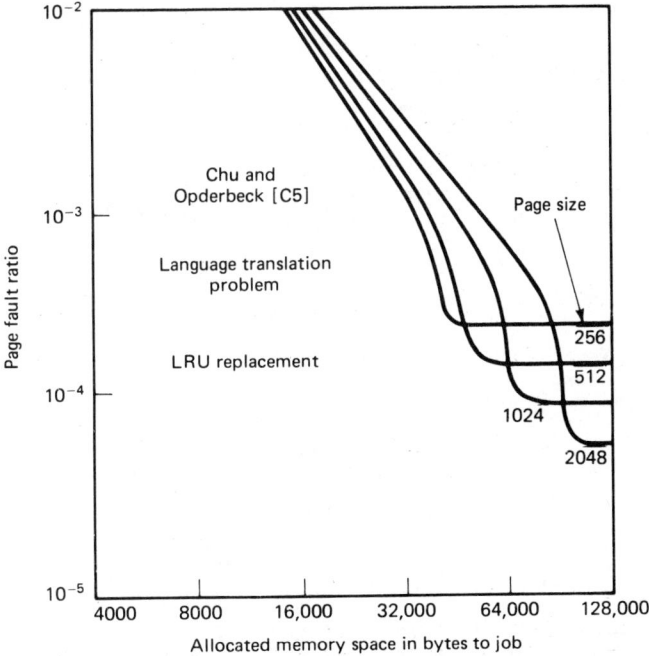

**Figure 5.28.** Page Fault Ratio Versus Allocated Memory.

ratio data from Chu and Opderbeck [C5] and Mattson [M10] for a single job environment. The experimental results indicate considerable variability in the memory demanded by a job. In general, as the number of pages allocated to a job is increased, the page fault ratio falls off abruptly until a minimum value is reached. This minimum value characterizes the number of faults required to bring in the job, execute it, and dispatch the results. As noted in Figure 5.28 as pages are made smaller, the minimum fault rate increases; more faults are required to bring in and dispatch the job. However, if main memory space is limited, small pages make more effective use of main memory.

### 5.8.3 Page Fault Generation Rates and Modeling

Both misses in a buffer and page faults in a main memory can be reasonably modeled by a modified independent reference model [E2]. In this model, once a block or page is selected, there is a high probability that it will be immediately reselected. Eventually, a new block or page will be selected in an independent fashion, with a probability in proportion to a page's frequency of use. Thus a processor's page fault activity can be approximated as an exponential server generating an average number of page requests per second at a rate proportional to the processor memory request rate multiplied by the miss ratio. A typical processor requires about two memory requests per instruction; consequently, $\lambda_p$, the average rate at which page requests are generated, can be given as follows:

$$\lambda_p \begin{bmatrix} \text{processor} \\ \text{page} \\ \text{request} \\ \text{rate} \end{bmatrix} = IPS \times Mrp \times 2(1 + g)Fy$$

where

$IPS$ = instruction per second

$Mrp$ = page fault ratio

$g$ = fraction of pages written that must be swapped

$Fy$ = fraction of time the processor is busy

To keep a multiprogrammed processor busy ($Fy \cong 1$), the paging disk must be able to service page requests at a rate equal to or greater than the rate at which they are generated. Figure 5.29 depicts the queuing arrangement normally used with a queue per sector and with jobs serviced on a shortest latency time first; that is, the jobs that arrive first at the

## 5.8 Virtual Memory Systems

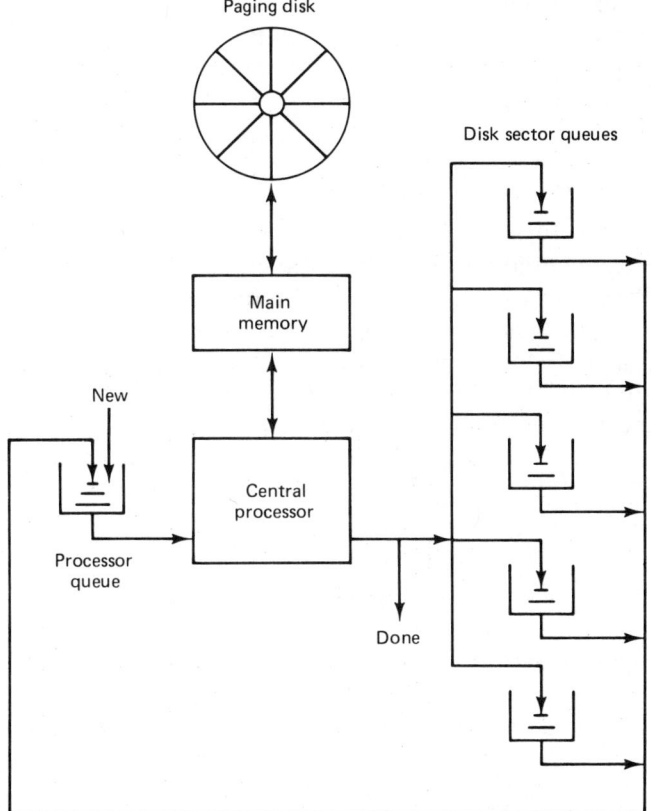

**Figure 5.29.** Disk-Process Queuing Arrangement.

read-write heads are serviced first [F3]. (A sector is assumed equal to one page.)

### 5.8.4 Balancing Page Service and Request Rates

To give two realistic examples, let us first assume a paging disk with ten sectors where each sector holds one 4096-byte page. Furthermore, assume that the disk is rotating at 3600 rpm and that there are a total of 400 tracks. In terms of general parameters, the values are summarized as follows:

$$s = \text{number of sectors} = 10$$
$$tr = \text{rotational delay} = \frac{1}{60} \text{ sec}$$

If one had a single job in the processor, the processor would cease to perform useful work when a page fault occurred and would wait for the new page to arrive. The average time required by the paging disk to service the request is

$$t_{av} = \frac{tr}{2} + \frac{tr}{s}$$

To make the analysis simple and intuitive, the disk also will be assumed to be an exponential server with an average service rate equal to the inverse of its average service time. The disk is obviously not an exponential server, because service always takes at least $tr/s$ seconds and never exceeds $tr(1 + 1/s)$ seconds. A precise analysis would have to take into account the distribution in disk service times, the number of jobs in the system, and the nature of the processor as a server.

As a numerical example, let the processor have an instruction rate of $2 \times 10^6$/s and let $Mrp$ and $g$ have the following values:

$$Mrp = 10^{-4} \text{ page fault ratio}$$

$$g = 0.25 \text{ fraction of pages written}$$

The average processor request rate then is

$$\lambda p = 2 \times 10^6 \times 2 \times 1.25 \times 10^{-4} \, Fy = 500 \, Fy/s$$

The average disk service rate $\lambda d$ for the disk assumed is

$$\lambda d = \frac{1}{t_{av}} (1 - Fy) = \frac{600 \times 20}{(60 \times 2) + (60 \times 10)} (1 - fy)/s$$

$$= 100(1 - Fy)/s$$

The two average rates for the exponential servers assumed must be equal in equilibrium, so one obtains

$$500 Fy = 100(1 - Fy)$$

$$Fy = \tfrac{1}{6}$$

Thus, the disk service rate is a limiting factor, and the processor is busy only one-sixth of the time.

If the processor is multiprogrammed, the sector queues on the disk can be filled, so the disk service rate can be increased and the processor can be kept busy a larger fraction of the time.

## 5.8 Virtual Memory Systems

For the multiprogrammed case $\lambda dm$, the service rate of the paging disk can be roughly approximated by the following expression [F3]:

$$\lambda dm = \frac{s}{tr}\left[1 - (e)\,exp - \frac{(J_d + 1)}{(s + 1)}\right]$$

where

$$\begin{pmatrix} J_T \\ \text{total number} \\ \text{of active jobs} \end{pmatrix} = \begin{pmatrix} J_P \\ \text{time average} \\ \text{number of jobs in} \\ \text{processor queue} \end{pmatrix} + \begin{pmatrix} J_d \\ \text{time average} \\ \text{number of jobs} \\ \text{in disk queues} \end{pmatrix}$$

is an expression relating the total number of jobs ($J_T$), processor jobs ($J_p$), and the disk jobs $J_d$.
This approximate model gives the best values for $1 < J_d < 10$.

Because the processor behaves as an exponential server, the processor will not be totally busy even when there is the average one job in the processor queue. Sometimes there will be none; other times there will be two or more. Figure 5.30 illustrates the fact that, on the average, three or four jobs need to be in the processor queue to have the processor busy

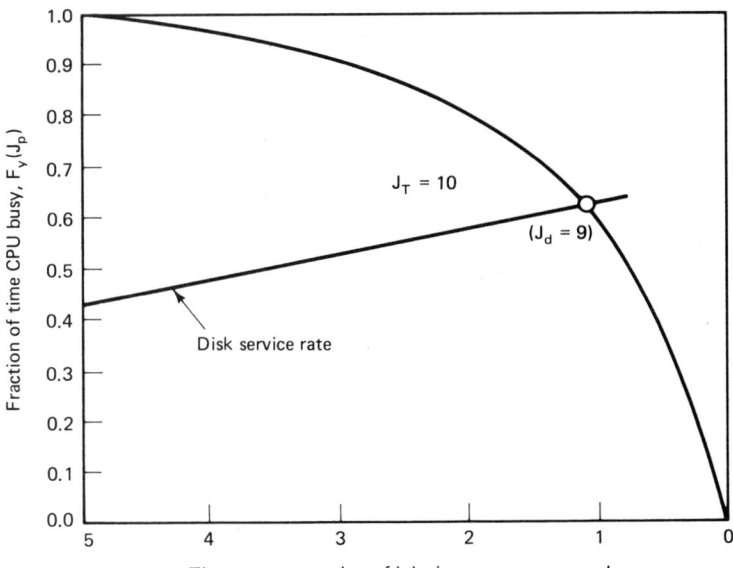

**Figure 5.30.** Disk-Processor Queue Equilibrium.

90% of the time. An accurate analysis obviously must take into account the statistical nature of both the requests and service replies.

If a very large number of requests are placed in the queues of the paging disk, a request can be serviced as each sector rotates by. For the sampling paging disk assumed, this would give a maximum rate of (10 × 60) or 600 requests serviced per second. For a smaller, more practical number of jobs, the service rate is reduced.

Let one assume that the processor is multiprogrammed at a level of ten. Time average equilibrium between the processor and disk occurs when the page request rate and page service rate are equal:

$$IPS \times Mrp \times 2 \times (1 + g) \, Fy \, (J_p) =$$

$$\frac{s}{tr}\left[\left(1 - (e) \exp - \frac{J_d + 1}{s + 1}\right)\right] \text{ per second}$$

$$500 \, F_y \, (1) = 600 \left[\left(1 - (e) \exp - \frac{9 + 1}{10 + 1}\right)\right] \text{ per second}$$

Equilibrium occurs for the simplified queuing model assumed with about one job in the processor and nine in the disk queues. The equilibrium is shown in Figure 5.30; the processor is busy 60% of the time.

It is very important to note that a reasonably low page fault ratio of $10^4$ was assumed. This could be achieved only by allowing considerable memory space to each job—on the order of 128,000 bytes. If the processor were working on interactive jobs in which the page fault ratio was much higher, say $5 \times 10^4$, the processor would be busy only 15% of the time, and almost all of the ten jobs would be continuously in the disk queues.

A gap memory technology that provides at a suitable price a block access time between 10 and 1000 $\mu$s would be ideal for such applications. At the moment, the problem is resolved by using very large main memories and having a multiplicity of paging disks. If such a gap memory were available, the system would be optimized with a reduced level of multiprogramming and smaller main memories [P2].

### 5.8.5 Page Replacement Strategies

Because performance depends critically on the page fault ratio, which, in turn, is dependent on the amount of memory allocated, there is a strong motivation to use main memory as efficiently as possible. A given job has varying main memory needs as it is executed, so a fixed allocation of memory sometimes will be wasteful and at other times will be inadequate. As a consequence, replacement strategies other than LRU have been developed.

## 5.8 Virtual Memory Systems

If an LRU strategy is used, a job is allocated a fixed amount of memory, and when space is needed, the least recently used page is removed or overwritten. Obviously, an updated list is necessary to identify which page was least recently used.

The working set strategy [D1] maintains, in essence, a counter for each page of a job, which is incremented each time a reference is made to another page associated with the job and is reset if a reference is made to the page itself. If the count exceeds a particular value $\tau$ (called the working set parameter), the page is made available for replacement. Jobs having a high page fault rate can make use of inactive page space of other jobs. The counters associated with pages for a particular job are incremented only by page requests arising from that job.

The page fault frequency strategy [C5] measures the number of page requests between page faults. If the count falls below a specified value $I$, the referenced pages that are causing the faults are brought into the main memory, thereby reducing the fault rate. On the other hand, if the count exceeds the threshold, all pages in main memory not referenced since the last fault are made available for replacement. The page fault frequency strategy thus provides rapid response to the changing memory needs of a job.

In real systems these strategies are often simplified. In addition, a choice is sometimes made to satisfy local requirements.

## PROBLEMS

1. Compare the memory system throughput for a single 16K word cache servicing a single memory of 16 modules against that of 16 caches of 1K words servicing 16 modules. Assume the caches have a .1-$\mu$s cycle time, the modules have 1.0-$\mu$s cycle time, a simple flagged swap algorithm ($X = 0.1$), and random ordering of memory requests. Use the hit ratio values indicated in the chapter.
2. Design an electronic element suitable for constructing a cross bar switch for connecting four processors to eight modules.
3. A three-level hierarchy uses memories with cycle times of 50 ns, 500 ns, and 500-$\mu$s. The prices are 0.1¢, 0.04¢, and 0.005¢/bit. Determine a nearly optimum ratio for the resources allocated between the first- and second-level memories.
4. The expression for optimum allocation of resources assumed that the miss ratio was given by $M_r = a_1/(a_0 + W)$. Determine the expression for the case in which the miss ratio is given by $M_r = \alpha\, e^{-\alpha W}$.
5. Consider 16 processors working on a single bus. Assume the service request rate from each processor if busy is one-twelfth of the bus

service rate. Determine the fraction of time the bus is busy and the fraction of time each processor is busy. Model the bus and processors as exponential servers.

6. In the sample cache design, the data portion of the cache used memory cells with common I/O and used the chip select signals to gate the data out or in during read and write operations. Determine how much shorter the access time would be if cells similar to the directory were employed and 6-ns gates were used to couple from the memory to the bus in place of the chip select gating.

7. Assume the processor indicated in problem 5 cost $5000 and the bus and central memory cost $50,000. Would adding two additional processors increase or decrease the total throughput per total dollars spent?

# Chapter 6
# Error-Correcting Codes and Reliability for High-Speed Memories

## 6.1 INTRODUCTION

Semiconductor memories are now used for a great variety of computer systems and computer-related equipments: large computers, minicomputers, microcomputers, add-on memories, peripheral devices and their controllers, remote terminals, and buffer memories. A main reason for the wide acceptance of semiconductor memories has been the rapidly decreasing ratio of price to performance. Although continuing cost and performance improvements have occurred, individual semiconductor chips still are not as reliable as desired for larger memory systems. Because a large memory system requires many chips, the reliability of the whole system diminishes as the system is made larger. Hence a wide variety of low-cost fault detection and correction techniques are used in these systems to improve reliability. These techniques obviously are important in large memory systems using cache techniques as well. In the following material, error detection and correction techniques are reviewed and related to cache memory systems.

## 6.2 ERROR-DETECTING AND ERROR-CORRECTING CODES

The theory and methods of implementation of error detection and correction (EDAC) techniques are well developed. The use of EDAC with semiconductor memories enables the design engineer to retain the device

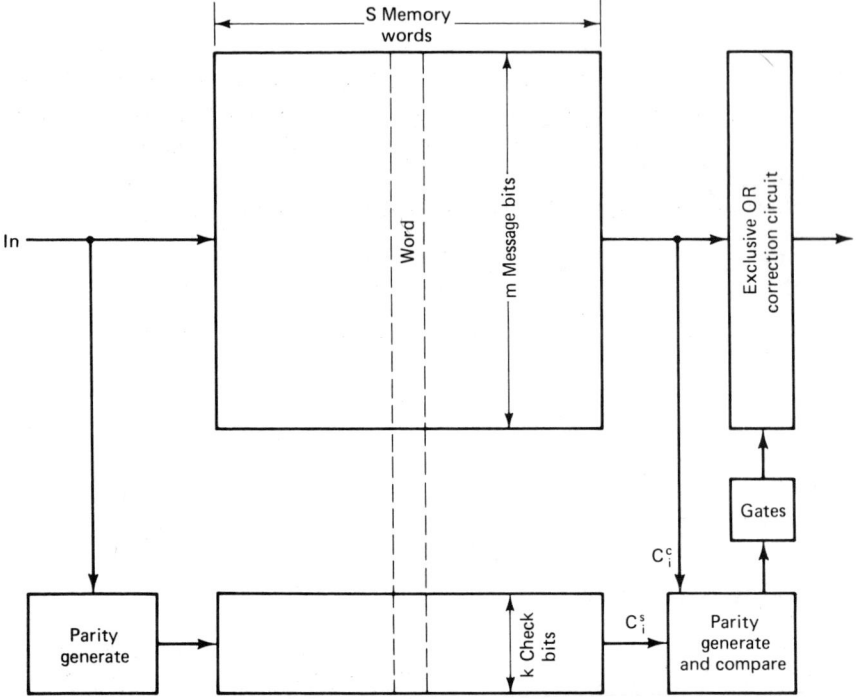

**Figure 6.1.** Block Diagram of Memory with SBEC.

advantages of low cost, high density, low power, and high speed while still achieving acceptable levels of memory systems reliability. The type of EDAC codes most commonly used in semiconductor memory systems is based on Hamming's single-error correcting (SEC) codes [H1]. Multiple-error correcting codes are quite complex and therefore are not generally used in semiconductor memories [P1].

Error corrections and detections are basically achieved by adding additional (redundancy) bits to the data field. Figure 6.1 shows the EDAC circuitry block diagram for a memory system. As seen, a data word of $m$ bits is received from the CPU, a field of $k$ check parity bits is generated, and both the data bits and the parity bits ($m + k$) or $n$ bits are stored in memory. Thus $k$ check parity bits are appended to the information bits.

All these $n$ bits are stored in memory where they are subjected to errors due to failure of memory subsystem components. When data are read back from memory, another field of $k$ parity bits is generated over the same subset of the $m$ information bits. These $k$ regenerated parity bits are compared to the $k$ parity bits read from memory, and the result of the comparison is $k$ syndrome bits. If there are no errors, then all these $k$ syndrome bits are zero. If there is any error, the $k$ syndrome bits provide

## 6.2 Error-Detecting and Error-Correcting Codes

information about the bit position that is in error so that the error can be corrected and correct data transmitted, thus improving the reliability of the system.

Lin [L8] and Peterson [P1] have treated exhaustively the theory of error-correcting codes. Here we shall confine ourselves to the following three cases:

Single-error detecting (SED) codes
Single-error correcting (SEC) codes
Single-error correcting plus double-error detecting (SECD) codes

Before these are discussed, let us define the following terms:

*(n, m) code:* An ordered pair descriptor of an error detection and correction (EDAC) code, where $n$ is the total number of bits per code word and $m$ is the number of information bits. $n - m(k)$ is the number of redundancy bits.

*Redundancy ratio (R):* Ratio of the number of the total number of bits (digits) per code word $(m + k)$ to the original word without parity bits. Thus,

$$R = \frac{k + m}{m}$$

*Code efficiency (CE):* Code efficiency is another measure of data redundancy. It is formally given as

$$CE = \frac{m}{n} = \frac{m}{m + k}$$

assuming all original $2^m$ messages are equally probable.

*Code word:* A member of the set of all legitimate words defined in the code space. The code space can be defined to be the subgroup that contains $2^m$ words of the $2^n$ words that are possible in the vector space of a code consisting of $n$ bits. The words that are not code words are defined to be the error words.

*Distance:* The minimum distance of bit positions that differ between two code words. It is also referred to in the literature as the Hamming distance. (Distance is determined by the number of bits in one message that must be toggled to map into another.)

### 6.2.1 Single-Error Detecting Codes

Single-error detecting (SED) codes are capable of detecting a single error in the transmitted information. Single bit parity checking is used extensively for single-error detecting facility. A parity check method consists of adding an extra bit of information to the unit of data. If the data consist of $n - 1$ bits, a parity bit of either 0 or 1 is used in the $n$th place so that the entire $n$ positions have either an even or odd number of 1.

The value of the parity bit (0 or 1) depends on whether the sum of the bits with value 1 in the unit of data being checked is odd or even. If the total number of bits with value 1, including the parity bit, is even, the unit of data is said to have even parity; if it is odd, it is said to have odd parity. All the subsystems of a system usually use either even or odd parity to maintain consistency.

Obviously, a single bit parity checking method is a single-error detecting code, since any single error in transmission leaves an incorrect number of 1s in the code word.

The redundancy ratio of single-error detecting codes with the single parity check method is $R = n/(n - 1)$. We see that to achieve low redundancy $n$ should be large. However, with large $n$, the probability of an error also increases. We also see that in the single bit parity check method the parity check involves all the bits of the code word.

### 6.2.2 Single-Error Correcting Code

In single-error correcting (SEC) Hamming codes, $k$ parity bits instead of a single parity bit are assigned to the $m$ information bits. These $k$ parity bits check parity for certain positions of the $m$ information bits and are determined by an encoding process.

Because the $k$ syndrome bits must give the position of a single error, the $k$ bits must describe $m + k + 1$ different things. So the requirement on the size of $k$ parity bits is that

$$2^k \geq m + k + 1$$

*or*, writing $m + k = n$,

$$2^m \leq \frac{2^n}{n + 1}$$

Using this inequality, Table 6.1 gives the maximum $m$ and $k$ for a given $n$. Table 6.2 illustrates the redundancy ratio and code efficiency for common word lengths.

Because the error code bits or check bits ($k$) must increase in increments of 1 bit, and since each added bit provides error correction and detection for a range of data bits, the redundancy ratio ($R$) and the coding efficiency (CE) are discontinuous functions of each change in $k$. From

## 6.2 Error-Detecting and Error-Correcting Codes

**Table 6.1 CODE LENGTH MESSAGES AND HAMMING DISTANCE**

| Code Bits $n$ | Information Bits $m$ | Check Bits $k$ |
|---|---|---|
| 1 | 0 | 1 |
| 2 | 0 | 2 |
| 3 | 1 | 2 |
| 4 | 1 | 3 |
| 5 | 2 | 3 |
| 6 | 3 | 3 |
| 7 | 4 | 3 |
| 8 | 4 | 4 |
| 9 | 5 | 4 |
| 10 | 6 | 4 |
| 11 | 7 | 4 |
| 12 | 8 | 4 |
| 13 | 9 | 4 |
| 14 | 10 | 4 |
| 15 | 11 | 4 |
| 16 | 11 | 5 |
| 17 | 12 | 5 |
| 18 | 13 | 5 |
| 19 | 14 | 5 |
| 20 | 15 | 5 |
| 21 | 16 | 5 |
| ... | ... | ... |

**Table 6.2 REDUNDANCY RATIO AND CODE EFFICIENCY**

| Check Bits | $k$ | 4 | 5 | 6 | 7 | 8 |
|---|---|---|---|---|---|---|
| Information bits, max = $2^k - k - 1$ | $m$ | 4–11 | 11–26 | 26–57 | 57–120 | 120–247 |
| Total code word bits $n = m + k$ | | 8–15 | 16–31 | 32–63 | 64–127 | 128–255 |
| Redundancy ratio, $R = n/m$ | | $\frac{8-15}{4-11}$ | $\frac{16-31}{11-26}$ | $\frac{32-63}{26-57}$ | $\frac{64-117}{57-120}$ | $\frac{128-255}{120-247}$ |
| Code efficiency, CE = $m/n$ | | $\frac{4-11}{8-15}$ | $\frac{11-26}{16-31}$ | $\frac{26-57}{32-63}$ | $\frac{57-120}{64-127}$ | $\frac{120-247}{128-255}$ |

Tables 6.1 and 6.2 we see that as word length increases the redundancy ratio decreases and the code efficiency increases rapidly.

The redundancy ratio is a fairly good measure of the cost increase and increase in overhead resulting from the addition of error detection and correction to a memory system. Because these extra check bits have to be shared in memory, the redundancy ratio represents the relative cost of the additional storage required to store the check bits. Besides the cost of these additional storage bits, the overhead for these extra bits is the cost of parity generators, decoders and comparators, and error correction logic. As the redundancy ratio is high for smaller word lengths, intuitively we would expect the cost of EDAC circuitry to be a large percentage of the total cost for short-word-length memory systems and the cost of EDAC to decrease for long-word memory systems.

### 6.2.3 Positioning of Check Bits and Circuitry

The $k$ parity bits check certain positions of $m$ information bits and generate correction information in case of an error. Let us call the $k$ parity bits

$$c_1, \ldots, c_k$$

and the $m$ information bits

$$I_1, \ldots, I_m$$

The check bits can be positioned in several different ways. The check bits can be dispersed within the bits or collected at the end. The manner in which the parities are computed also can be changed in numerous ways.

If a bit in an $m$-bit data word is in error, two or more syndrome (error) bits will be 1 for a normal assignment. On the other hand, if one of the stored parity bits is in error, it will simply cause one syndrome bit to equal 1 when compared with the recomputed parity bit.

In Figure 6.2(a) an arbitrary assignment has been made in which every bit in the original 16-bit word has been assigned as an input to either two or three of the $k$ check parities ($C_i$). The particular selection was made on an arbitrary basis, and the bits involved in computing each check parity are illustrated in Figure 6.2(b). Each check parity bit is formed by simply connecting the appropriate set of data bits into a parity network as illustrated. As an example, parity check bit $C_1$ involves data bits $b0$, $b1$, $b2$, $b3$, $b4$, $b5$, $b6$, $b7$, and $b11$. Other check bits or parity bits would involve a different combination of the data bits. The 16-bit data word is illustrated as a square array simply to highlight the overlapping check-bit fields.

Figure 6.3 shows the circuitry required to implement a single-error correcting code. In this example it is assumed that the parity or check bits are computed by a set of five parity circuits. The same parity network might be used to generate the parity bits when the word is orginally stored

## 6.2 Error-Detecting and Error-Correcting Codes

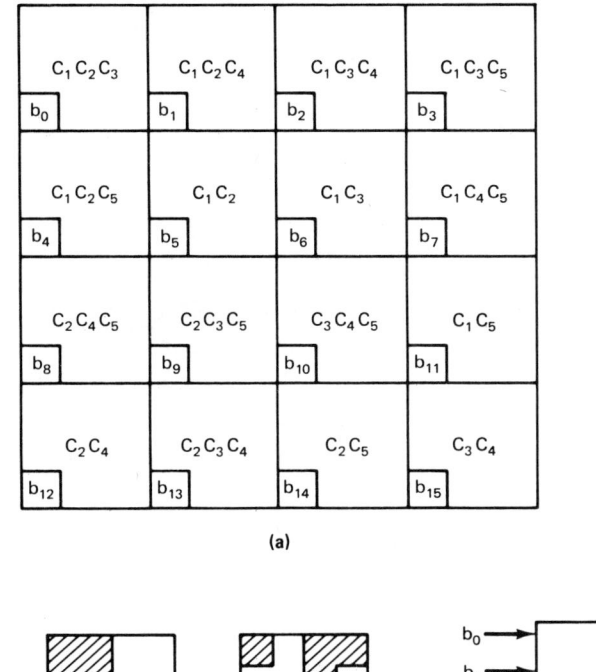

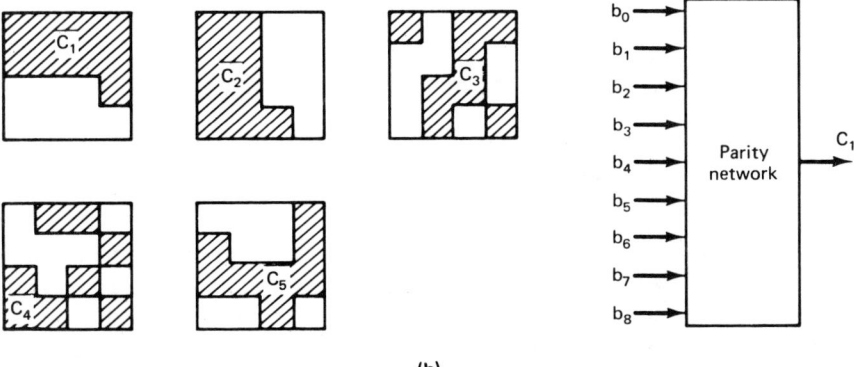

**Figure 6.2.** (a) Assignment of Data Bits to Check Parities; (b) Data Bits Involved in Various Parity Computations: Assignment Maps.

and also when the parity is recomputed for checking. For convenience, the stored check bits have been labeled with a superscript $s$ and the recomputed check bits are labeled with a superscript $c$ in Figure 6.3.

To generate the syndrome bits, the corresponding stored check bit and recomputed check bit are connected into an exclusive OR circuit. If the two check bits agree, the resultant output is a 0 (the syndrome bit is 0). On the other hand, if they differ, the syndrome bit will be 1. In Figure

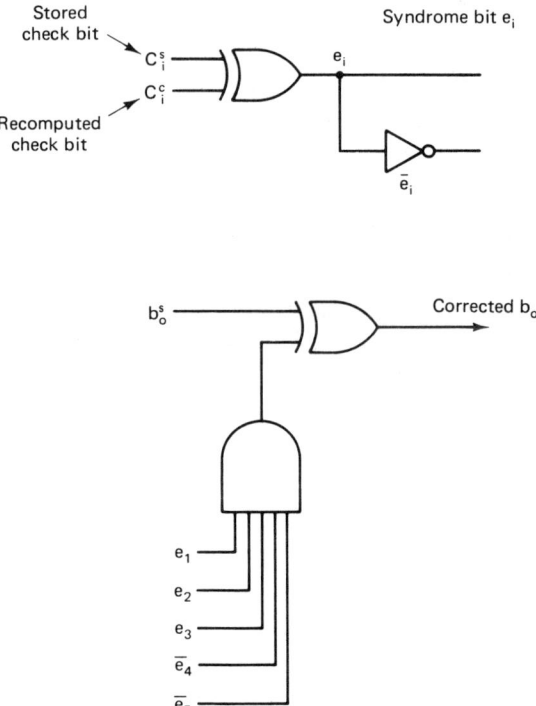

**Figure 6.3.** Error Correction Circuitry.

6.3 the syndrome bits are labeled $e$. To correct a specific bit in the original data word, it is only necessary to use the available information. For example, if $b_0$ were in error, syndrome bits 1, 2, and 3 would all be 1, and syndrome bits 4 and 5 would be 0. If syndrome bits $e_1$, $e_2$, $e_3$, $\overline{e_4}$, and $\overline{e_5}$ are connected to a five-input AND gate, the resultant output would uniquely identify bit 0 as being in error. If the stored bit ($b_0$) is connected into an exclusive OR circuit along with the signal from the gate circuit, the resultant output is corrected or toggled back to its original value. If the gate signal is zero, the bit is not altered. Each bit in the original data word requires generation of a control signal and use of an exclusive OR to correct the result in case of error. The amount of circuitry involved, however, is not large. Because, typically, four or eight exclusive OR circuits are found in a package and several AND gates are in a package, the number of integrated circuits required to implement the logic is modest.

It also is true that the performance penalty introduced by the error-checking circuitry is not very large, particularly if the circuitry is made with very fast logic. Assuming that the parity network has a delay of two or three unit gate delays, a total of five to six gate delays is required to correct a word. If, for example, high-speed Schottky or ECL circuits are used, the additional access delay may be no more than 10 to 30 ns. In many systems this additional delay may be unimportant.

The fraction of additional bits required for error correction to the number of bits in a data word becomes progressively smaller as the word length is made long. As a consequence, it is desirable to organize memories, as far as error correction is concerned, with long word lengths. If the memory is of any substantial size, this is conveniently done.

By the addition of another check bit for the 16-bit data word example given, double-bit error detection can be achieved as well as single-bit error correction. This property can be illustrated in the following way.

Let every data bit be involved in three of the six check bits with every data bit involving a unique combination of check bits. (Note three items out of six without regard to order can be chosen 20 ways, which is greater than the 16 needed.) Thus a failure of a single data bit will cause three syndrome bits to be logical 1s, whereas if a check bit failed, only one syndrome bit would be a logical 1.

If two bits involved in computing a parity both fail, the syndrome bit would indicate no error. Thus the number of syndrome bits that would be a logical 1 would be reduced. This results in having an even number of syndrome bits that are logical 1s when two bits are in error. The number can be 2, 4, or 6 as indicated next in the example. Distinct and different from the three in case of single data error.

$$\begin{matrix} \text{bits} \\ \text{in} \\ \text{error} \end{matrix} \begin{cases} \text{bit \# 1} & \widehat{e_1} \, e_2 & \widehat{e_4} \\ \text{bit \# 2} & e_1 & e_3 \, e_4 \end{cases} \leftarrow \begin{matrix} \text{syndrome bits in} \\ \text{case of single errors.} \end{matrix}$$

syndrome bits removed by double errors.

An error in one or two check bits also leads to an even number of syndrome bits.

## 6.3 RELIABILITY ANALYSIS

Error detecting and correcting codes greatly improve the data integrity of a memory subsystem. In this section we shall quantify the improvement through reliability analysis of various codes that are implemented in memory systems. We shall (1) examine traditional reliability theory, and (2) analyze the impact of error detecting and correction on memory system reliability.

### 6.3.1 Traditional Reliability Theory

Reliability is usually defined as the likelihood that components or equipment will continue to operate successfully for a time ($t$). It is specifically the probability of survival of the equipment or the system over some specified time interval. It also indirectly indicates the probability of failure of a system during its normal operating life. Since a system consists of some number of components, the reliability of the total system is affected by the reliability of its elements.

The classical approach develops a functional relationship between component reliability and system reliability by categorizing the impact of reliability of components on the system. It partitions the system into the following three categories:

> *Series system:* If a failure in any one of the components can cause the entire system to fail, the system is classified as a series system.
>
> *Parallel system:* If failure only in all the components causes the entire system to fail, the system is classified as a parallel system.
>
> *Binomial system:* This is a special case of a parallel system where $n$ components operate in parallel, but $m$ out of the $n$ components need to be functional for the system to operate.

### 6.3.2 General Reliability Equation

Before we attempt to estimate the reliability of the whole system, we must first consider the failure rate of individual components. Suppose the system consists of a large (ideally infinite) number of components and $N$ of these components are operating after time $t$ (starting from some arbitrary point of reference). As time $t$ increases, $N$ would obviously decrease, so $dN/dt$ is negative (or zero) for all $t$ equal or greater than 0.

From this, we observe that the failures per unit time are also dependent on $t$. The ratio of the rate of decrease of $N$ to $N$ itself at any time $t$ is defined as the failure rate; at the time $t$ it is denoted by

$$\lambda(t) = \frac{dN/dt}{N} \qquad (1)$$

Rearranging this equation

$$\frac{dN}{N} = -\lambda(t)\, dt \qquad (2)$$

## 6.3 Reliability Analysis

If the failure rate $\lambda(t)$ is assumed to be constant, $\lambda$, rather than a function of $t$, then

$$\frac{dN}{N} = -\lambda dt$$

Integrating this expression, we get

$$\log N = -\lambda t + \text{constant}$$

or $\qquad N = Ke^{-\lambda t},$

where $K$ is constant and $e$ = base of the natural log (2.71828). If $K = N_0$, the initial value of $N$, then

$$N = N_0 e^{-\lambda t} \qquad (3)$$

Since $N$ of the components, starting with $N_0$, are operating at time $t$, the probability of a particular item not failing during the time $t$ is given by

$$\frac{N}{N_0} = e^{-\lambda t}$$

This can be thought of as the probability of survival *or* the reliability of the system.
Hence

$$R(t) = e^{-\lambda t} \qquad (4)$$

If we define

$$\tau = \frac{1}{\lambda} \qquad (5)$$

where $\tau$ is the mean time between failure (MTB), we can write

$$R(t) = e^{-t/\tau} \qquad (6)$$

This relationship is usually known as the exponential reliability law *or* exponential failure law.

Figure 6.4 shows the curve of failure rate against operating time for a typical component. This is commonly known as the "bathtub" curve. Note that the failure rate is highest during the early life of the device and

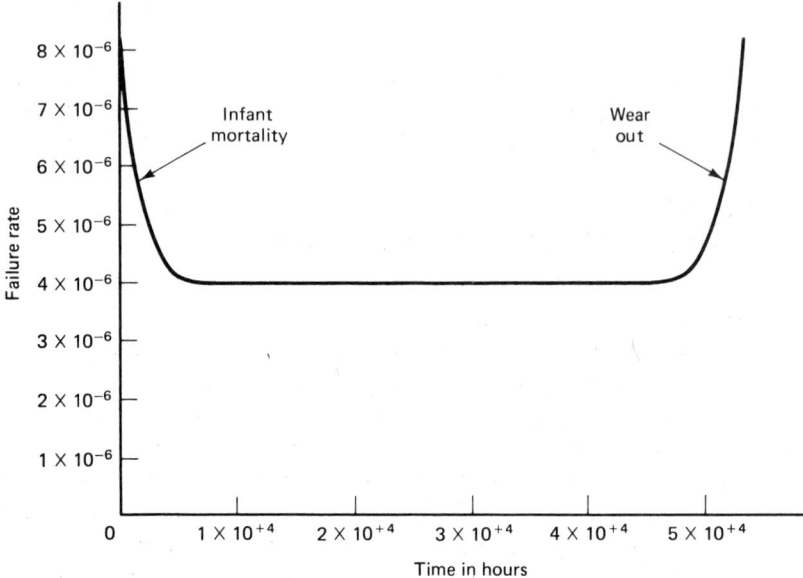

**Figure 6.4.** Hypothetical Component Failure Rate.

is in the "Infant mortality zone." During the useful life or normal operating life, the failure rate is constant and corresponds to random and independent failures; it is only during this period that the reliability estimation of a system using the $N$ components can be made. We see that the failure rate increases again when the device grows old, or in the wear-out zone if one exists.

### 6.3.3 Basic Reliability Distribution Theory

If we define $R(t)$ as the probability of success and $F(t)$ as the probability of failure, then

$$R(t) \cup F(t) = 1$$

and

$$R(t) \cap F(t) = 0$$

The failure probability $F(t)$ can actually be defined as

$$F(t) = \int_0^t f(t)\, dt$$

## 6.3 Reliability Analysis

where $f(t)$ is the failure density function, and the probability of success as

$$R(t) = 1 - F(t) = 1 - \int_0^t f(t)\, dt$$

The probability of failure between two time intervals $t_1$ and $t_2$ can be computed from the probability function

$$P = \int_{t_1}^{t_2} f(t)\, dt$$

and since all the devices of a system have finite lifetimes,

$$P = \int_0^\infty f(t)\, dt = 1$$

Since

$$R(t) = 1 - \int_0^t f(t)\, dt$$

the density function $f(t)$ can be computed from the preceding by differentiating; or

$$f(t) = \frac{dR(t)}{dt}$$

The mean time to failure (MTTF) is given by

$$\text{MTTF} = \int_0^\infty t f(t)\, dt$$

The failure rate $\lambda(t)$ can be determined from any probability distribution by taking the ratio of the failure density function $f(t)$ to the reliability function $R(t)$ or

$$\lambda(t) = \frac{f(t)}{R(t)}$$

For a device that obeys exponential failure law or

$$R(t) = e^{-\lambda t}$$

the failure density function

$$f(t) = \frac{dR(t)}{dt} = \lambda e^{-\lambda t}$$

$$\text{MTTF} = \int_0^\infty t f(t)\, dt$$
$$= 1/\lambda$$

That is, the MTTF of a device following exponential failure law is equal to the reciprocal of the failure rate. This also is often called *mean time between failures* (MTBF).

The failure rate of a device with an exponential reliability is then:

$$\lambda(t) = \frac{f(t)}{R(t)} = \frac{\lambda e^{-\lambda t}}{e^{-\lambda t}} = \lambda$$

Very often, as a first approximation, it is assumed that electronic components follow an exponential distribution. One of the basic properties of the exponential distribution is that failure is independent of time. This property allows one to vary the combination of devices and hours in unit hours of reliability testing $i$; for example, if 20,000 unit hr are required for testing certain components, then either 100 components can be tested for 20 hr or 10 components can be tested for 2000 hr to demonstrate a given reliability. Failure rates are then usually expressed as percent per 1000 hr. If the exponential distribution does not apply, which means the failure rate is not constant with time, reliability cannot be expressed by percent per 1000 hr.

When the failure rate is constant, it can be represented in various ways as follows: Failure rate equivalent statements:

$$0.00001 \text{ failures/hr} = 10 \text{ failures}/10^6 \text{ hr}$$
$$= 0.1\%/100 \text{ hr}$$
$$= 1\%/1000 \text{ hr}$$

So

$$\text{MTTF} = 1/0.00001 = 100{,}000 \text{ hr}$$

To predict the reliability of a general system, the following assumptions must be made [B16]:

## 6.3 Reliability Analysis

1. All the components have constant failure rates; that is, the equipment is operating in its useful life period.
2. The failure of any one component is independent of all other components.
3. Failure rate data are available for all components and pertain to the actual environment to be used.
4. All the components must be functioning for the system to operate.

### 6.3.4 Reliability for a Series System

If the system has $n$ components that are functionally independent of one another, then the system reliability

$$R(t) = \prod_{j=1}^{n} R_j(t)$$

where $R_j(t)$ is the reliability of the $j$th component; that is, the system reliability is the product of the reliability of its individual components.

If these components obey exponential failure distributions and have failures rates of $\lambda_1, \ldots, \lambda_n$, then the system reliability

$$R(t) = e^{-\lambda_1 t} e^{-\lambda_2 t} e^{-\lambda_3 t} \ldots e^{-\lambda_n t}$$

$$= (e) \exp\left[-\sum_{j=1}^{n} \lambda_j t\right]$$

and the MTTF for a series system is

$$\text{MTTF} = \int_0^\infty t(e) \exp\left[-\left(\sum_{j=1}^{n} \lambda_j t\right) dt\right]$$

$$= \frac{1}{\sum_{j=1}^{n} \lambda_j}$$

If all the components have identical or the same failure rate, then the system reliability is given by

$$R(t) = e^{-n\lambda t}$$

and

$$\text{MTTF} = \frac{1}{n\lambda}$$

### 6.3.5 Parallel System Reliability

For a parallel system, all the components of the system must fail in order for the system to fail. Again, if we assume that components are functionally independent, then the probability of system failure is

$$P(F) = \prod_{j=1}^{j=n} P(R_j)$$

where $P(R_j)$ is the probability of failure of $j$th component. So, if $Q(t)$ is the system unreliability and $Qj(t)$ is the unreliability of the $j$th component,

$$Q(t) = \prod_{j=1}^{j=n} Qj(t)$$

and system reliability

$$R(t) = 1 - Q(t)$$

$$= 1 - \prod_{j=1}^{j=n} Q_j(t)$$

$$= 1 - \prod_{j=1}^{j=n} [1 - R_j(t)]$$

Hence, if there are $n$ components with exponential reliabilities and failure rates of $\lambda_1, \lambda_2, \ldots, \lambda_n$ and they operate in parallel for the system, the system reliability equation becomes

$$R(t) = 1 - \prod_{j=1}^{j=n} (1 - e^{-\lambda_j t})$$

And if all the components have the same failure rate, $\lambda$, then

$$r(t) = 1 - (1 - e^{-\lambda t})^n$$

and the MTTF for a parallel system is

$$\int_0^\infty t\,[1 - (1 - e^{-\lambda t})^n]dt$$

### 6.3.6 Binomial System Reliability

For the binomial system, $n$ components operate in parallel, but $m$ out of $n$ components must be functional for the system to operate properly. So, if the probability of a single device operating successfully is

$$R(t) = e^{-\lambda t}$$

then

$$Q(t) = 1 - R(t) = 1 - e^{-\lambda t}$$

So the probability of success and failure for all combinations of $n$ devices is given by the binomial expression $(R + Q)^n$, which is equal to

$$(R + Q)^n = R^n + nR^{(n-1)} Q + \frac{n(n-1)}{2!} R^{(n-2)} Q^2 + \frac{n(n-1)(n-2)}{3!} R^{(n-3)} Q^3 + \ldots + Q^n = 1$$

The first term of the binomial expression is $P_0 = R^n$, which is the probability of all devices operating successfully. The second term, $P_1 = nR^{n-1} Q$, is the probability of only one device failing, the third term $P_2 = [n(n-1)/2!] R^{(n-2)} Q^2$, is the probability of two devices failing ..., and the last term $P_n = Q^n$ is the probability of all devices failing.

The general binomial distribution equation is given by

$$R(t) = \sum_{i=m}^{n} R^m (1 - R)^{n-m}$$

where $R = e^{-\lambda t}$ for components with exponential reliability functions and is the failure rate.

$$\text{MTBF} = \int_0^\infty t \left[ \frac{-d}{dt} \sum_{i=m}^{n} R^m (1 - R)^{n-m} \right] dt$$

## 6.4 IMPACT OF EDAC CODES ON MEMORY SYSTEM RELIABILITY

Reliability improvement in memory subsystems resulting directly from the application of EDAC codes was initially considered by Allen [A5] in 1966. Allen realized that the physical organization of the memory components is very important in obtaining the benefit of EDAC. Allen noted that the organization of conventional core memories was not suitable for simple application of EDAC. To be most effective, the failure of a single device should cause only a single bit to be in error during a read or write operation. In a core memory, failure of a word driver causes many of the bits in a word to be in error. Allen proposed that a physically distinct core memory be used for each bit in a word. That is, for a memory word of $n$ bits, physically there would be $n$ distinct submemories. In such an arrangement, every bit of a word is retrieved independently from a distinct submemory and contains its own address decoding, drivers, and sense circuitry. The greatest advantage of such an organization is that single failures in either the cell, the sense circuitry, or the drive circuitry can be constrained to affect a single bit of this data at most. Because of the physical separation, two errors in a memory word would require that error-enduring failures exist in two submemories with independent groups of components. Allen also proposed that with this type of memory organization the application of single-error correcting codes would tremendously extend the reliability of the memory.

Semiconductor memories usually are organized for application of EDAC codes. Typically, semiconductor memory ICs are arranged so that any one IC contains a certain bit for a group of words. This arrangement ensures that a single IC failure does not cause a failure of 2 or more bits in a word.

### 6.4.1 Semoconductor Memory Organization with SBEC

Semiconductor memory chips usually are organized with $m$ words with word lengths of $n$ bits, usually 1, 2, 4, or 8 bits. For simple error correction, word lengths of 1 are preferable. If the memory size is $S$ bits, then $k = S/m \times n$, chips are used to form this memory. The minimum number of words in a memory will vary with the number of data bits in the device. For example, if a memory is constructed from 4K × 1 RAM and if it has a 32-bit word, then at least 32 4K × 1 RAMS are required if words are to be read or written in a single cycle. Except for small microcomputer

## 6.4 Impact of EDAC Codes on Memory System Reliability

applications, memories involve many more than the minimum number of chips.

Figure 6.5 provides a convenient means of determining the MTBF for memories from the ICs alone for a wide range of memory sizes in terms of the device failure rates when error correcting is not used.

Figure 6.5 is a log/log plot relating the number of memory devices to the mean time between failures, with device failure rate as a parameter. This nomograph is based on simple equation,

$$\text{MTBF} = \frac{1}{d\lambda}$$

where  $d$ = number of devices

$\lambda$ = failure rate of the chip

It should be noted that Figure 6.5 is simply based on RAM devices and does not include other components making up the total memory. It simply illustrates variation of MTBF for various-sized memories over a range of device failure rates.

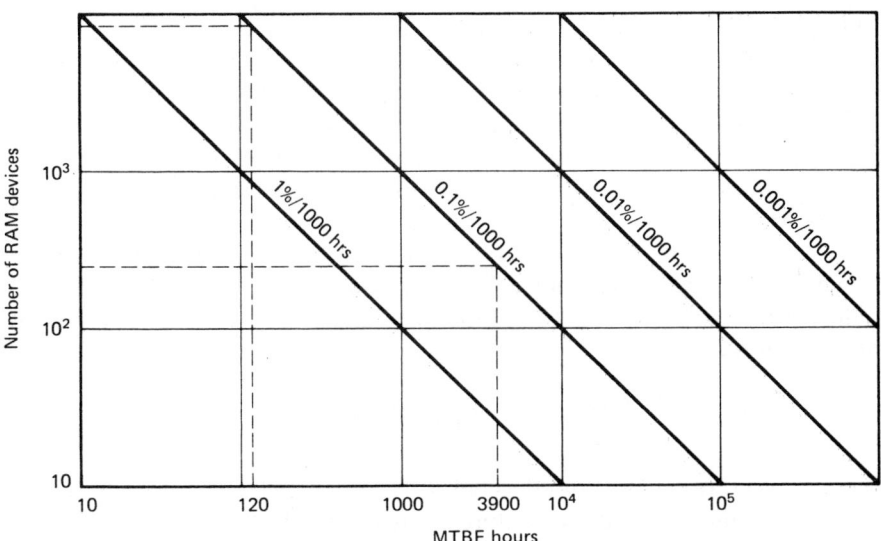

**Figure 6.5.** Relation of Memory Size in Devices to Mean Time between Failures.

## 6.4.2 Reliability Enhancement with SBEC

Error-correction codes can enhance reliability of memories and offset errors that might arise from device failure or from bit errors. For example, experimental results indicate that some 16K dynamic random access memory devices have soft error rates of $10^{-6}$ per hour ($10^{-6}/16{,}384$ per bit per hour). If a 1 million byte memory was organized with 128K 64-bits words and was made from 512 of these memory devices, the soft failure rate, assuming statistical independence, would be

$$512 \times 10^{-6} = 5.1 \times 10^{-4}/\text{hr}$$

The mean time to a soft failure would be 2000 hr or about two and a half months. If the memory were organized with 64-bit words with 7 check bits, and if all locations were read every hour to correct any soft failures that might occur within the hour, the failure rate would be about

$$128{,}000 \times \frac{71 \times 70}{2} \times \left(\frac{10^{-6}}{16{,}384}\right)^2 \left(1 - \frac{10^{-6}}{16{,}384}\right)^{568 \times 16{,}384}$$
$$\approx 1.2 \times 10^{-12} \text{ per hr}$$

(words)   (2 out of 71)   (2 failed)   (good)

This calculation assumes two soft errors in the same word in an hour would be the dominant cause of failure and that the detection logic would not contribute to failures. If the memory were not checked and corrected for soft errors for 100 hours, the chance of failure each hour in the interval would be 100 times greater than if it were checked hourly. Note the dramatic improvement in failure rate in either case over a memory without redundancy.

The same error-correction circuitry can be used for device failure, as well as soft errors, assuming the devices are bit organized. If the device failure rates were $10^{-6}$, the total memory failure rate due to the memory device failure would be

$$512 \times 10^{-6}/\text{hr} \cong 5 \times 10^{-4}/\text{hr}$$

If error correction were added as before, bad devices were replaced within an hour of failure, and the failures caused by the correction logic neglected, the memory failure rate due to device failure would be

$$8 \times \frac{71 \times 70}{2} (10^{-6})^2 (1 - 10^{-6})^{566} = 2 \times 10^{-8} \text{ per hr}$$

(columns)   (2 bad devices)   (good devices)

This calculation again assumes statistically independent device failures; it also assumes that for the memory to fail the two failing devices must hold bits for the same words. The case of three or more devices failing is neglected. Again note the dramatic improvement in failure rate. This advantage diminishes if failed devices are allowed to accumulate in the system and are not replaced. Without maintenance the system with redundancy would have a 50% chance of operating 2000 hr without failure. The nonredundant system would have a 50% chance of operating 1400 hr without failure.

The mean time to a 50% chance of failure ($TM_{50}$) can be computed in the following way, assuming the maintenance interval is much less than the failure time. Let $b_m$ be defined as the maintenance inverval. Then

$$P\left\{\begin{matrix} \text{OK in} \\ b_m \end{matrix}\right\} = P\left\{\begin{matrix} \text{no failures} \\ \text{in } b_m \end{matrix}\right\} + P\left\{\begin{matrix} \text{one device} \\ \text{failure in } b_m \end{matrix}\right\} + P\left\{\begin{matrix} \text{two not} \\ \text{in same} \\ \text{column} \\ \text{in } b_m \end{matrix}\right\}$$

$$P\left\{\begin{matrix} \text{OK} \\ \text{in } b_m \end{matrix}\right\}^s \approx 0.5$$

$$TM_{50} = s \cdot b_m$$

Figure 6.6 is a plot of the reduction in the mean time to failure as the maintenance time is extended.

## 6.5 COMMERCIAL SBEC CIRCUITS

A variety of semiconductor manufacturers make integrated circuits that implement SBEC for memories. The following specifications are for the Advanced Micro Devices AM 2960. It is designed so that single or multiple units can be used for words of 16, 32, 48, or 64 bits. By using more check bits than the minimum required, the code provides for double-error detection as well.

# Am2960
## Cascadable 16-Bit Error Detection and Correction Unit

### ADVANCED DATA

### DISTINCTIVE CHARACTERISTICS

- **Modified Hamming Code**
  Detects multiple errors and corrects single bit errors in a parallel data word. Ideal for use in dynamic memory systems.

- **Expandable**
  One Am2960 provides EDC on 16-bit data words.
  Two Am2960s provide EDC on 32-bit data words.
  Four Am2960s provide EDC on 64-bit data words.

- **Syndromes provided**
  The Am2960 makes available the syndrome bits when an error occurs, so the location of memory faults can be logged.

- **Microprocessor compatible**
  The Am2960 is designed to work with Z8000 microprocessor systems as well as high performance 2900 designs.

- **Advanced circuit and process technologies**
  Newest 2900 LSI techniques provide very high performance.
  Data-in to error detection typically 30ns
  Data-in to correct data out typically 50ns

- **Built-in Diagnostics**
  Extra logic on the chip provides diagnostic functions to be used during device test and for system diagnostics.

### GENERAL DESCRIPTION

The Am2960 Error Detection and Correction Unit (EDC) contains the logic necessary to generate check bits on a 16-bit data field according to a modified Hamming Code, and to correct the data word when check bits are supplied. Operating on data read from memory, the Am2960 will correct any single bit error and will detect all double and some triple bit errors. For 16-bit words, 6 check bits are used. The Am2960 is expandable to operate on 32-bit words (7 check bits) and 64-bit words (8 check bits). In all configurations, the device makes the error syndrome available on separate outputs for data logging.

The Am2960 also features two diagnostic modes, in which diagnostic data can be forced into portions of the chip to simplify device testing and to execute system diagnostic functions. The product is supplied in a 48 lead hermetic DIP package.

### BLOCK DIAGRAM

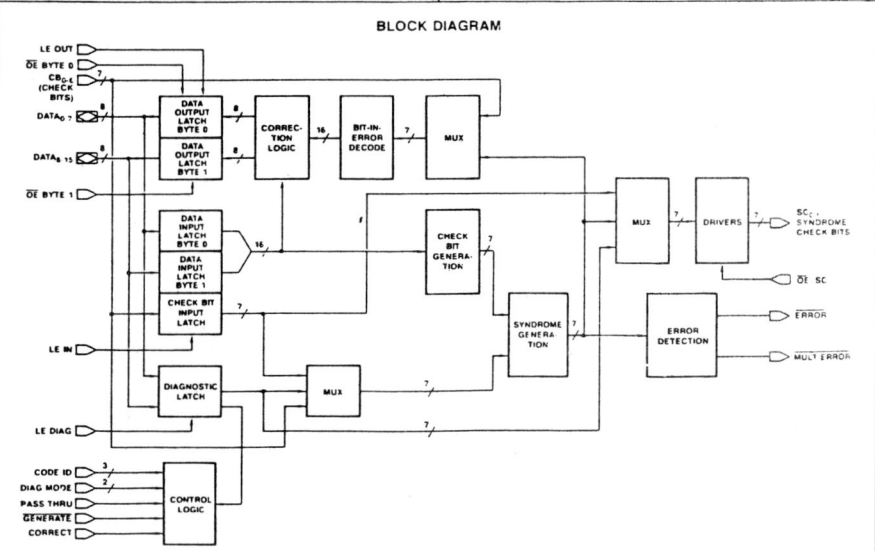

## 6.5 Commercial SBEC Circuits

### EDC Architecture

The EDC Unit is a powerful 16-bit cascadable slice used for check bit generation, error detection, error correction and diagnostics.

As shown in the block diagram, the device consists of the following:

- Data Input Latch
- Check Bit Input Latch
- Check Bit Generation Logic
- Syndrome Generation Logic
- Error Detection Logic
- Error Correction Logic
- Data Output Latch
- Diagnostic Latch
- Control Logic

### Data Input Latch

16 bits of data are loaded from the bidirectional DATA lines under control of the Latch Enable input, LE IN. Depending on the control mode the input data is either used for check bit generation or error detection/correction.

### Check Bit Input Latch

Seven check bits are loaded under control of LE IN. Check bits are used in the Error Detection and Error Correction modes.

### Check Bit Generation Logic

This block generates the appropriate check bits for the 16 bits of data in the Data Input Latch. The check bits are generated according to a modified Hamming code.

### Syndrome Generation Logic

In both Error Detection and Error Correction modes, this logic block compares the check bits read from memory against a newly generated set of check bits produced for the data read in from memory. If both sets of check bits match, then there are no errors. If there is a mismatch, then one or more of the data or check bits is in error.

The syndrome bits are produced by an exclusive-OR of the two sets of check bits. If the two sets of check bits are identical (meaning there are no errors) the syndrome bits will be all zeroes. If there are errors, the syndrome bits can be decoded to determine the number of errors and the bit-in-error.

### Error Detection Logic

This section decodes the syndrome bits generated by the Syndrome Generation Logic. If there are no errors in either the input data or check bits, the $\overline{ERROR}$ and $\overline{MULTI\ ERROR}$ outputs remain HIGH. If one or more errors are detected, $\overline{ERROR}$ goes LOW. If two or more errors are detected, both $\overline{ERROR}$ and $\overline{MULTI\ ERROR}$ go LOW.

### Error Correction Logic

For single errors, the Error Correction Logic complements (corrects) the single data bit in error. This corrected data is loadable into the Data Output Latch, which can then be read onto the bidirectional data lines. If the single error is one of the check bits, the correction logic does not place corrected check bits on the syndrome/check bit outputs. If the corrected check bits are needed the EDC must be switched to Generate Mode.

### Data Output Latch

The Data Output Latch is used for storing the result of an error correction operation. The latch is loaded from the correction logic under control of the Data Output Latch Enable, LE OUT. The Data Output Latch may also be loaded directly from the Data Input Latch under control of the PASS THRU control input.

The Data Output Latch is split into two 8-bit (byte) latches which may be enabled independently for reading onto the bidirectional data lines.

### Diagnostic Latch

This is a 16-bit latch loadable from the bidirectional data lines under control of the Diagnostic Latch Enable, LE DIAG. The Diagnostic Latch contains check bit information in one byte and control information in the other byte. The Diagnostic Latch is used for driving the device when in Internal Control Mode, or for supplying check bits when in one of the Diagnostic Modes.

### Control Logic

The control logic determines the specific mode the device operates in. Normally the control logic is driven by external control inputs. However, in Internal Control Mode, the control signals are instead read from the Diagnostic Latch.

TABLE IV. 16-BIT MODIFIED HAMMING CODE — CHECK BIT ENCODE CHART.

| Generated Check Bits | Parity | Participating Data Bits | | | | | | | | | | | | | | | |
|---|---|---|---|---|---|---|---|---|---|---|---|---|---|---|---|---|---|
| | | 0 | 1 | 2 | 3 | 4 | 5 | 6 | 7 | 8 | 9 | 10 | 11 | 12 | 13 | 14 | 15 |
| CX | Even (XOR) |   | X | X | X |   | X |   |   | X | X |   | X |   | X |   |   |
| C0 | Even (XOR) | X | X | X |   | X |   | X |   | X | X |   | X |   |   |   |   |
| C1 | Odd (XNOR) | X |   |   | X | X |   |   | X |   | X | X |   |   | X |   | X |
| C2 | Odd (XNOR) | X | X |   |   |   | X | X | X |   |   | X | X |   |   |   |   |
| C4 | Even (XOR) |   |   |   | X | X | X | X | X |   |   |   |   |   |   | X | X |
| C8 | Even (XOR) |   |   |   |   |   |   |   |   | X | X | X | X | X | X | X | X |

The check bit is generated as either an XOR or XNOR of the eight data bits noted by an "X" in the table.

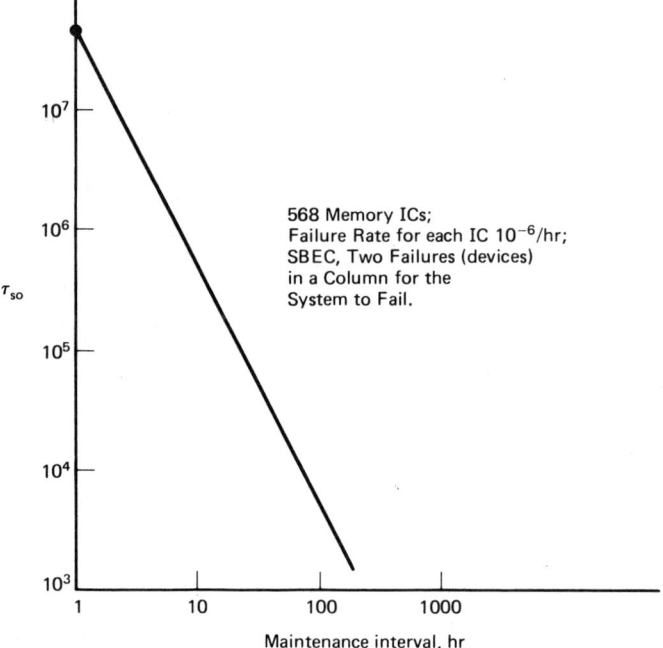

**Figure 6.6.** Effect of Maintenance Interval on Time to 50% Chance of Failure ($T_{50}$).

## PROBLEMS

1. A memory has a 120-bit word length. How many check bits are required to implement single-bit error correction?
2. A memory has a 40-bit word length. Determine the number of check bits required to provide single-bit error correction and double-bit detection.
3. A room has four light bulbs each with an MTBF of 1000 hr. What are the chances that two or more bulbs will be working after 500 hr?

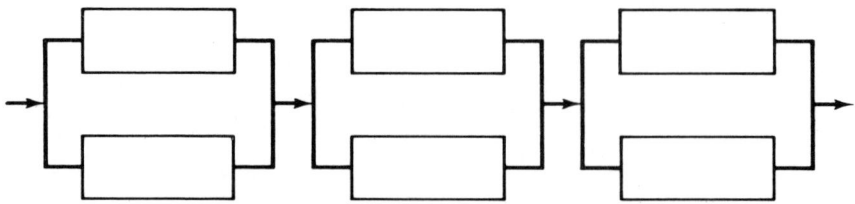

## 6.5 Commercial SBEC Circuits

4. A dual redundant system is composed of the serial parallel arrangement indicated. Determine the probability that the system is working as a function of time; each block has a failure rate of $10^{-6}$ hr. To work, there must be a completed path through the network.
5. A memory with a 48-bit word is to have SBEC with double-error detection. Seven check bits are to be used. Assign the 7 check bits to the various 48 data bits. Design the logic to indicate double errors.
6. Consider a memory that uses 4096 × 1 memory ICs and is organized as 65,536 words of 48 + (7) data bits. Determine the chance of failure in 1000 hr of operation with and without error correction. Assume the IC failure rate is $2 \times 10^{-7}$ and two must fail in the same column for the memory to fail. Neglect the failure rate of the gates in the correction logic.
7. Single-bit error correction becomes more efficient as word length is increased. Determine the efficiency of a 1024-bit word with error correction.
8. For problem 6, assume single failed devices are replaced every 100 hr. Determine the chances that the system has failed in 1000 hr.

# Chapter 7
# Historical Evolution of Hierarchical Memories and Cache Systems

## 7.1 THE HISTORY OF MEMORY HIERARCHIES

The concept of employing transparent memory hierarchies for matching the speed discrepancy between the CPU and memory and giving the user the idea of an infinite-sized memory, has been known for a long time. The first large-scale Electronic Numerical Integrater and Calculator (ENIAC) built at the University of Pennsylvania had a simple hierarchy consisting of 20 temporary storage registers of 10 decimal digits (vacuum tubes) and 312 words of alterable read-only memory, all backed by a storage function of punched cards for storing intermediate results. Here the speed of the calculation was limited by the speed of the punching. Also, as early as 1947, Manchester University in England had designed a first-generation computer using fast index registers, Williams tube memory, and magnetic drum auxiliary storage. Both the main memory and auxiliary storage were organized into fixed-length pages, which were transformed into electro-static storage during program execution.

In 1948, the Selective Sequence Electronic Calculator (SSEC) of IBM also had a hierarchial memory system, which consisted of 20,000 words of paper storage, 150 words of relay memory, and 8 words of electronic memory, each word consisting of 19 digits and a sign [B13]. SSEC was actually IBM's first stored program computer capable of treating its own stored instructions exactly like data, modifying them and acting on the result [A7].

In 1956, the Ferranti Mercury Computer [L5] had used a hierarchical memory system consisting of a small core memory of 40K bits backed by a 640K bit drum store. The memory management responsibility of this system was essentially on the programmers, who had to insert overlay routines for initiating all memory transfers between storage levels. Because efficient memory management required detailed knowledge of the system, it was found that experienced programmers could use the system efficiently, whereas many other programmers spent most of their time doing inefficient transfer of information between two levels.

Suitable interpretive coding for permitting the two-level system to appear as one level has been proposed by Brooker [B15]. This was, however, accompanied by an effective loss of machine speed.

In 1958, Bucholz [B12] had proposed a two-level memory hierarchy scheme consisting of 512 fast words, (0.5-microsecond ($\mu$s)) backed by a large, slow backing store (8K, 12-$\mu$s core blocks) for the IBM stretch computer. The stretch computer had the goal to achieve two orders of performance improvements over the then-existing 704. To achieve this, the CPU was organized into two asynchronous units: an instruction unit and an execution unit with separate instruction and operand memories. By partitioning memory into independent asynchronous units that could be accessed independently, and by placing the instructions and operand in different memory modules, it was possible to overlap instruction and operand fetch memory cycles and to achieve a high-instruction execution rate [B14].

The UNIVAC Larc-1 system [E3,E4] also used a simple memory hierarchy system consisting of a 4-$\mu$s main memory with a 1-$\mu$s buffer, and a complex pipelining scheme of four macroinstructions. In Larc-1, while instruction $I_n$ was being fetched, the operand address of instruction $I_{n-1}$ was being modified (indexed), the operand for instruction $I_{n-2}$ was being fetched, and instruction $I_{n-3}$ was being executed. This overlap control logic for maintaining an orderly execution of instructions through the pipeline was quite complex. Besides providing overlapped memory operation, Larc-1 provided 99 fast-access registers to minimize memory reference.

The storage organization scheme of these first-generation computers had tremendous impact on the second-generation computers, starting with ICL Atlas.

## ICL Atlas Virtual Memory System

Even though the concept of *virtual memory,* a technique that gives the illusion of an infinite memory to the user and that automates all memory

## 7.1 The History of Memory Hierarchies

management problems, had been known for quite some time, it was only in 1961 that this idea was implemented for the first time. ICL Atlas computer was the first successful implementation of a "user transparent, completely automated, one-level, virtual memory system" [K8]. Even though this system employed a storage hierarchy, to the user it appeared as a single, one-level monolithic storage structure. The Atlas machine actually consisted of a three-level storage hierarchies, a private store, a central store and a backing store (as shown in Figure 7.1).

The private store was strictly visible to the internal machine architecture only; it was completely transparent to the user. The private store actually consisted of two subunits, a fixed store and a subsidiary store. The fixed-store concept used in Atlas was analogous to the concept of microprogram store prevalent in machines today. This fixed store pro-

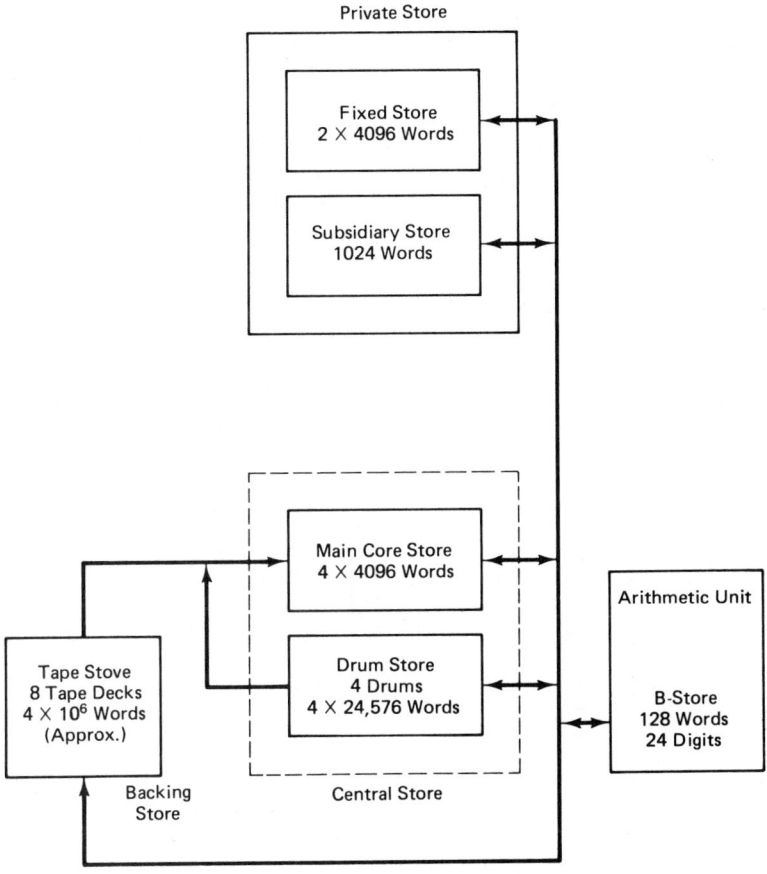

**Figure 7.1.** Atlas Memory Hierarchy System

vided permanent read-only storage functions for frequently needed, complex mathematical functions, I/O conversion routines, and storage management routines.

This fixed store was organized in two separate units; each unit consisted of 4096 words (each word being 50 bits), organized into 16 columns of 256 words (Figure 7.2). The access time to a word in a particular column was 0.4 $\mu$s and access to a word involving column change was 1.4 $\mu$s. The subsidiary core store consisted of 1024 words of temporary storage, which provided working space for fixed-store programs.

The central store consisted of a core and drum store combination with a maximum address capability of $10^6$ words. The core store was organized into four stacks, with each stack being 4096 words, and the drum capacity was 96,000 words organized in 4 drums. Both the core and drum were partitioned into fixed page size of 512 words, and the basic unit of data transfer between core and drum was 512 words. The tape store provided very large capacity (4 million words) basic storage for the machine. The data were transferred between the tape and control store also in units of 512 words.

The main core store address was provided by either the central machine, the drum or the tape system. The access to core was controlled with a fixed priority, with the drum having the highest priority, then the tape, and then the processor with the lowest priority.

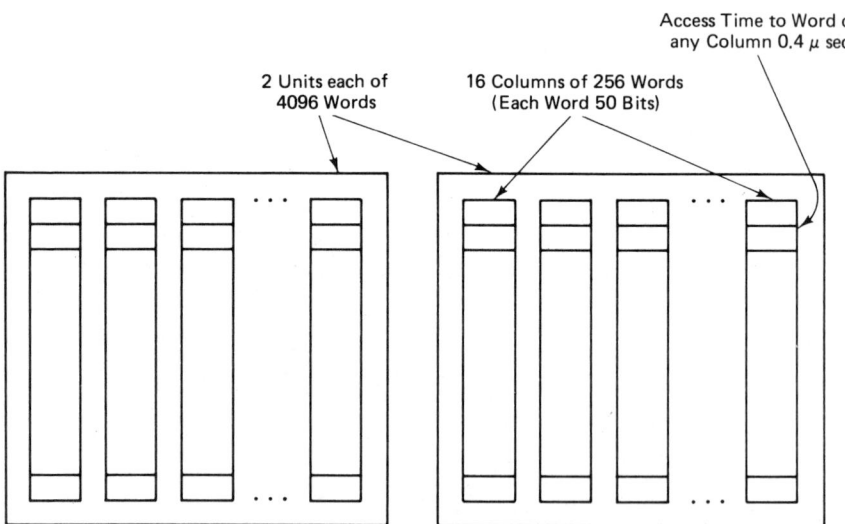

**Figure 7.2.** Atlas Fixed Store

## Core Arrangement

The core store was split into four independent stacks (each with its own individual address decoding and read/write mechanism), which could be accessed simultaneously. The stacks were arranged in two pairs, the first pair containing the first addressable half of the core store and the second pair containing the other half. These stack pairs were, in a way, interleaved; that is, the contiguous physical addresses were arranged across alternate stacks, which permitted the accessing of a pair of instructions in a single-store cycle with one store request. A pair of instruction buffer registers and address buffer registers were provided to minimize the number of accesses to the core and improve the overlapping of one address equivalencing with another.

The greatest effort made to alleviate the speed disparity between the CPU and the core store was the provision of 128 fast B registers (index registers) from which CPU could obtain half-word operand at approximately the matching speed of the CPU. These registers had dedicated usage; some were used by the system routines and some were available to the user.

These registers were used as follows:

Eight registers were special-purpose registers, used for organization procedures.

Eight registers were used to hold the addresses of main instructions, extra code and interrupt controls to permit rapid switching of procedures.

Some registers were specifically used solely by system routines.

Some were of limited utility to the user.

Some were used by different compilers for storing indexes and addresses of data descriptions for address modifications.

However, it was found that, except in some hand coded programs, these explicitly used registers were inefficiently used in the compiled code of programs written in high-level languages. Consequently, the provision of these registers did not really significantly reduce the number of actual main store accesses or alleviate the mismatch between the CPU speed and the main store.

## Memory Management of Atlas

The storage hierarchy was managed automatically as a single "one-level" storage structure by the system. The user did not have to worry about overlay problems; the data-transfer mechanism was completely transparent to the user. Both the core store and the drum store were partitioned into logical page size of 512 words. Even though the system had a physical storage capacity of only 32 pages (core store of 16K words) and drum store of 96K words, the total local addressing capability for all users was 20 bits, allowing a maximum of $10^6$ words. Thus, the primary store had a capacity of only 32 pages, while the secondary store had a capacity of 2048 pages.

Since each logical page could reside in any of the 32 physical pages, to expedite the address translation mechanism, the system provided a set of 32 associated page address registers (PAR), one address register for each physical page; and address translation was provided by a simple *tag* search mechanism.

The higher-order 11 bits of the logical address served as the logical page number or tag, which was compared in an associative fashion with the tag contents of all 32 registers. If there was a match, the matched PAR provides the proper decoded physical page number, which was concatenated with the word offset within the page to generate proper physical address. If there was no match, an interrupt routine was invoked to initiate some proper data transfer between drum and core.

An intelligent drum transfer *learning program* was devised to minimize the data transfer time between the core and drum and to maximize the page hit ratio. This learning program is equivalent to the familiar replacement algorithms. One track, on each drum, was used to identify absolute block positions around the drum periphery. Efforts were made to minimize the time of writing a transfer to drum by writing the required block into an available empty block position on any drum, and the transfer was controlled by referencing the subsidiary directory. This subsidiary directory was updated only when an actual data transfer took place.

Upon entry to the drum transfer program, the first action was to decide the absolute position on a drum of the required page or block. This drum transfer program was initiated as soon as it received a request for a read transfer from drum. Furthermore, to expedite data transfer between core and drum and also to overlap the time for the learning program into the wait period for the read transfer or into the transfer time itself, an empty *or* vacant page position was provided in the core. As soon as the absolute position of the required block was determined in the drum, order was given to carry out data transfer from drum into this empty page position in core, with the transfer occurring automatically as soon as the drum reached the correct angular position. The page address register in the vacant position was set to an appropriate block number for drum transfer.

The data transfer from the drum to the empty page location in core completed half of the learning programs replacement activity. As soon as

## 7.1 The History of Memory Hierarchies

this data transfer from drum to the empty page location in core was complete, the learning program was activated to select a proper page in the core to transfer to drum. This was to ensure an empty page slot for the next read request to the drum. This appropriate block selection was very carefully chosen by the learning program to minimize data transfer time and maximize hit ratio. In order for this learning program to have some data to operate on and not to select its page replacement decision on a completely random basis, usage history (in the form of a use digit) was maintained for each page. This use digit was set to 1 whenever any word of that page was accessed. The learning program could read all the 32 use digits (of all the PARs), with the reading automatically resetting them to zero. However, the frequency with which these use digits were read was controlled by a clock, which measured not real time but the number of instructions executed in the operation of the main program. These use bits were read every time 1024 instructions had been executed.

Besides the page usage digits, two other dynamic parameters associated with each page were maintained: (1) the total length of usage of that page ($t$), and (2) the total period of inactivity of that page ($T$). The frequency with which the usage digits were inspected determined the accuracy of the values of $t$ and $T$.

The page to be transferred from the core to the drum was selected based on the following three simple tests (in order of priority): remove the page that has

1. $t > T + 1$
2. the page with nonzero $t$ ($t \neq \phi$) and maximum $(T - t)$
3. maximum value of $T$ with all $t = 0$

$t = 0$ implied that the page was in use.

The first rule selected the page that had been out of use for the longest time (and least likely to be used by the program). The second rule ignored all pages that were in current use *and* selected the page that was not needed for the longest time. If it could not find a page in this category, it selected a page from all the pages that were being used with a maximum $T$ (total period of inactivity). If the same page was required again, $T$ was set to $\phi$ and it was hoped that the same mistake would not be repeated again.

Even though Atlas was not a true multiprogrammed machine, it demonstrated the feasibility of implementing a simple and elegant one-level automated storage mechanism. Even though the store had the capability of storing many programs, the CPU did not switch to a separate program during address mismatch. The CPU basically remained unproductive during program transfer and thus represented a very serious performance limitation. While it was true that an experienced programmer, knowledgeable about the internal details of the machine, could organize an efficient data-transfer scheme, it represented a tremendous burden on the user and often resulted in inefficiency. From Atlas experience it was learned that the system should be designed to permit multiple users with mechanisms provided to switch CPU between users wherever CPU became idle during long operations (especially during I/O activity and page transfer). Also, it was realized that, instead of partitioning the storage into the size of fixed natural units (page), the partitioning should be allowed to be varied (should be partitioned into segments).

Atlas architecture had tremendous impact in the second- and third-generation machines of the 1960s. Before Atlas, the solutions to memory hierarchy problems had been either too expensive or too inefficient. Memory hierarchy problems were solved either by the provision of a very large and expensive core store, for example, 2.5-Mbit store at MIT [P7] or by the use of user manageable two-store hierarchy, that is, a small core store (40,000 bits) expanded to 640,000 bits by a drum store, as in Ferranti Mercury. In the later system, the user had to worry about all the data-transfer problems.

What is impressive about the Atlas machine is that, even though the machine was designed about two decades back, the designers had provided a clever, cheaper scheme for implementing an efficient virtual memory system. Although it was not realized at the time the machine was designed, the machine had features of the microprogrammed, cache, paged virtual memory system found today. Issues of mechanisms and policies were very clearly thought out, and a very elegant virtual memory solution to the memory management problem was provided.

From Atlas experience, Kilburn and others suggested the use of a tunnel diode-fast core store combination *or* even the use of a faster-slower core store combination for high-performance systems. This had a direct impact on ETL-MK6 systems.

The ETL-MK6 computer [T1] also employed a three-level memory hierarchy and was characterized by its special use of high-speed memories. On the lowest level it had magnetic drums with 258,048 words (48 bits each). At the intermediate level it had two ferrite core memories of 4096 words each with a 2-$\mu$s cycle time, and at the top level it had two tunnel diode memories of 64 words each with 250-ns cycle time (Figure 7.3). The tunnel diode memories were further divided into three sections: 32 words of program stack, 64 words of arithmetic stack, and 32 index registers. The arithmetic stack and the index registers were available to the programmers, whereas the program stack was not available. Even though from the logical designer's point of view, ETL-MK6 had three levels of memory, it gave the illusion of a single-level memory of $2^{18}$ words. The 32 words of program stack were of very high speed and were

## 7.1 The History of Memory Hierarchies

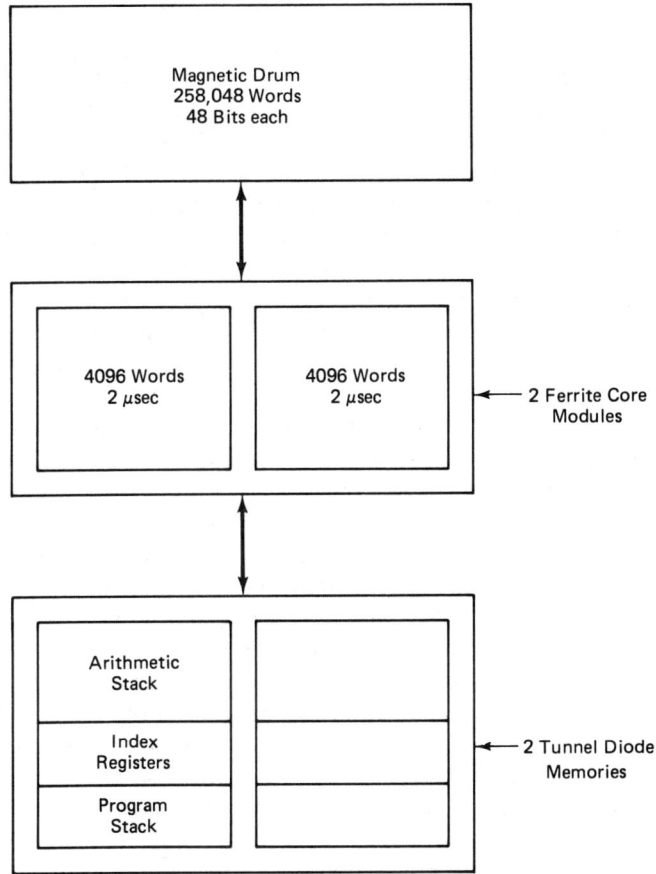

**Figure 7.3.** Three-level Memory Hierarchy of ETL-MK6 System

essentially used for storing 64 steps of program currently under execution and accumulating instructions as they were taken out of memory. Just by storing a few instructions and utilizing the large loop behavior of programs, it was possible to achieve significant performance improvements for program execution.

### Look-Aside Memory

To deal with the problem of high logic-to-memory speed ratio, Bloom, Cohen, and Porter [B1] proposed the scheme of a look-aside, instead of look-ahead, memory. Based on the locality principle of observed program behavior, they proposed the provision of a small, fast associative storage.

This associative storage consisted of a set of high-logic speed registers and was completely transparent to the programmers (i.e., it was never directly addressable by the programmers), even though philosophically it was part of the main memory. This associative storage basically served as an information accelerator. Each look-aside register consisted of three sections: (1) memory or cell address, (2) data or cell contents, and (3) usage indicators (control part), as shown in Figure 7.4.

The store address portion of the look-aside registers was connected to a logical comparator, which had the capability of comparing simultaneously the memory address in the look-aside register with the memory address requested by the processor. If the address match took place, the contents of the cell were made available to the processor immediately, thus obviating the need for a memory transaction. Only when the data requested by the processor were not found in the cells or the look-aside registers were memory transactions initiated and the contents of the cell along with the cell address placed on their respective places in the look-aside registers.

To implement an effective replacement algorithm to decide which look-aside register to displace to memory, Bloom and others departed from the classical digital approach and used analog usage indicators by associating a condenser with each look-aside register. The condenser was charged each time the corresponding look-aside register was accessed. Thus, at any given time the charge residing in the condenser decided the most recent usage of that particular look-aside register, and the condenser associated with the lowest amount of voltage was associated with the register not referenced by the processor for the longest time. They also discussed a more sophisticated approach of using two condensers per each register, one of which was charged to full voltage and the other charged with a constant increment each time the register was accessed.

Using a very complex command and index register structure, they were able to drastically reduce the number of instructions in a loop, thus reducing the number of look-aside registers. It was realized by them that the number of look-aside registers directly affected the speed of the machine. They also concluded that the number of look-aside registers should be at least equal to the number of instructions in the loop plus the number of accumulators and index registers used by the loop in order to be efficient.

Lee [L1] also proposed an improved version of this look-aside memory. He had realized that the gain in this look-aside memory system performance depended on four things: (1) the size of the fast associative memory, (2) the speed ratio of the associative memory to the main memory, (3) the replacement algorithm, and (4) the object program that was being run on the system. To improve the performance, he proposed a

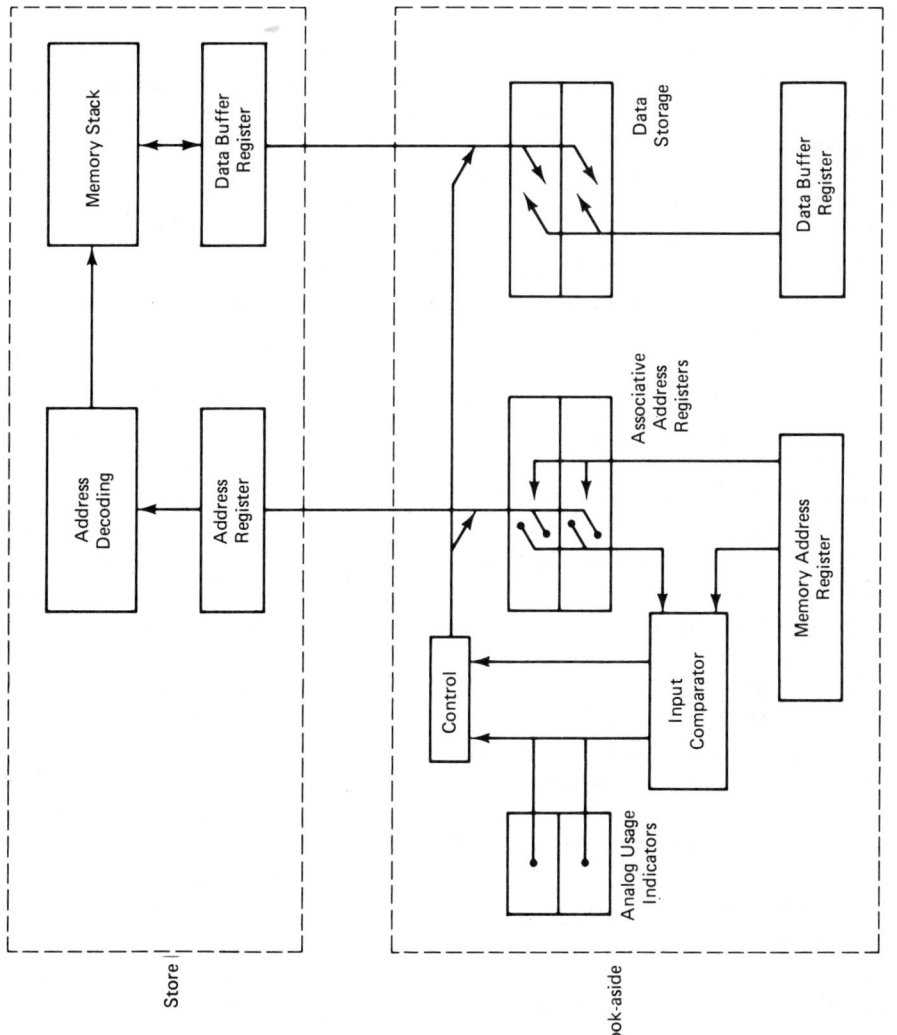

**Figure 7.4.** Bloom, Cohen, and Porter's Look-Aside Store

slightly different scheme. Like the look-aside memory structure of Bloom and others, Lee's memory consisted of three parts: an address part, a data part, and a control part. But the control part was organized a little differently. Lee's control part consisted of a bit that indicated whether the data had been altered since their last transfer from the main memory, and another bit that was used as a pointer. The cell with 1 bit at its pointer position was the one to be purged or replaced when the transfer of a new word from the main memory had to take place. It was made sure that, of all the words in the associative store, only one word could have a 1 bit at the pointer position, the rest of them being zero.

## Wilkes's Slave Memory

M. V. Wilkes [W1], in 1965, discussed the use of a fast core memory of 32K words serving as a *slave* memory to a larger and slower core memory of 1 million words, as a scheme of implementing dynamic storage allocation and to achieve the effective cycle time of the fast core. By a slave memory, he implied a scheme that allowed the fast memory to accumulate automatically. The information that came from the slower memory made it available to the processor for subsequent use; this avoided the penalty of incurring main memory accesses. Wilkes outlined the basis for a satisfactory two-level storage system without involving a high degree of complexity in the hardware. He considered various schemes for a computer system that had a working memory of 32K words and 1-$\mu$s access time, backed up by a large core memory of 1 million words and with an 8-$\mu$s cycle time.

In the simplest scheme, Wilkes considered the splitting of programs into 32K word blocks with each user making use of one or more blocks for his program. A base register was provided for the large core memory and contained the starting address of the currently active 32K block of core memory. Also, each base register was associated with two tag bits; the first tag bit indicated whether the block (word) had been copied in the fast memory or not, and the second tag bit indicated if the block (word) since copies had been changed. He operated the slave memory on the principle of locality of program behavior and used a flagged swap algorithm to transfer information between the fast and slow stage to minimize the traffic and improve efficiency. Also, he advocated the need of avoiding transferring of all of 32K words of data from the store to the slave, because only a small fraction of 32K words was actually going to be used.

Upon any reference to the memory, the fast memory was accessed first, and if the first tag bit was a 1, no reference was made to the slow memory. This was true for both read and write operations. If a word in

## 7.1 The History of Memory Hierarchies

the fast memory was changed, the second tag bit was changed from 0 to 1 (Figure 7.5). Thus, gradually the fast memory accumulated all the words of program in active use. When a new program became active, the number in the base register was changed to correspond to the corresponding 32K words of block, and a FS algorithm was used to displace information from the slave memory to the slow store. All the registers having a 0 in their first tag bits were not affected at all and neither were all the other registers having 10 in their tag bits; only the registers having 11 in their tag bits were affected. Since this scheme did not use the write-through (WT), algorithm, there was a need of transferring changed block from the fast memory to the slow memory.

Wilkes also proposed some schemes for organizing a memory serving as slave to various blocks of main memory. Most of the concepts advocated by him are used in modern-day cache systems; for example,

1. IBM 360/85 validity bits associated with blocks are the same concept of dynamic tag bits suggested by Wilkes.
2. The desire to transfer partial amount of buffer rather than the whole buffer was also suggested by Wilkes and used in the IBM 360/85 system.

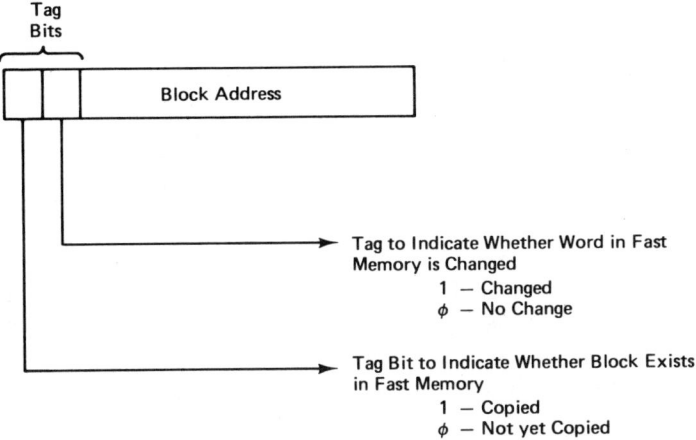

**Figure 7.5.** Wilkes's Tagged Bits Scheme

### Anderson and Glaser's System

Anderson and Glaser [A1] also discussed systems philosophy for the use of a hierarchical memory in kilomegacycle computer systems. The hierarchy considered by them consisted of the following:

1. A relatively small, very high speed fixed-access memory matched to state-of-the-art logic.
2. A much larger and slower fixed-access-time secondary storage.
3. Even slower, a fixed-random access time tertiary store such as discs, drums, or photographic storage.
4. If desired, an additional level of memory consisting of tapes, cards, and so on.

The mechanism for making use of the hierarchical memory, as considered by them, was inextricably interwoven with the philosophy of basic program structure. Considering an ALGOL 60 block structured feature program, they pointed out that the very high speed store need only be large enough to contain the elements of a program (instruction and data) "active" at a given time, while the larger store could be used to contain those elements of the program that are logically in the immediate path of the computational flow, and consequently may be required less directly.

According to their tentative estimates, the minimum storage size for high-speed storage was between 128 and 256 words, while 512 to 1024 words was considered to be a reasonable upper limit; and they concluded that 1024 to 2046 words should be adequate to handle the active part of most programs.

While Wilkes had advocated the slave memory concept only for operands, Scarott [S1], also in 1965, extended the slave concept for both operands as well as instructions. Scarott advocated the slave memory organization from three major considerations: (1) nature of address sequence (instructions or data); (2) nature of operations on data (modified or not modified), and (3) need for matching storage hierarchy to a particular programming environment.

Instead of implementing a homogeneous slave store, Scarott advocated the use of heterogeneous slave stores—instructions and operands. Also, based on the nature of address sequences, he advocated that the sizes of the two caches be different. The instruction buffer was 16 words and the data buffer was 64 words. Both of these were backed by a homogeneous 16K-word store. To further improve the data-transfer operations, Scarott advocated that the instruction buffer be organized as read-only store, whereas the operand buffer could be organized as read/write.

Because the instructions were not modified by the CPU, there was no need to transfer back any information from the instruction buffer to the main store. However, the operand could be modified by CPU; hence it had to be organized as read/write buffer. To improve the data transfer, he maintained a modified bit along with each buffer location. This mod-

## 7.1 The History of Memory Hierarchies

ified bit was set only if the data associated with that particular buffer location were changed by the executing program. This modified bit later determined whether a particular word needed to be transferred back to the main store *or* not. This modified-bit scheme is similar to the one proposed by Lee and is also known as *write back* strategy today. Upon detection of a miss (write attempt by CPU to an operand location not found in operand buffer), only the operand store was modified. If this involved replacing a word from the fast store, some particular word had to be selected. If this word had its modified bit set, that particular word was transferred to the main store.

Scarott also argued that there was a strong correlation between particular programming environment, storage hierarchy structure, and buffer size. He pointed out that, while a small instruction buffer space might be adequate for scientific applications, commercial applications might necessitate larger buffer space. Scarott's concepts of modified bit, heterogeneous buffer space, and different-sized buffer spaces have had a tremendous impact on machines today.

In 1967, Gibson [G1] for the first time carried out an intensive investigation of the usefulness of multiword block transfer between the backing store and a local (buffer) store. He had intuitively recognized that by transmitting blocks of words, rather than a word at a time, and exploiting locality of program behavior, it was possible to prorate the penalty of initial access time due to physical distance, effective address mapping, and so on, over many words. Some of the fundamental questions that he wanted to answer were:

What should be the optimum block size?
What should be the size of the CPU's local buffer?
Which replacement algorithm should be used?
How does the running program affect the usefulness of block transfer?

To analyze these, he collected extensive addressing patterns from twenty 7000 series programs. Each program generated approximately 3 million address references, which were sliced into 200,000 reference sequences for the analysis purpose. For the simulation, Gibson varied the block sizes from 4 words/block to 248 words/block, the local buffer size from 32 words to 8192 words, and he tried 15 different replacement algorithms. Some of his important conclusions are as follows:

1. Block sizes of 4 to 16 words were most efficient in utilizing the local buffer storage space, the smaller being better. The useful-

ness of extra words in a block seemed to decrease with increasing block sizes. Also, he found that while the number of accesses outside local store increased for smaller block size, the number of words transferred to local store decreased for smaller block sizes.
2. Local buffer storage of 2K to 4K words was adequate for most of the programs to achieve a hit ratio close to unity.
3. Even though some sort of associative mapping replacement algorithm gave better performance than congruent mapping scheme, in general, replacement algorithms had negligible impact on the performance of the system.
4. Addressing pattern rather than program size was more important for achieving higher system performance.
5. Smaller block sizes resulted in better traffic density between the CPU and its local store, and it was extremely important to choose proper block size are local storage size to achieve desirable traffic rate.

Partitioning further the address streams into instruction streams and data streams, Sisson [S6] did further simulation studies and concurred with Gibson's results that small block sizes tended to give better performance. Also, she found that, maybe due to program locality behavior, instruction fetching resulted in better speed up than operand fetching, and she advocated separate buffer spaces for instruction and data.

In 1969, Lee [L4] formally published the result of his simulation studies for evaluating the performance improvement of 4- 256-word associative, look-aside memory scheme for the PDP-1 computer. Lee used three simple object programs: (1) roots, primarily a calculating program calling floating point subroutines and decimal binary conversion routines, (2) MACRO, a PDP-1 assembler macro assembling a short source tape, and (3) LOOK-ASIDE simulation program, a copy of the simulator itself. Lee found that for a memory speed ratio of 10 (i.e., assuming a main memory access time of 1 $\mu$s and buffer access time of 100 ns), and with 128-cell associative buffer memory, it was possible to achieve an effective speed of two to three times the speed of buffer address time, i.e., to achieve an effective cycle time of 250 to 400 ns.

Lee had further investigated the impact of two different purge (replacement) algorithms, the single activity bit algorithm and the round-robin algorithm. He found that the more complex scheme of removing stale information from the associative memory based on the cell activity resulted only in very little improvement over the simple round-robin method and argued that the complex replacement scheme might not be justifiable from a cost viewpoint. Actually, as early as 1964, Lee [L2] had proposed the possibility of transferring small blocks of words rather than single words or huge pages like Atlas (512 words) between the backing store and the local buffer; this scheme was formally simulated by Gibson.

## 7.2 LARGE CACHE SYSTEMS

### Cache Memory Systems of IBM

Even though the concept of a memory hierarchy and the use of a high-speed buffer for getting higher performance were known for a long time, the concept of a cache as known today was implemented for the first time in the IBM 360/85, a big mainframe commercial system [L3]. In the 360 model 85, a storage hierarchy consisting of relatively smaller and faster semiconductor memory (16K to 32K bytes, 80-ns cycle time) and a larger, relatively slower main memory (512K to 4096K bytes, 1.04-$\mu$s cycle time) was used to achieve high performance and high throughput. The small, fast semiconductor store was completely integrated with the CPU and was described as the cache memory. This memory was completely transparent to the user; that is, it was not addressable by the programmers (the term cache means hidden). By containing information that was most frequently needed by the CPU, the cache reduced the need for the processor to get data from the main memory. Thus, most of the memory appeared to the processor as a very high speed memory at the cost of main memory. Only when the data needed by the CPU were not in the cache was the main memory referenced and new data brought into CPU.

*Cache Organization*

In the 360 model 85, both the main memory and cache were divided into fixed-size logical sectors (or pages). Each sector consisted of 1K contiguous bytes, starting at 1K-byte boundaries. The cache consisted of 16 sectors (16K bytes), and the main memory consisted of 512 to 4096 sectors (512 to 4096K bytes). Since the cache consisted of only 16 sectors, at a given time only 16 main storage sectors could be present in the cache and only 16 main storage sectors could have cache sectors assigned to them. So, during program execution some sort of association had to be set up between main storage sector and the cache sector. This was achieved by providing 16 sector address registers, which served as the tag store for the main storage sectors and held the address of the main storage sectors to which the cache sectors were assigned (Figure 7.6).

The assignment of cache sectors to main storage sectors was dynamically adjusted and accomplished via a least recently used (LRU)

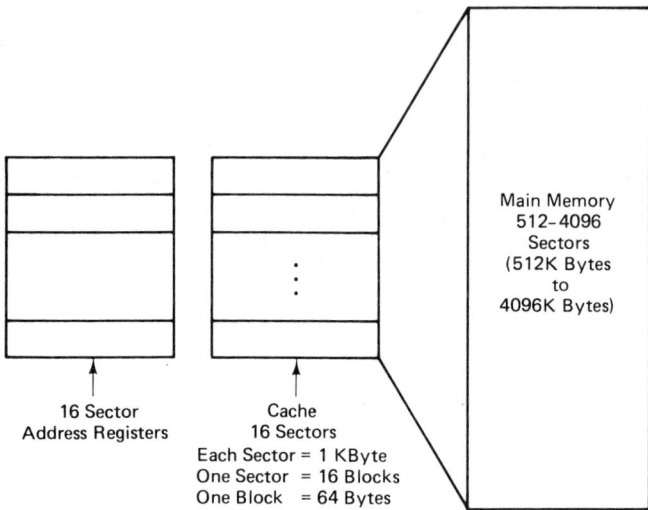

**Figure 7.6.** IBM System 360/85 Cache

algorithm. Efforts were made to assign the cache sectors to the main storage sectors that were being used by the program. A dynamically prioritized *activity list* was maintained, with the most recently referenced sector on the top of the list (implying the highest priority), and the least recently referenced sector on the bottom of the list (implying the lowest priority).

As long as the processor requests for the main memory were satisfied by the cache sectors, the pointers were manipulated simply by moving the priority pointers without manipulating any data. However, if the processor demanded a main storage sector that was not in the cache memory (i.e., it was the reference for an unassigned main storage sector), one of the cache sectors needed to be reassigned to the main sector. The cache sector selected for the reassignment was the one that was at the bottom of the list (implying it was the sector that had gone the longest without being referenced to and hence was probably least likely to be referenced in the future).

Particular reference to a particular cache sector caused it to be moved to the top of the list, with the intervening ones moving down one position. The cache sectors below it were not affected. Note that this did not involve actual movement of sectors within cache, but simply a reordering of pointers for new priorities.

Assignment of a cache sector to a main storage sector simply involved setting up an appropriate tag for cache. Furthermore, data movement did not occur at sector units. To minimize data movement time,

## 7.2 Large Cache Systems

each sector was organized as consisting of 16 blocks, each block being 64 bytes, and the blocks were loaded into cache on a demand basis.

Since each sector consisted of 16 blocks, some *validity* information was maintained to identify those blocks in the cache that belonged to the currently mapped sector. The validity bit of each block was turned on when that particular block was loaded and was turned off when the cache sector was mapped to a different sector. Since the cache size was 16 sectors (total of $16 \times 16$ blocks = 256 blocks), a 256-bit valid register was maintained (Figure 7.7).

### Address Translation

In 360 model 85, the sector size was designed large enough to minimize address mapping. It was realized that a large sector size might cause storage fragmentation and a smaller sector might imply a larger map table. A 1K sector size, partitioned into sixteen 64-byte blocks was thought to be quite adequate. Also, while it is true that fully associative mapping minimizes address contention and achieves higher hit ratios, it was realized that full associative memory mapping would imply either a large

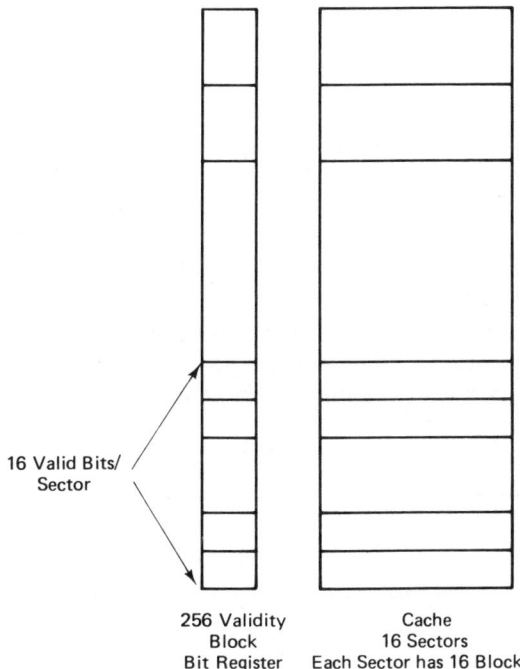

**Figure 7.7.** IBM System 360/85 Cache and Validity Block Bit Register

number of associative compares or a slow serial search, resulting in poor performance. Since a cache must be accessed at high speed, this sector mapping scheme with fully associative compares with 16 sector address registers was found to result in an optimum configuration.

An address for the 360/85 consisted of three components: the sector address, block address, and byte address (Figure 7.8). Each sector consisted of 16 blocks, each block consisting of 64 bytes. Since each sector consisted of 1K contiguous bytes, blocks were mapped in sequential order and the location of any byte in a particular sector was fixed. The low-order 6 bits of address specified byte address within the block, the next 4 bits specified block address within the sector, and the uppermost 14 bits specified the unique main storage and backing storage sector address. So, the lower-order 10 bits actually specified byte offset within a particular sector.

Since there were only 16 sectors in the cache, these 14 high-order bits had to be compared with the tags stored in the cache to see whether the particular backing store sector had been assigned any cache sector and, if so, where. If there was a match at any particular tag location, that encoded location specified the higher-order 4 bits of the cache storage. If there was a match, then these upper 4 bits along with the 4 bits of block address (in logical address) were combined to generate a particular cache block address (8 bits) to get the corresponding validity bit. If the corresponding valid bit was 1 (i.e., the block was valid), the right block had been located in the cache (Figure 7.9).

The least-order 6 bits specified the byte address of that particular block, which was provided to the CPU. However, if the block was invalid (i.e., valid bit was $\phi$), the particular block had to be reloaded into the cache. If the logical sector address did not match with any physical cache sector address, a *sector fault* was generated and then only a particular sector had to be reassigned.

To avoid the necessity of writing back a complete sector at replacement time, the cache in the 360/85 used a write through policy. So all write operations caused the main storage locations to be changed even if

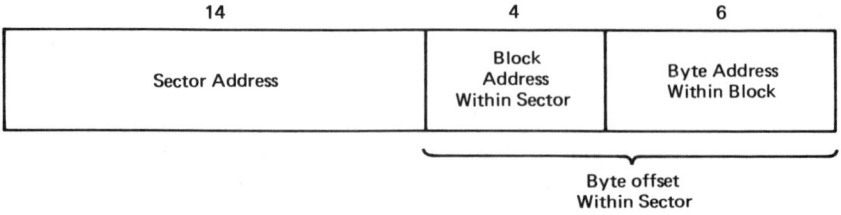

**Figure 7.8.** Logical Address of IBM System 360/85

## 7.2 Large Cache Systems

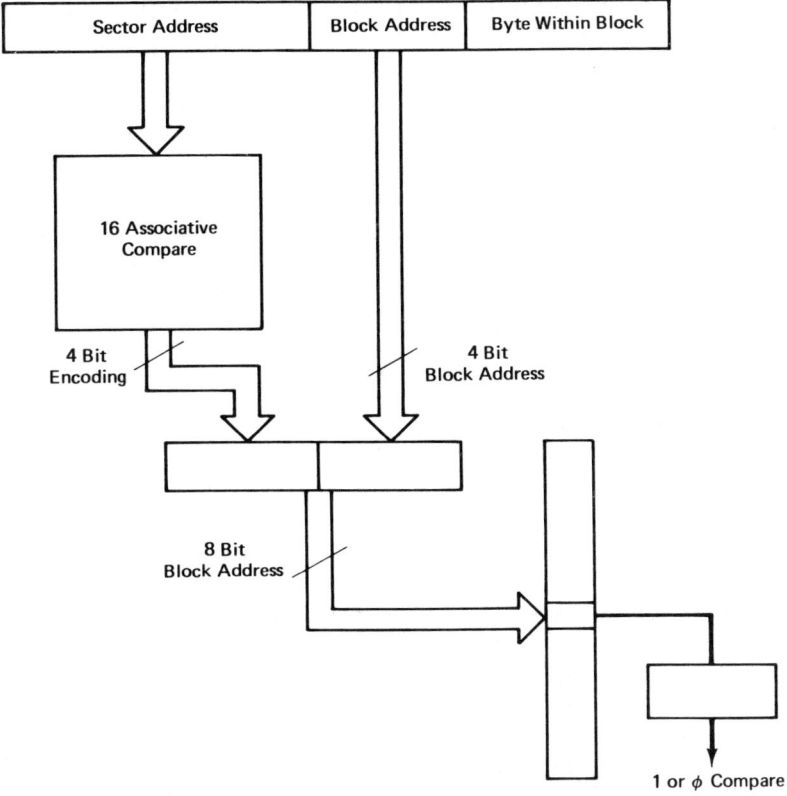

**Figure 7.9.** IBM System 360/85 Address Translation Mechanism

the main storage being written had a cache sector assigned to it. If the main storage sector had a cache sector assigned, the cache sector was also updated. If there was no cache sector assigned, there was no activity for the cache (i.e., neither the valid bit nor the activity list were updated). Since the main storage always contained a copy of good data, there was no problem of stale data, and there was no need to transfer any data from the cache to the main store. It was only the read operation that could cause a cache sector to be reassigned, blocks to be loaded, or the activity list to be revised. So, by maintaining a write through scheme, stack reassignment activity, block loading, and activity list updating were minimized for all write operations.

The CPU normally took two cycles to get data from the cache, one cycle to do tag search and validity checking and another to get data from cache. Provisions were made to overlap requests so that memory requests could be processed every cycle. If the data were not in the cache (for read operations), additional cycles were required to move data from the main memory to cache.

The basic storage word in the 360/85 was 16 bytes. So two 8-byte storage core modules were paired together and operated simultaneously. Besides this, a four-way interleaving was used to generate requests for 64 bytes, the whole block. To improve performance further, the first basic storage module referred to (during each block load) was the one containing 16 bytes of data wanted by the processor. So this module was started first, and data from this module, in addition to being loaded into cache, were sent directly to the processor so that the execution could proceed immediately.

*Performance Evaluation*

To measure the effectiveness of proposed cache, Liptay [L3] compared its performance against a postulated 360/85 system consisting of an integrated single-level storage operating at cache speed, which represented an upper limit on the performance of the model 85. They generated 19 trace tapes (containing about 250,000 instructions executed either by the problem programs or the operating systems), which served as input to the simulation program to evaluate the 360/85 and the postulated system. It was found that the real machine achieved a performance execution rate of 66% to 94% (with an average of 81%) of the postulated system. In addition, it was found that the average probability of finding data wanted by the processor in the cache memory was an incredible 96.8%. This was because programs tended to display some sort of "locality" behavior. It was observed that, if the addresses generated by a program were random, the probability of finding the data wanted in the cache would be much less than 1%.

Cache design parameters (cache size, sector size, block size, replacement algorithm, etc.) were decided upon after extensive simulation analysis. Figures 7.10 and 7.11 show the performance of different cache sizes with different numbers of sectors and different block sizes, relative to the postulated integrated single-level storage system. Based on these, the cache size was chosen to be 16K bytes, with each sector being 1K bytes, partitioned into 16 blocks of 64 bytes each. They also investigated the impact of two different replacement algorithms, varying from fully associative mapping to direct mapped scheme. All the parameters were finally decided to achieve best balance between cost and performance.

The 360/85 system implemented for the first time the concept of a cache as a nanosecond–microsecond memory hierarchy in a large-scale commerical system and legitimized this concept. After this, the cache

## 7.2 Large Cache Systems

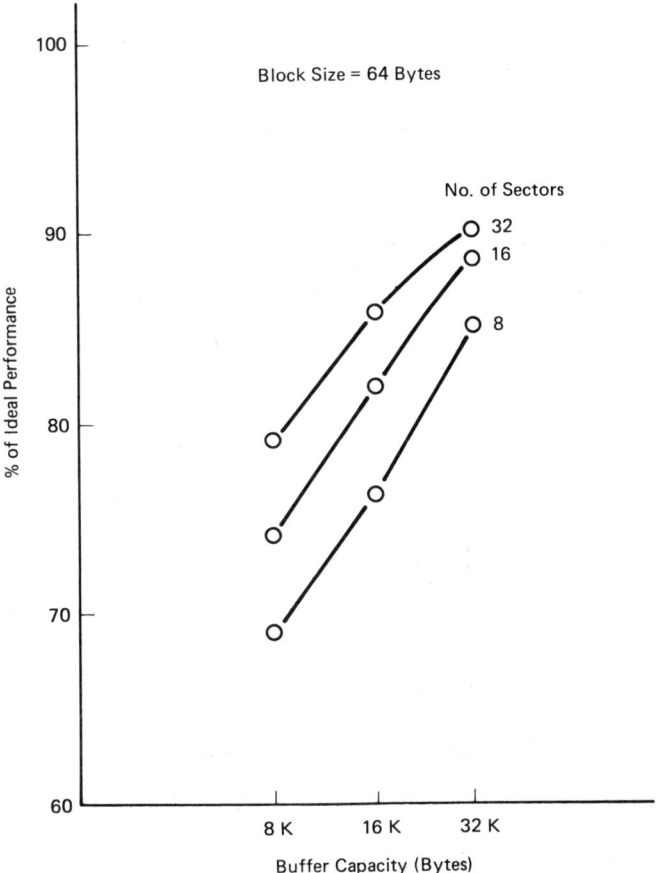

**Figure 7.10.** Liptay's IBM 360/85 Cache Data

concept became almost ubiquitous in all large-scale systems. The cache concept was used on the system 360 model 195, and the concept was included in the 370 series models 370/155 and 370/165; they are described by Katzan [K6].

### System/370 Model 155 Cache

The IBM System/370 Model 155 is a high-performance, 32-bit data-processing system designed for commercial, scientific, and real-time applications, with a machine cycle time of 115 ns and a main storage cycle time of 2070 ns (for an access width of 16 bytes). The speed discrepancy

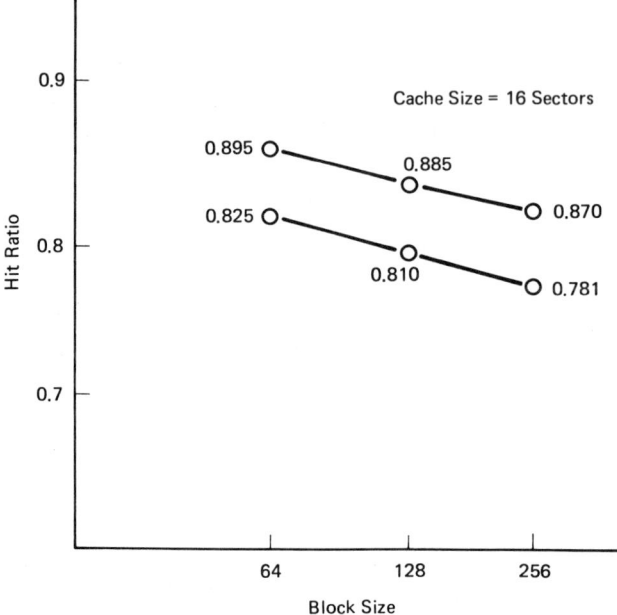

**Figure 7.11.** Liptay's IBM 360/85 Hit Ratio Data

between the CPU and main storage (factor of 18) is matched by a high-speed cache system. The cache for model 155 is 8K bytes with a cycle time of 115 ns (the same as CPU cycle time). The cache is designed in such a way that a fetch can be initiated by the CPU every machine cycle. The data path in the CPU and between CPU and cache is 4 bytes. The CPU can fetch 4 bytes of data from the cache in two machine cycles or 230 ns and 8 consecutive bytes in 345 ns.

Both the main storage and the data cache are divided into blocks of 32 bytes. Each block is further divided into 16-byte half-blocks. A 16-byte half-block (a quad word) is the basic unit of data transfer between the main storage and the cache.

*Cache Organization*

The system/370 computer generates a 32-bit effective address by adding the contents of the base register, the index register, and the displacement field. Since the model 155 can support physical memory up to 2M bytes, only the lower-order 21 bits of physical address (bits 11 to 31) are used, as shown in Figure 7.12. This physical address consists of three fields: bits 28 to 31 specify byte offset within the half-block, but 27 specifies the

## 7.2 Large Cache Systems

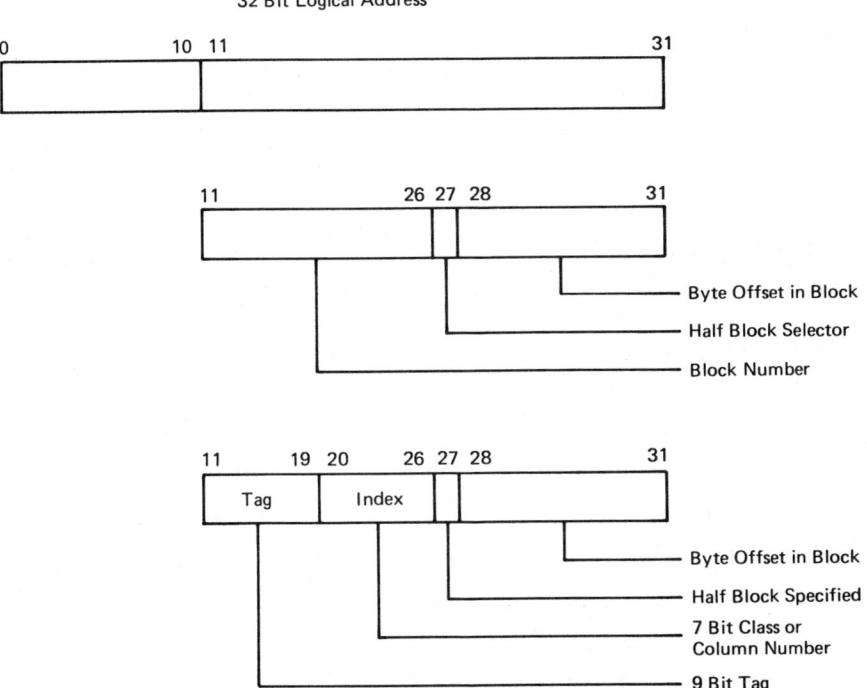

**Figure 7.12.** IBM System/370 Model 155 Addressing Scheme

particular half-block and bits 11 to 26 specify the block address. The block address conceptually consists of two subfields: an index field (column number of class number) and a tag field. Since the cache is organized into 128 classes (columns), bits 20 to 26 specify the index field and bits 11 to 19 specify the tag field.

The data cache is organized as 128 classes and 2 set associative caches set 0 and set 1. (The cache can be thought of as 128 columns and 2 rows.) Each set conceptually has two parts, an index (tag) array and a data array. Each set of index arrays has 128 entries (one per class) and so needs 7 bits of index address. Each set of data arrays also has 128 entries. However, since each entry of data array has space for a block of data (two half-blocks of data), the half-block bit (bit 27) is combined with the index field (bits 20 to 26) to generate the index address for the data array.

Each index array entry consists of three parts: tag field (bits 11 to 19) of the physical address, 2 valid bits (one for the high-order half-block and another for the lower-order half-block), and an OK bit to indicate that the corresponding positions in the data array and index array are functioning properly (Figure 7.13). The main storage is also partitioned into 128 classes with the number of blocks is each class depending on the size of the main store.

## Cache Operation

The cache is maintained on a half-block basis using index, tag, and the half-block indicators. The control unit for the cache also maintains a latch to determine which set of the two needs to be assigned.

The index field of the effective address, (bits 20 to 26) specifies a location in both sets of the index array. Once selected, the tags from both sets of the index array are compared with the tag field of the effective address, and corresponding half-block bits are compared. If there is a match between the tag field and the half-block bit of the effective address with the corresponding tag field and the half-block bit of either of the sets, the reference is considered to be a data hit and the requested half-block is sent to the CPU from the cache.

If the tag and half-block position do not match, the corresponding half-block is fetched from main storage, sent to CPU, and the appropriate cache location is updated using the following algorithm [K6]:

1. If space is available in both the sets for the corresponding block, the latch determines which set is to be assigned for the requested block.
2. If the corresponding block in one set is assigned and the other is available, the available set is assigned.
3. If the corresponding blocks in both sets have one half-blocks assigned, neither block is available and the latch determines which set should be assigned.

The cache storage is updated only if the index and tag for the half-block being altered agree with one of the two index entries for that class.

The buffer control unit for the cache is also designed to manipulate the latch, valid bits, and OK bits. When a particular set of a particular class cache block is referenced, the latch is set to indicate the other set (to indicate the set referenced last). Also, system reset initializes all index array entries to zero, resets all valid bits, and sets all OK bits of the index entries. Also, upon a particular buffer component failure, the OK bit of that block is set off and a machine check interruption is generated. The system also has the capability of disabling the cache by either console switch or under microprogram control, with some performance degradation.

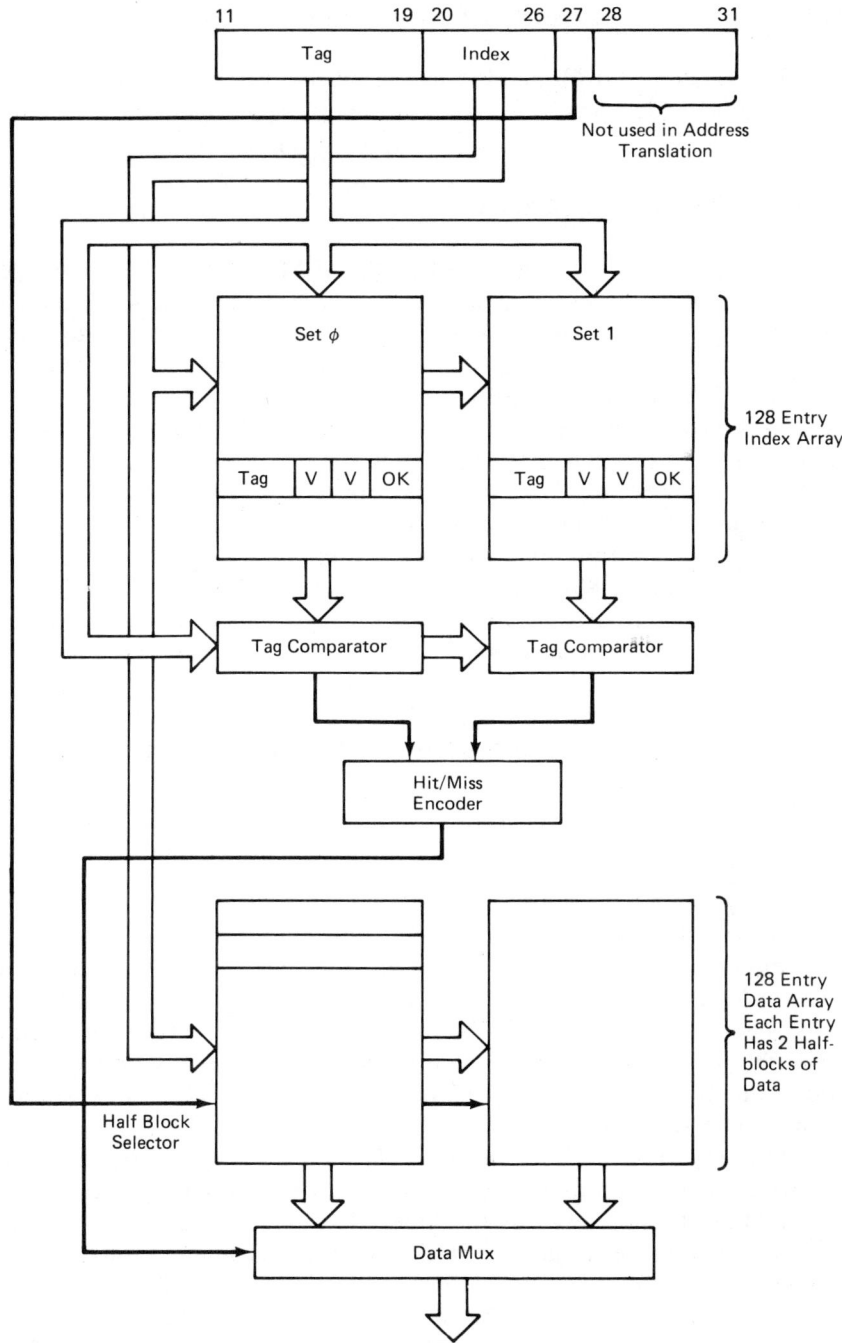

**Figure 7.13.** IBM System/370 Model 155 Cache (128 classes, 2 set Associative)

The System/370 Model 155 cache used a write through technique for minimizing the transfer between cache and main memory.

### System/370 Model 165 Cache

A high-speed cache was also used in the IBM System/370 Model 165, which is a high-performance system designed for large-scale scientific and business applications, with a CPU machine cycle time of 80 ns and a main storage cycle time of 2 $\mu$s (for an access with 8 bytes). The data path within the CPU and between the CPU and storage is 8 bytes wide. However, to achieve higher performance, the storage is four-way interleaved, and the CPU is designed in such a way that it can reference storage every machine cycle. The speed discrepancy between the CPU and main storage (a factor of 25) is matched by a high-speed cache system.

The cache for the model 165 is available in either 8K or 16K bytes with a cycle time of 80 ns. The cache is designed in such a way that a fetch can be initiated by the CPU every machine cycle. The CPU can fetch 8 bytes of data from the cache in two machine cycles or 160 ns and 16 bytes in 240 ns.

Both the main storage and the data cache are divided into blocks of 32 bytes. A 32-byte block is the basic unit of data transfer between the main storage and the cache.

*Cache Organization*

The system/370 generates a 32-bit effective address, but since the model 165 supports a maximum physical address space of 16MB, it uses the lower-order 24 bits (bits 8 to 31) as shown in Figure 7.14. This effective address consists of three fields: bits 29 to 31 specify byte the offset within the double word, bits 27 to 28 specify a particular double word within the block, and bits 8 to 26 specify the block address. The block address consists of two subfields: an index field and a tag field.

The size of the index field depends upon the cache size and cache organization. For the 8KB cache, organized into 64 classes (columns), bits 21 to 26 (6 bits) serve as the index field (class or column number). For the 16KB cache, organized into 128 classes (columns), bits 20 to 26 (7 bits) serve as the index field. For the 8KB cache, bits 8 to 20 serve as the tag; and for the 16KB cache, bits 8 to 19 serve as the tag.

For both the 8KB and 16KB cache, the cache is organized as a four-set associative cache, sets 0, 1, 2, and 3. These four sets can be visualized as four rows. So the cache can be thought of as organized either in 64

## 7.2 Large Cache Systems

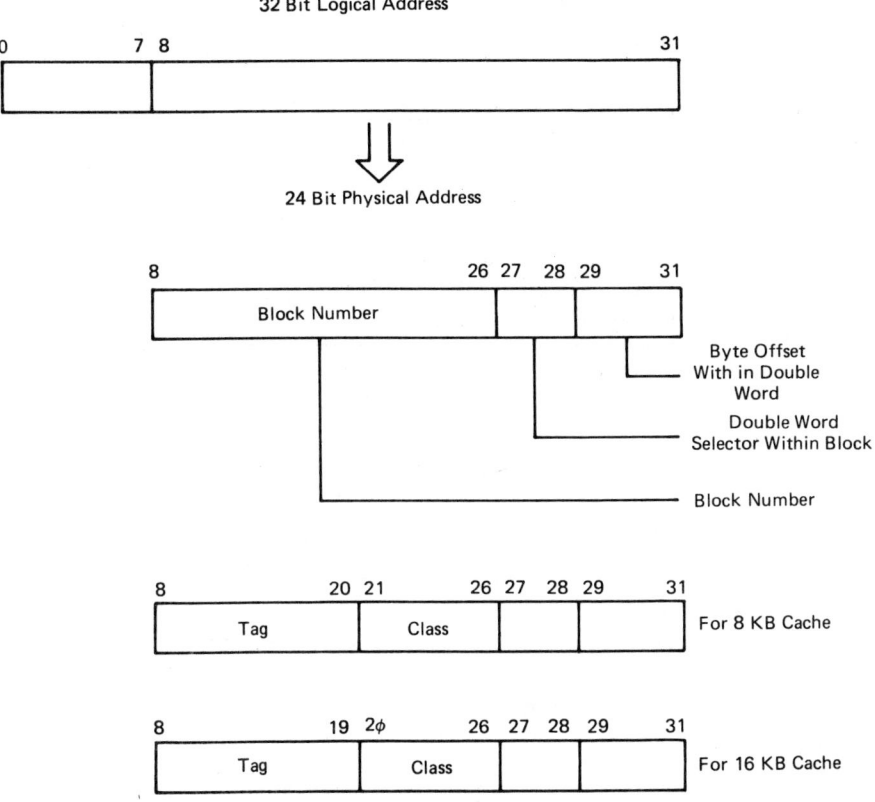

**Figure 7.14.** IBM System/370 Model 165 Addressing Scheme

columns × 4 rows (for 8KB) or 128 columns × 4 rows (for 16KB) (Figure 7.15). Each set (row) conceptually has three parts: an index (address tag) array, a replacement array, and a data array. Since a block (four double words, 32 bytes) is the basic unit of information transfer between the main storage and the cache, each index array entry of the data cache corresponds to one data array entry consisting of a block of data.

Each set of the index array has 64 entries for the 8KB (128 entries 16KB) cache and needs 6 bits for its address. Each set of the data array also has 64 entries (128 for 16KB). However, since each data entry has space for four double words, each set of the data array has space for 56 double words and needs 8 bits for its address. Bits 27 to 28 of the effective physical address are concatenated with bits 21 to 26 (bit 20 to 26 for 16KB cache) to generate the index address for data array (Figure 7.16).

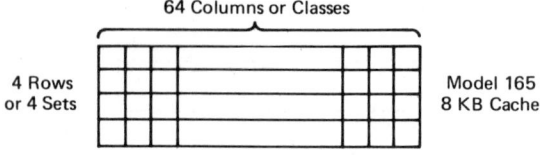

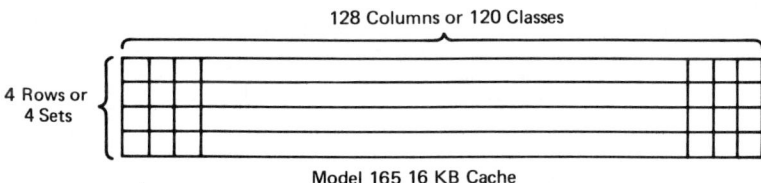

**Figure 7.15.** Cache Organization of 370 Model 165

Each class in the data cache is also associated with a four-entry replacement array that controls cache replacement activity. When a particular cache block is referenced by the CPU, it is put at the top of the list for the particular class, and when a particular block needs to be reassigned for a class, the entry at the bottom of the list for that particular class is selected for replacement.

## Cache Operation

The index field of the effective address for the index array, bits 21 to 26 (bits 20 to 26 for 16KB cache), specifies a location in all sets of the index array. Once selected, the tags from all the four sets of the index array are compared with the tag of the effective address bits 8 to 20 for the 8KB cache (bits 8 to 19 for the 16KB cache). If there is a match between the effective address tag field and any of the tag sets, the reference is considered to be a data hit and requested the double word from the corresponding block of the corresponding set is provided to the CPU. The physical double word specified along with the byte offset within the double word can be concatenated with the output of the index array to select any specific byte of desired data. Note that, since a single cache is used for both instruction and data, the data from the cache can either be the data desired by the CPU or even by the instruction, which can be loaded into the instruction buffer.

However, if the requested block is not found in the index array, the corresponding data block has to be fetched from the main storage, sent to CPU, and also stored in the cache for future reference. The cache, like the 360/85, uses a load through scheme for passing data to the CPU (i.e., the particular double word requested by the CPU is the first one that is fetched from the main storage and sent to the CPU. The rest of the double words of the block are fetched from the main storage in subsequent cycles. The cache block on the bottom of the replacement array of the particular class is assigned this new block of data, and the index array is updated accordingly.

The cache also uses a store through scheme for updating main memory. The data cache is updated only for write bits. For write misses, only the main memory is updated. Since the write through scheme always maintains a valid copy of information in the main storage, there is no need to transfer any information from cache to main storage.

Besides model 155 and 165, the cache was implemented in models 168, 168-3, and 195. Actually, the cache concept has been used in almost all the large models. Table 7.1 summarizes cache sizes and cycle times for all 360 and 370 models [B13]. The cache concept was used also in model 303X series.

## IBM 3033 Cache

A high-speed, relatively large sized cache has been used in model 3033. The IBM 3033 is one of the large-scale processors in the 370 family, with the capability of supporting up to 32MB of main storage, with a processor cycle time of 57 ns and executing about 5 million instructions/second. The design of the 3033 is similar to the 370 model 168.

The 3033 has a 64KB high-speed data cache for both instructions and data. This large, high-speed cache is one of the main reasons for the high performance enhancement of the 3033. The cache has the same cycle time as the CPU (57 ns).

The main storage cycle time for model 3033 is 285 ns. The main storage is divided into eight logical storage elements (LSE) and interleaved in eight ways. A double word (8 bytes) is the basic unit of data access from each LSE, and eight double words (64 bytes block) can be requested from eight LSEs concurrently.

The speed discrepancy between the CPU and the main storage (factor of 5) is matched by a high-speed cache system. The cache for model 3033 is a 64KB, high-speed cache for both data and instruction, with 57-ns cycle time. The cache is designed in such a way that a fetch can be initiated by the CPU every machine cycle. The CPU can obtain a double word from cache in two cycles (114 ns) and 16 bytes in 171 ns.

Both the main storage and the data cache are organized and divided into blocks of 64 bytes. A 64-byte block is the basic unit of data transfer between the main storage and the cache.

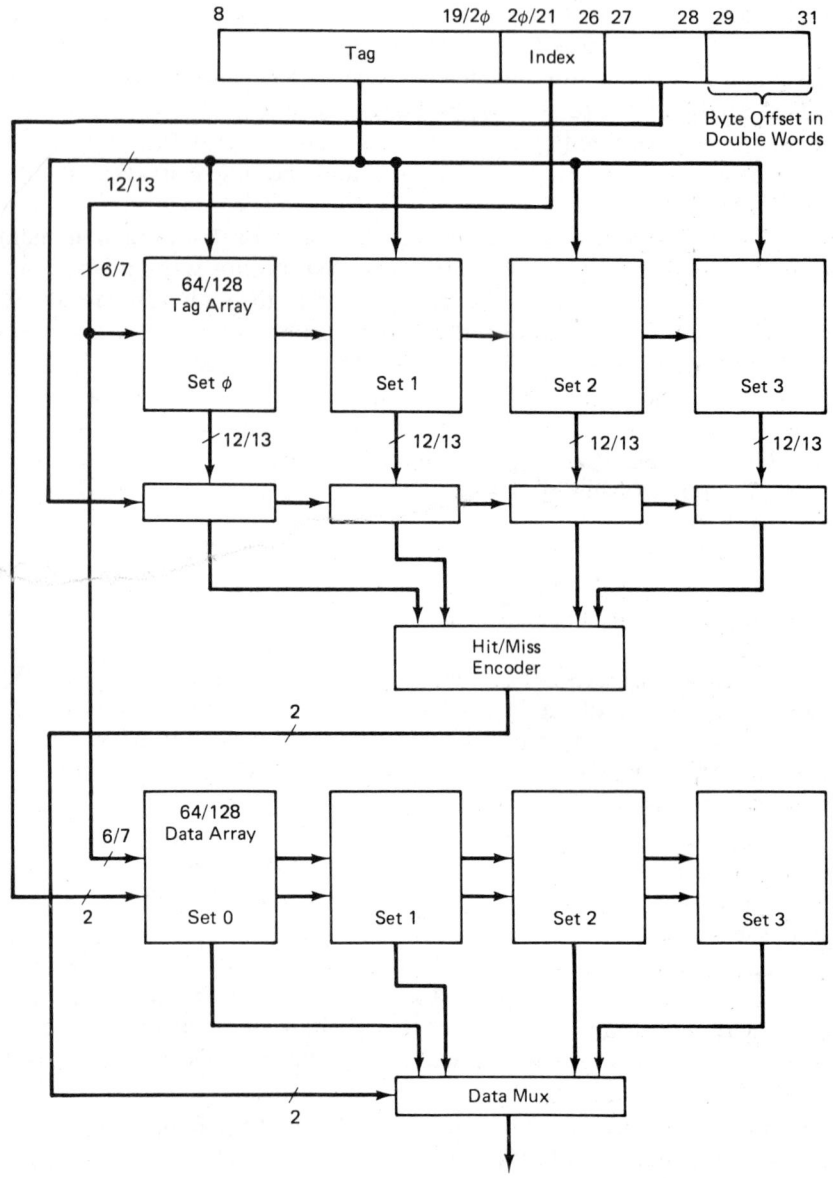

**Figure 7.16.** Data Cache Organization of System 370 Model 165 (8 or 16KB cache)

Table 7.1 CPU CYCLE TIME AND CACHE CONFIGURATIONS FOR 360 AND 370 SYSTEMS

| Model | CPU Cycle Time (ns) | Processor Storage (ns) | Size | Cache Block | Cycle Time | Writing | Assoc. |
|---|---|---|---|---|---|---|---|
| 360/85 | 80 | 960 | 16–32 | 16 × 4 | 80–110 | ST* | 16 |
| 360/195 | 54 | 756 | 32 | 8 × 8 | 54–112 | ST | 4 |
| 370/155 | 115 | 2070 | 8 | 16 | 115–230 | ST | 2 |
| 370/155 II | 115 | 2070 | 8 | 16 | 110–230 | ST | 2 |
| 370/158 and 158-3 | 115 | 1035R 920W | 8 | 16 | 115–230 | ST | 2 |
| 370/165 and 165 II | 80 | 2000 | 8–16 | 8 × 4 | 80–110 | ST | 4 |
| | 80 | 2000 | 8–16 | 8 × 4 | 80–160 | ST | 4 |
| 370/168 and 168-3 | 80 | 320 | 8–16 | 8 × 4 | 80–160 | ST | 4–8 |
| | 80 | 320 | 32 | 8 × 8 | 80–110 | ST | 8 |
| 370/195 | 54 | 756 | 32 | 8 × 4 | 54–162 | ST | 4 |
| 3031 | 115 | 345 | 32 | 8 × 4 | 115–230 | ST | 8 |
| 3032 | 80 | 320 | 32 | 8 × 4 | 115–230 | ST | 8 |
| 3033 | 57 | 285 | 64 | 8 × 8 | 57–114 | ST | 16 |
| 3033N | 57 | 285 | 16 | 8 × 8 | 57–114 | ST | 8 |
| 3033S | 57 | 285 | 0.5 | 8 × 4 | 57–114 | ST | 8 |
| 3081 | 26 | 312 | 32 | 8 × 16 | 26–52 | SW** | 4 |
| 4331-1 | 300–1600 | 900R/1300W | — | | 200 | SW | 4 |
| 4331-2 | 200–1600 | 2600R/3100W | 8 | 4 × 16 | 225 | SW | 4 |
| 4341-1 | 150–300 | 2400 | 8 | 8 × 8 | 120R 180W | SW | 8 |
| 4341-2 | 120–240 | 1440 | 16 | 16 × 4 | | | |

*ST, store-through
**SW, simple swap

## Cache Organization

Since the model 3033 supports a maximum physical address space of 32MB, it uses the lower 25 bits of the effective address (bits 7 to 31) as shown in Figure 7.17. This effective address consists of three fields: bits 29 to 31 specify byte offset within the double word, bits 26 to 28 specify the particular double word within block, and bits 7–25 (19 bits) specify the block address. The block address consists of two subfields.

Since the cache for the model 3033 is organized as 64 classes (64 columns) of 16 set associative (16 rows) write, bits 20 to 25 (6 bits) of the effective address serve as the index field and bits 7 to 19 (13 bits) serve as the tag field. Each set (row) of the cache consists of three parts: an index (address tag) array, a replacement array, and a data array. Since a block (8 double words, 64 bytes) is the basic unit of information transfer between the main storage and the cache, each index array entry of the data cache corresponds to the data array entry consisting of a block of data.

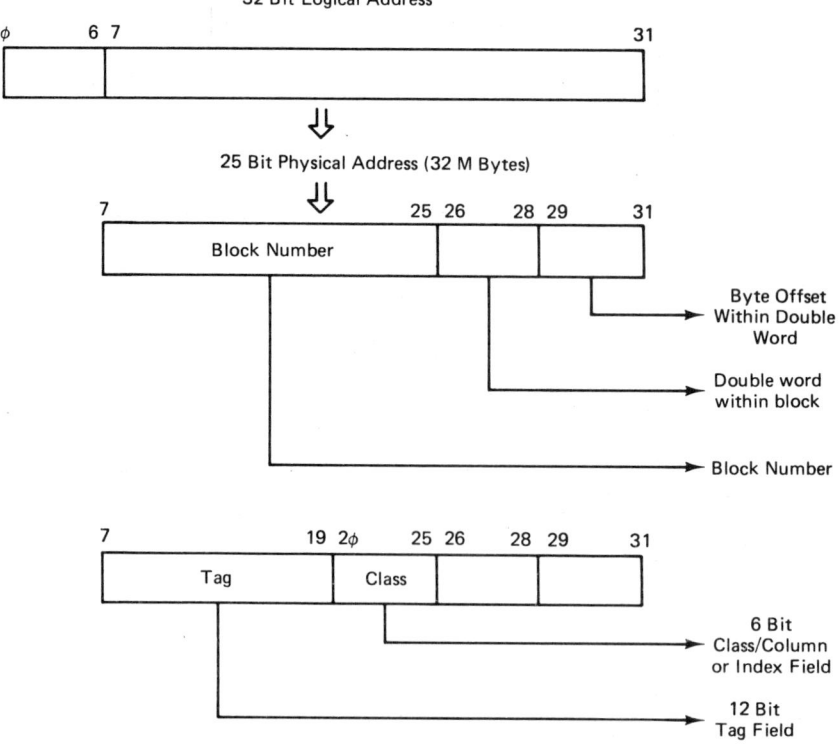

**Figure 7.17.** IBM 3033 Addressing Scheme

## 7.2 Large Cache Systems

Each set of the index array has 64 entries and needs 6 bits for its address. Each set of the data array also has 64 entries. However, since each data array entry has space for 8 double words, each set of the data array has space for 512 double words and needs 9 bits for its address. Bits 20 to 28 serve as the index address for data array.

Each class in the data cache is also associated with a 16-entry replacement array, which controls cache replacement activity. When a particular cache block is referenced by the CPU, it is put at the top of the list for the particular class, and when a particular block needs to be reassigned for a class, the entry at the bottom of the list for that particular class is selected for replacement.

### Cache Operation

The index field of the effective address for the index array (bits 20 to 25) specifies a location in all sets of the index array. Once selected, the tags from all the 16 sets of index array are compared with the tag of the effective address bits 7 to 19. If there is a match between the effective address tag field and any of the set tags, the reference is considered to be a data hit and the requested double word from the corresponding block of the corresponding set is provided to the CPU. The physical double word specific along with the physical byte offset from the effective address can be concatenated with the output of the index array to select any specific byte of desired data (Figure 7.18). Note that since a single data cache is used for both instructions and data, the data from the cache can either be the data desired by the CPU or may even be the instruction that can be loaded into the instruction buffer. However, if the requested block is not found in the index array, the corresponding data block has to be fetched from the main storage and also stored in the cache for future reference.

The cache uses a load through scheme for passing data to the CPU; that is, the particular double word requested by the CPU is the first one that is fetched from the main storage and sent to the CPU. The rest of the block is fetched from the main store subsequently. The cache block on the bottom of the replacement array of the particular class is assigned this new block of data, and the index array is updated accordingly.

The cache also uses a write through strategy for updating its data cache and main memory. The data cache is updated only for write hits. For write misses, only the main memory is updated. Since the write through scheme always maintains a valid copy of information in the main storage, there is no need to transfer any information from cache to main storage.

The main processor storage for the 3033 can also be viewed as logically partitioned into 64 classes, with the number of blocks per class

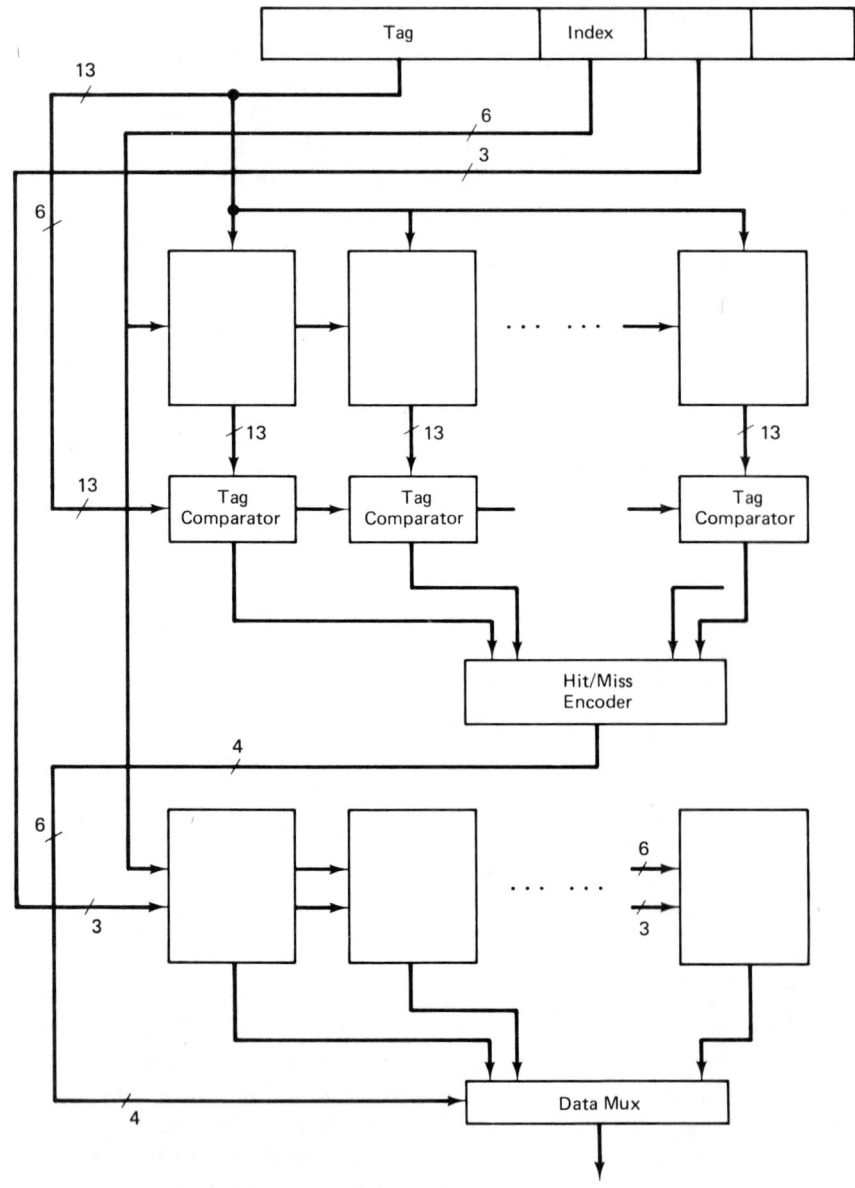

**Figure 7.18.** IBM 3033 Data Cache Organization

## 7.3 Other Cache-Related Studies

depending upon the storage. For 4MB of main storage, blocks per class will be 1024, and for 32MB of storage, there will be 8K blocks per class. Since the cache is organized as 16 set associatives, any block of any particular class of main storage can reside in any of the 16 sets of corresponding class.

## 7.3 OTHER CACHE-RELATED STUDIES

The successful implementation of the cache concepts in IBM 360/85, 195, and 370 series stimulated a great deal of interest in further application and investigation of this concept in the late 1960s and 1970s. In 1969, Conti (C1), in an excellent review, addressed the issue of different memory

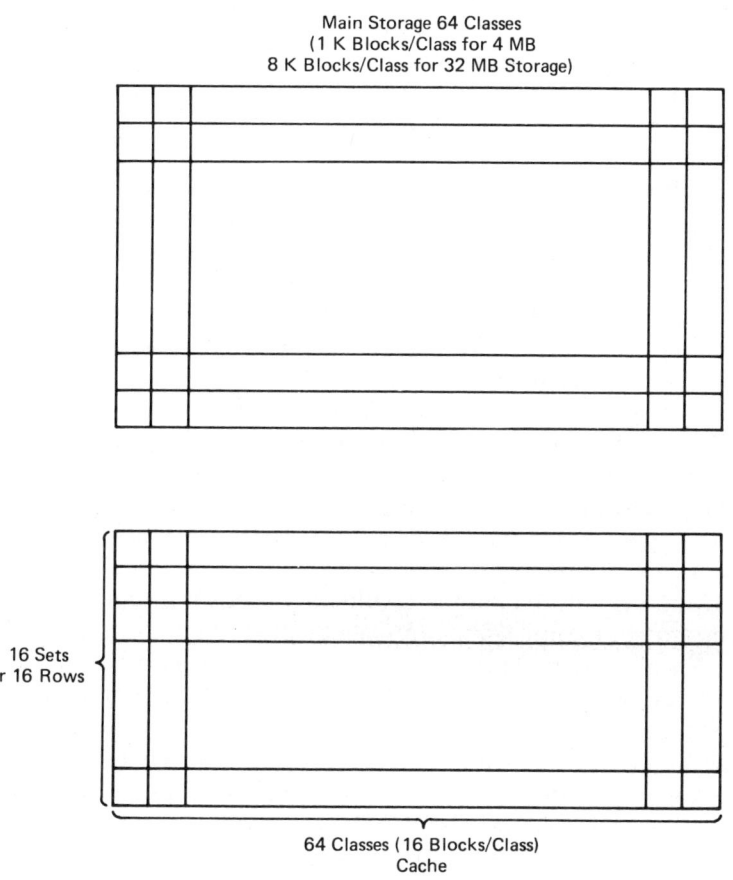

**Figure 7.19.** IBM 3033 Main Storage and Cache Organization

mapping techniques and the issues of various writing and replacement algorithms. He explained in detail the operation of four basic types of mapping techniques: sector or paged, direct mapping, fully associative, and set associative mapping. These four techniques are still the most commonly used buffer mapping techniques. He pointed out the advantages and disadvantages of each type of mapping. Conti illustrates that the sector mapping scheme with each sector divided into blocks, close to the optional transfer size and with their associated valid bits (as implemented in the 360/85), has the advantage of requiring relatively fewer tags and results in the possibility of simultaneous comparison of all tags. The direct mapped approach obviated the need for associative compare and led to the simplest hardware and fastest possible cache access time at the expense of increased block contention within the cache. The fully associative mapping scheme, even though it was the best approach for minimizing contention and achieving high hit ratio, did not seem to be practical for implementation with the existing technology. It also resulted in a long access time (due to long serial search), compared to the direct mapping scheme or even sector organized buffer (which could get away with full association on a very small number of tags). Conti showed that set associative techniques represented advantages over both the fully associative and direct mapped scheme and was most likely to yield the most cost-effective performance within the constraints of available technology.

For writing algorithms, Conti illustrated that a store through algorithm was appropriate for sector mapping schemes. A sector mapped cache was not very conducive to swapping, because at the time of replacement of a sector it was possible that a sector could contain many blocks that had to be swapped, thus possibly resulting in a very large swap time and tying up the backing storage for a long time. The IBM 360/85 sector mapped cache had used a store through writing scheme. The swapping scheme was adequate for the other three mapping techniques. In fact, it appears that they give better performance than the store through techniques.

Conti also illustrated the results of various replacement algorithms, ranging from a totally random replacement strategy to very sophisticated ones. An algorithm that appeared to give satisfactory results was the strategy of replacing the blocks that had not been referenced for the longest time. This scheme, however, necessitated keeping track of activity bits with each block. Conti also pointed out the advantage of the load through mode of operation, where the requested data from the CPU not found in the cache was provided to the CPU from the main store as quickly as possible. These schemes have been used later on most of the IBM models.

## 7.3 Other Cache-Related Studies

In 1970, Meade (M1) addressed the issue of memory hierarchy in general, justifying the need for an adequate memory hierarchy to get better performance. He addressed various critical buffer design parameters and classified all the parameters into two major categories: intrinsic and extrinsic. Cache access time and cost were classified as the intrinsic factors, whereas block size, buffer capacity, control algorithm, and information transfer rate were classified as the extrinsic parameters. Like Gibson and Sisson, Meade found that for a given buffer size there was an associated optimum block size. For any given buffer size, the miss ratio (1-hit ratio) tended to decrease first as the block size was increased and then increased sharply after the optimum was achieved. For buffer sizes of 2K to 128K bytes, he found that optimum block size was 64 bytes. After the optimum, the miss ratio seemed to increase with increasing block size because the block was becoming so large that the buffer contained too few blocks. However, if the buffer capacity was increased to contain the same number of blocks, then the miss ratio seemed to decrease. Meade also showed that traffic between a buffer and the next level was the product of miss rate and block size, and since a block was the basic granular unit of data transfer, larger block sizes resulted in increased traffic. Larger blocks necessitated larger buffers to maintain an adequate number of blocks, longer total block transfer time, and greater backing store bandwidth.

Meade showed that, for a given buffer capacity, given block size, and algorithm, there was a corresponding distribution of references for a set of programs. A larger buffer capacity seemed to result in a better hit ratio. He pointed out that buffer capacity must be based upon performance and cost-performance analysis and showed that buffer size for a large system had to be at least 8K bytes to get a decent hit ratio (close to 99%). Also, since the buffer size seemed to be independent of memory size, the memory hierarchy with a cache seemed to be more appealing than a single-level memory with high capacity. Meade strongly advocated the need for a properly designed memory hierarchy for achieving a better performance–cost ratio of the total memory system, and he also stated qualitative rules for two- and three-level memory hierarchy systems.

In 1971, Meade (M2) illustrated design particulars, logic implementations, control algorithms, and partitioning for fully associative and set associative cache sizes varying from 4K to 16K bytes. He considered a machine with an addressing range of 16M bytes. Both the cache and the main memory were partitioned into blocks of 64 bytes; each block consisting of eight 8-byte words. Meade suggested various ways of implementing the association design, such as a push down list or a simple numbering counter scheme. Finally, he chose a numbering counter scheme. The cache consisted of a tag array, a random access data array, a numbering array, and replacement control logic. Meade specified the designs in enough detail to make some comparisons between the two approaches. He found that a simple two-set associative controller had approximately three-fourths the delay of the fully associative version (25% faster). Also, Meade showed that, while for smaller cache sizes (4K bytes, 64 blocks) the control cost for both the alternatives was approximately equal, for larger cache sizes, the fully associative cache was about four times more expensive than the set associative cache. Meade predicted wider use of fully associative algorithms with the advancement of technology and the availability of larger content addressable memories.

In 1972, Meade (M3) again made an attempt to explain the mystery of a cache and the ground rules of good cache design, and investigated the possibility of using a cache for multiprocessors and multiprogramming systems. He pointed out the need for choosing cache capacity and backing memories by an adequate analysis of performance and cost. A backing memory was characterized as having a fixed size with variable cost and performance, whereas a cache was characterized as a memory with variable size with fixed cost and performance. Comparing cost-performance analyses of various hypothetical machines, Meade showed that cache memory was more cost effective in a larger computer system than a small one. In large systems, the cache cost was insignificant compared to the total cost of the machine, whereas in small machines the cost of cache constituted a significant portion of the total cost and was not thought to be cost effective. He pointed out that for intermediate systems the justification of a cache can only be made when the cache plus the backing memory costs less than a single main memory fast enough to permit equal throughput. Meade extended the cache concept to microprogramming, multiprocessing, multiprogramming, and virtual memory systems. He was hopeful that advancement of technology would produce fast bipolar cache buffers (16 to 20 ns) with 240- 320-ns MOS main memories and would make the cache concept applicable in a wide variety of systems.

The successful implementation of the cache concept in System/360 models 85 and 195 and various system/370 models such as 155 and 165 created an increasing interest in memory hierarchy systems. In the early 1970s there was an increasing amount of interest in the successful implementation of multilevel memory hierarchy systems, with emphasis on automatic, optimal storage hierarchy management and selection of proper technologies for optimal computer storage systems.

To address the issue of optimal, multilevel memory hierarchy systems, Mattson and others (M8), in 1970, devised a technique known as stack processing for determining performance measures for a large class of demand paged, multilevel storage systems utilizing a variety of mapping schemes and replacement algorithms in one pass of the address space.

## 7.3 Other Cache-Related Studies

They found conventional simulation techniques to be too slow as tools for determining adequate selection of technology, implementation of each technology, and management of data flow in the hierarchy. The stack processing technique, as devised by them, was a technique for efficient cost-performance evaluation of a large class of storage hierarchies and yielded processing of hit ratio data 1000 times faster than before. For a multilevel memory hierarchy, the various design parameters that needed to be considered were the following:

1. Cost and speed of CPU
2. Buffer technology
3. Memory technology
4. Buffer capacity
5. Page size
6. Number of blocks per page
7. Number of classes
8. Buffer page frame per class
9. Replacement algorithm
10. How the stores are handled

Miss ratio data of Mattson illustrate that, for a given buffer capacity and a given number of classes, the miss ratio tends to decrease with increasing page size, and there is an optimum miss ratio for a given buffer size. After the minimum is reached, the miss ratio tends to increase with the increase of the page size. Also, for a given page size, the hit ratio seems to improve with larger buffer capacity. From Mattson's data, 64 to 128 bytes seem to be the optimum block size.

Mattson used these hit ratio data along with technology parameters and timing cost parameters to calculate the cost performance in dollars time seconds per access for different designs. The technology parameter included CPU cost, buffer technology, and memory technology. The timing and cost assumptions included directory search time, priority list update time, data access time, memory cycle time, page move times, parity list check and update time, directory update time, and average memory system response time. The system cost figure included CPU cost, buffer cost, directory cost, priority list cost, and memory cost.

Lin and Mattson [L7] used the stack processing method to compare the cost performance between two- and three-level hierarchies and hierarchies using random access and serial access devices. They found that system cost performance was very strongly affected by the bus bandwidth between levels in the hierarchy. The access time ratio (between the backing store capacity) influences to lesser degree the total system cost performance. Also, they found that for a given hierarchy there was an optimum access time ratio, which seemed to increase with an increase of backing store capacity and decreased appreciably as the bus width narrowed. They found that, unless the access time ratio between the backing store and buffer exceeded about 50, the two-level hierarchies had better cost performance than three-level hierarchies. They also examined the feasibility of using bubble domain memories as backing store and concluded that, for memory capacity of less than 1M byte, a random access stores appeared to be favorable over serial access devices, and for capacities of 4M bytes and 16M bytes, serial access stores with shift register lengths of 256 bits and 1024 bits appeared to be more favorable.

In 1972, Haltfield and co-workers [H4] carried experiments to determine the best page size for a virtual memory system and concluded that the general assumption about virtual memory systems (that as the overhead time—time for access, page management decreases, the page size should be decreased) was not always a good one. With the various experiments conducted, they provided evidence that larger page sizes tended to provide better performance for programs that made highly localized use of memory space. They concluded that the relation between page reference pattern and page replacement algorithm gave rise to behavior that was not yet quite well understood.

In 1972, Chu and Opderbeck [C5] developed a new replacement strategy called page fault frequency replacement algorithm. This algorithm used the measured page fault frequency as the basic parameter. This scheme did not require prior knowledge of program behavior. It allocated memory according to the dynamically changing memory requirements of each process. From various simulation results, they found that the performance of this algorithm appeared to be better than the LRU algorithm and comparable to the working set replacement algorithm of Denning (D1). Also, the implementation of the PFF replacement algorithm appeared to be less complicated than that of the LRU and far less complicated than that of the working set replacement algorithm.

In 1972, Kaplan and Winder [K2] also studied the design problem of a computer system employing a cache memory hierarchy and proposed a new measure of effective cache performance. This new measure was defined as

$$u = (1 - HR)r$$

This new measure was normalized to instructions rather than references and measured misses instead of hits. They believed very strongly in the advantages offered by $u$ as a cache parameter, because $u$ provides

## 7.3 Other Cache-Related Studies

impact on performance and most importantly $u$ was insensitive to cache design parameters (such as width of the bus between processor and cache, the specific way instructions are implemented, and the instruction fetching algorithm).

They defined two new parameters: $u$, or misses per instruction, and $k$, the cost in extra misses from a switch of tasks. The use of $k$ allowed substantial independence from certain relationships between performance and cache design parameters. They also provided new performance data based on sampling of a data-processing system with numerical examples of how this might be used by the designer of a new system.

In 1973, Pohm and others (P4) investigated the feasibility of a multiclass buffer memory system with a flexible segmented directory and update list structures constructed from fast memory cells. The system was designed in a modular form such that the number of words per block, blocks per class, and classes could be conveniently varied and allowed the system to be conveniently tailored for intended use. They demonstrated that the use of buffer increased the cost of 500,000 bytes memory by about 8%, while decreasing the effective cycle time by a factor of 3.

In 1974, Agrawal [A6] investigated the applicability of cache concepts to SYMBOL-2R-like unconventional computing structures. His specific goals were to analyze the effects of architectural organization of an unconventional computing structure on the design management of its cache memory, to investigate whether in a multidedicated nonhomogeneous time-sharing system the cache should be organized as a homogeneous unit or a heterogeneous unit, and to determine whether the cache should be partitioned into equal sizes for different classes or whether the amount of cache allotted to a class would vary depending upon its need and demand.

It was shown that for SYMBOL-2R-like computing structures, the address referencing pattern and total amount of memory activity of different dedicated processors were highly affected by the storage organization and management of its virtual memory system. From the experimental data it was observed that each processor had a cache need characteristic of its special function rather than the particular problem being run. From this he concluded that the overall hit ratio would not be affected very much by the variation of user environments. The concept of small dedicated cache memories for a multidedicated processor of SYMBOL-2R-like structure was found to be very effective, because the memory space for a processor was exclusive for a time slice and consequently did not generate any interference for other processors when directory search occurred.

In 1974, Chow [C8] treated the optimization of storage hierarchy as a geometric programming problem and formulated a very simple model.

He assumed the hit ratio function to be representable by power functions and developed explicit formulas for the minimum hierarchy access time. He showed that the optimal number of storage levels in the hierarchy was proportional to the logarithm of the system's capacity with the constant of proportionality depending on technology and hit ratio characteristics. Also he showed that the optimal cost ratios of adjacent storage levels, storage capacities of adjacent level, and ratios of device access times were constant.

For quickly assessing many of the technological and structural alternatives in storage hierarchies, Gecsei and Lukes [G7] developed a model based on a cyclic queuing model of computer systems and its programming environment. Their goal in formulating this model was to create a computationally efficient technique for evaluating the gross effects on performance of variations in computing work load and hierarchical components.

Gecsei in 1974 [G8] extended the concept of stack processing developed by Mattson and others, called a joint stack processing technique for determining hit ratios for a class of multilevel hierarchies (called staging hierarchies). The staging hierarchies concept, as introduced by Slutz and Traiger (S9), allowed for an arbitrary number of memory levels using different block sizes of various levels and for multiple copies of the same block in the system.

In 1975, Pohm and others [P3] identified four writing policies: (1) write through (WT), where the main information is always updated for write operations; (2) simple swap (SS), where information was written back into main memory when it was removed from cache; (3) flagged swap (FS), where only information that was changed was written back to main memory; and (4) flagged-register swap (FRS) by which a block of information that was changed and was to be written back was swapped into a register first and then written to the memory later. They derived the relation for computing effective access time and cycle time for different cases. They demonstrated that the FRS algorithm was superior to all other algorithms. They showed that for a 50-ns buffer with a 750-ns backing store and a 200-ns buffer with a 1500-ns backing store, even with hit ratio as low as 0.80 to 0.82, it was possible to achieve a 4 to 1 increase in speed over the backing store speed. They also considered the effect of interleaving for improved performance. They considered two alternative designs, involving four memory modules. In one, a 200-ns, 500-word buffer was attached to each single 700-ns access time, 1500-ns cycle time backing store module. In the other alternative, a 2000-word buffer was attached to the four models operating simultaneously to transfer four words of block at a time. The equivalent effective cycle time for the four independent modules was 100 ns and for the single system it was 215 ns.

7.4 Cache for Minicomputers                                                      189

It was shown by them that interleaving individually buffered main memory modules can achieve very high system performance not achievable in a single buffer. The cost, however, was larger than for a single buffer scheme.

## 7.4 CACHE FOR MINICOMPUTERS

In 1971, Bell and Casasent [B3] investigated the feasibility of using a small cache for the PDP-8/E to get about five times improvement in performance. The PDP-8/E had 4K words of main memory with a cycle time of 1 $\mu$s. Using a fast cache of 100 ns, they illustrated the possibility of getting an effective cycle time of 200 ns. They pointed out that, due to ease of implementation, the simple direct mapping scheme was most appropriate for the minicomputer. Simulation results were obtained for three different assembly language programs for cache sizes ranging from 64 to 512 words.

They also investigated three different write back strategies: (1) to always write the word in cache and main memory (WT), (2) to write the new word in cache first and always write into the main memory when the word has to be replaced (simple swap), and (3) to use a control bit to indicate whether the word has been modified or not, and do the writing based on the flag control bit (flagged swap). They further investigated the effect of splitting the cache into separate instruction and data buffers. For an undivided cache, they considered the one cache to be organized one word wide and for divided cache, they considered two ways of organizing the cache, both one word and two words wide. They found that the undivided cache gave better performance in all cases.

Trying to show the technical feasibility of a cache memory with a small minicomputer, they demonstrated that it was possible to get a performance gain of 5 or more at a cost increase of 2 or less.

In 1974, Bell and others [B4] described again further simulation results carried out on a minicomputer PDP-8E. They considered detailed investigation of three different writing strategies: write through, conflicting usage write back (CUW), and conflicting usage write back with a modified bit (CUX). The modified bit kept track of whether the word in the cache was modified or not. If the word was not modified, the cache data were not written back into main memory during replacement time. It was found that the CUX scheme gave considerably improved performance over simple write through strategy (Figure 7.20).

To collect traces, three different programs generating traces of 1 million addresses each were chosen. One program was a numerical computation in FOCAL, an interactive interpreter that was widely used. The

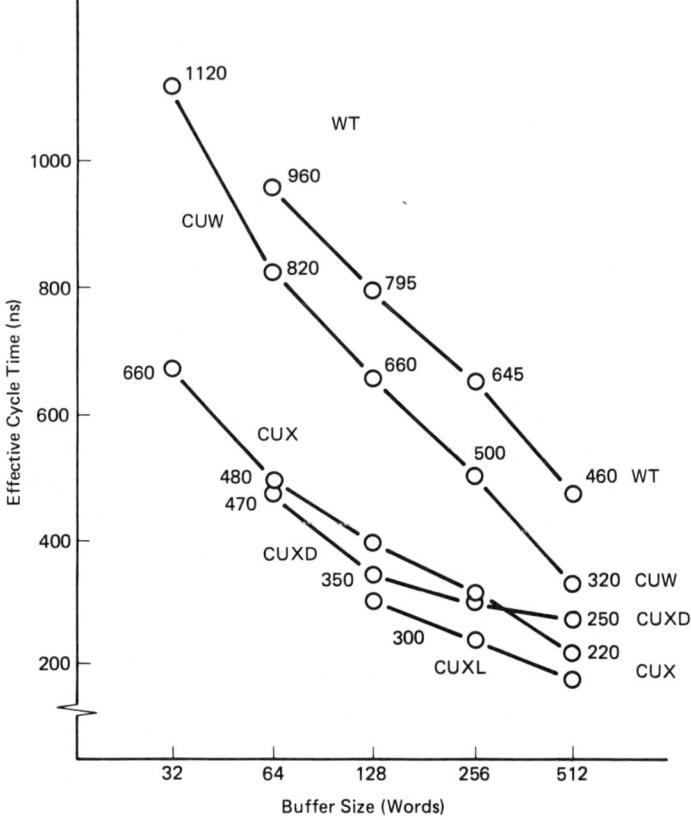

**Figure 7.20.** Bell, Casasent, and Bell's Data

second program was FFT, which was the most commonly requested program from the program library, and the third was an assembly program. Like the previous study, they also investigated the possibility of organizing the cache as a collection of heterogeneous cells—instructions and data.

For a divided cache, the best performance was obtained when it was divided into two equal halves, one for instruction and another for data. However, this performance was still worse than that obtained from an undivided homogeneous cache. Also, like the mainframe philosophy, this investigated the possibility of a cache with look ahead (CUXL). In this scheme, everytime a word was brought in from main memory, the next consecutive word was also brought into the next consecutive cell at the

## 7.4 Cache for Minicomputers

same time. Even though this scheme seemed to give better performance than without the look-ahead feature, because of complexity it was not thought to be worthwhile to add to the cache.

In 1975, Pucknell in England [P5, P6] investigated cost-effective performance enhancements of small processors operating in real-time engineering environments. He concluded that, out of all the techniques that had been used in large computer systems, the cache store concept was the most promising scheme for improving performance.

Tredennick and Welch [T7] in 1977 investigated cache buffering schemes for variable-length operand processing. They demonstrated that interposing three small direct-mapped cache stores between the slow memory and the serial arithmetic unit obviated the need for variable-length, general-purpose registers in the ALU.

In the commercial minicomputer field, the Eclipse, a high-performance 16-bit CPU featuring microprogrammed control, floating-point arithmetic, and up to 256K bits of error-correcting MOS memory, was the first minicomputer to employ a cache system. With all these integrated features, Eclipse was designed as a high-performance machine for high-level language and operating system [D2, D3].

A high-speed, content addressable, bipolar cache memory of 16 words was integrated along with each memory board of 8K words. This distributed cache buffer approach enabled the CPU to get 2 bytes of data every 200 ns and to achieve an overall system bandwidth of $10^6$ bytes/second. Since the cache was local to the memory board, the ratio of bipolar cache to MOS memory remained constant no matter how many boards were used. This allowed very easy memory expansion. For a CPU request, first the content addressable memory was checked to see if the data were in cache. If there was a match, data were made available to the CPU in 200 ns; otherwise they were retrieved from MOS memory in 700 ns.

The 16-word cache had room for four blocks with each block being four words. The cache controller used a least recently used algorithm to replace any particular block from the cache. It continuously assigned the most recently used, next to most, next to least, and least recently used tag to each block in cache and flagged invalid data, making those data the next candidate for replacement.

Furthermore, the memory was interleaved two, four, or eight ways to reduce effective memory cycle time. With four-way core memory interleaving, it was possible to achieve an effective cycle time of 600 ns (rather than 800 ns), and with eight-way interleaving it was possible to reduce core cycle time to 500 ns. Eclipse was an attempt at very innovative design with conservative techology [W7].

## PDP-11/70 MMU and Cache

The PDP-11/70 was introduced by DEC in 1976 as the most powerful member of the 16-bit PDP-11 family. This computer was designed to operate in very large, sophisticated, high-performance systems, varying from high-speed real-time applications to multiuser, multitask time-shared applications [P9]. Extending the physical address space to over 2M bytes, this computer embedded the notion of three separate address spaces: a 16-bit program virtual address space, an 18-bit unibus space, and a 22-bit physical address space (Figure 7.21). The 22-bit physical address space enables the CPU to reference a unique 2M-byte memory location. For this machine, the physical address space (22 bits) was much bigger than its virtual address space 16 bits). A memory management unit (MMU) integrated within the CPU converted a 16-bit program virtual address to 22-bit physical address, and a separate unibus map was provided to map an 18-bit address to the 22-bit physical address.

### Memory Management Unit

The memory management unit (MMU) integrated within the CPU provided the hardware facility for memory management and protection. Memory management functions include allocation and reallocation of memory for various users in a multiuser, multiprogramming system environment and valid access checking to protect any user program from malicious use of memory.

The MMU of PDP-11/70 consisted of three sets of 32 sixteen-bit registers (a total of 96 sixteen-bit registers), one for kernel mode, one for supervisor, and one for user mode. The mode filled in the processor status

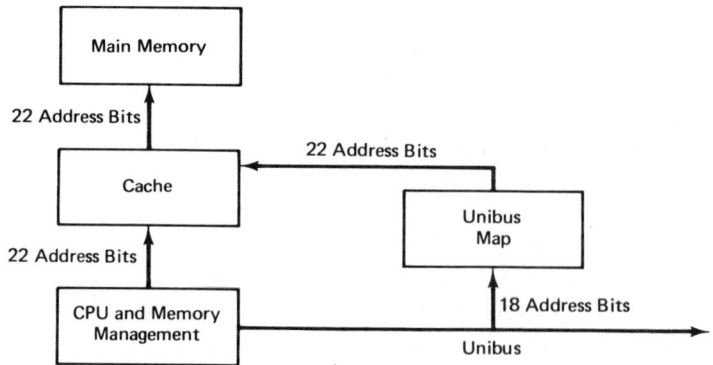

**Figure 7.21.** Address Space of PDP-11/70

## 7.4 Cache for Minicomputers

word, which specified the set of registers to be used. Each set of dedicated registers was further partitioned into two groups of registers, one for instruction and one for data space. Each of these groups was further subdivided into two parts of eight registers. One part was called page address register (PAR) and the other, page descriptor register (PDR), the PAR and PDR being selected as a pair. Both the I space and the D space had eight PARs and eight PDRs in each mode of the CPU operation—kernel, supervisor, and user (Figure 7.22). The I space was used for all instruction fetches, index words, absolute addresses, and immediate operands; D space was used for all other references.

A PAR/PDR pair contained all the information needed to describe and locate a currently active page. In the PDP-11/70, the memory is allocated dynamically in pages, which varies from 32 words to 4K words, (64 bytes to 8K bytes) and can be located anywhere in physical memory. Each page is composed of 1 to 128 internal blocks of 32 words, and the starting physical address of each page is an integral multiple of 32 words (64 bytes) (i.e., pages are allocated on a 64-byte boundary). The page

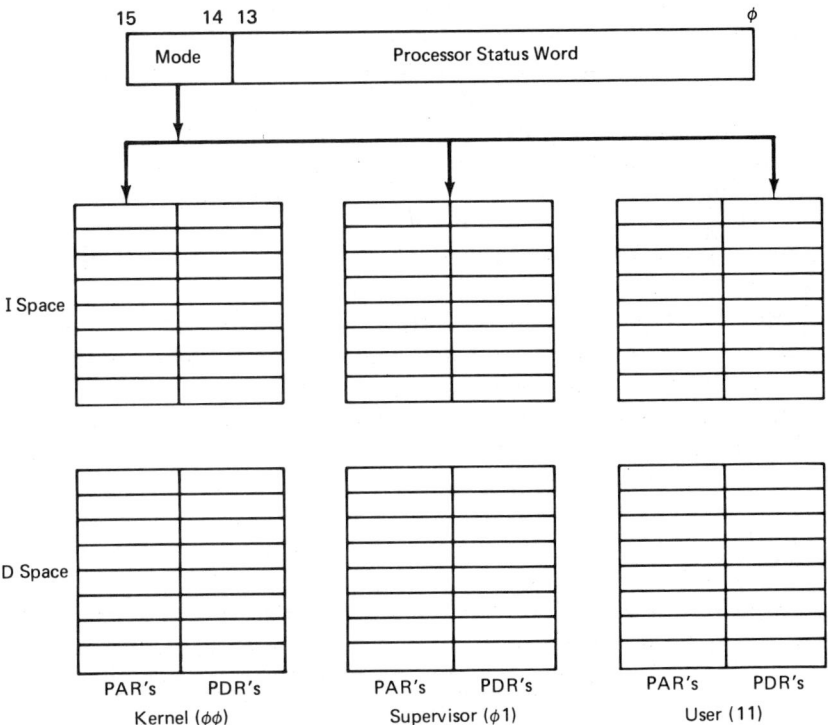

**Figure 7.22.** Memory Management Unit of PDP-11/70

address register (PAR) contains the starting address of the page as a block number in physical memory, whereas the page descriptor register contains the information relative to page length access control and page expansion. This scheme allows pages to be dynamically relocated in physical memory in a manner completely transparent to the programmer by merely changing the PARs.

*Address Translation*

The virtual address of the PDP-11/70 consists of three fields: two 3-bit active page field (APF), which selects a particular PAR/PDR pair, a 7-bit block number in the current page, and a 6-bit offset within the block (Figure 7-23).

The logical sequence for constructing the physical address from the logical address is as follows: the 3-bit APF of the virtual address selects a particular PAR/PDR pair from the corresponding space (I or D space) of the corresponding mode (kernel, supervisor, user). The block number from the virtual address is compared against the page length field (PDF 8-14) to detect any possible bound or length errors. An error can exist in two ways, when expanding upward if the specified block number in the virtual address is greater than the one in the corresponding page length field of the PDR, and when expanding downward if the block number is less than the page length field. If there is no error, the block number of VA (virtual address) is added to the page address field (of the PAR) to generate the block number which will contain the physical address of the block. The offset within the block from the VA field is concatenated with the physical block number to yield a true 32-bit physical address (Figure 7.24).

Besides the page length field, the PDR contains some access control and access information bits. It also contains a bit that can specify the direction of page expansion for either program space or stack space. To provide a powerful memory management scheme, the system has also used four separate memory management registers or fault recovery registers.

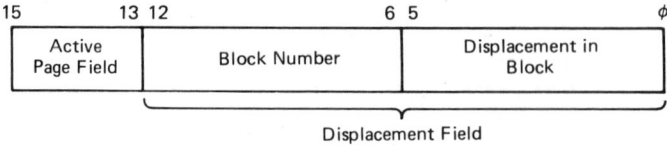

**Figure 7.23.** PDP-11/70 Virtual Address (16 Bits)

## 7.4 Cache for Minicomputers

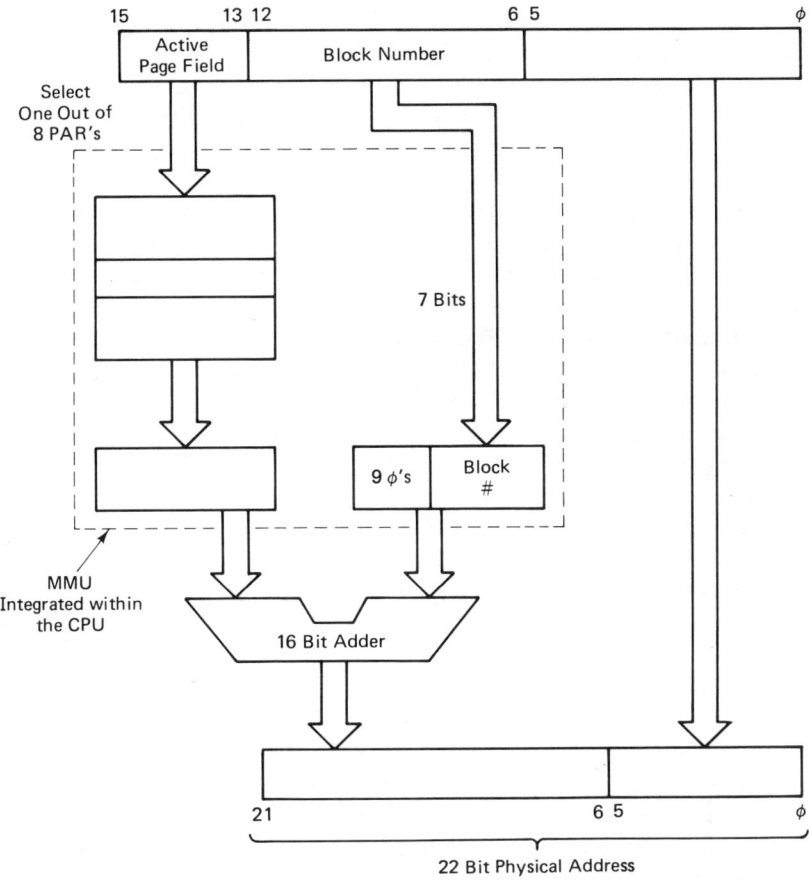

**Figure 7.24.** PDP-11/70 Virtual to Physical Address Translation

### Data Cache

Besides a powerful memory management unit, the PDP 11/70 also has a 2K byte high-speed data cache to provide faster access to frequently needed data. After an extensive amount of simulation and modeling, the cache size was chosen to be 1K words organized as a two-set associative cache. A block of two words (4 bytes) was the basic unit of data transfer between the main memory and the data cache. Hence, the data cache consisted of 512 blocks of data with each set consisting of 256 blocks.

The physical address of the PDP-11/70 consists of three fields: bit 0 specifies the byte within a word, bit 1 specifies within the blocks, and bits 2 to 21 specify the block address. The block address consists of two subfields: index field and tag field.

The data cache is organized as 256 classes, two-set associative cache: set 0 and set 1. Bits 2 to 9 (8 bits) of the physical address serve as the index (class) address and bits 10 to 21 (12 bits) serve as the tag address. Each set of the data cache has conceptually two parts: an address (tag) array and a data array. Both the tag array and data array have 256 entries. Bits 2 to 9 serve as the index for the tag array. However, since each entry for the data array has a block of data *or* two words, each set of data array has room for 512 words and needs 9 bits for its address. Bits 1 to 9 serve as the index address for the data array.

The index field for the tag array (bits 2 to 9) specify a location in both sets of the index array. Once selected, the tags from both the sets of index array are associatively compared against the tag portion of the physical address (PA) (bits 10 to 21). If there is a match between the PA tag field and either of the tag sets, the reference is considered to be a data hit and the requested word or block is obtained from the corresponding set of the data array. These physical data are 16 bits wide. The physical byte portion of the physical address can be concatenated with the index portion for the data array to select any specific byte of data desired. Also, since the cache is for both data and instruction, data fetches from the cache can either be the physical data desired by the CPU or the instruction.

However, if there is no match between the tag field of the physical address and either of the tag entries (of the address array), the data reference are considered to be a miss and the requested data block has to be retrieved from the main memory. The read request is initiated for the desired block from the main memory, sent to CPU, stored in the cache, and the proper index array entry updated. If both sets of the index entry for the corresponding class are valid, some sort of replacement devision has to be made to select appropriate sets. The cache uses a random replacement, rather than an LRU or FIFO, as its replacement strategy for updating its sets.

The cache uses a write through strategy as its writing strategy. For write hits, both the cache and the main memory are updated. However, for a write miss, the referenced location is updated in main memory only, leaving the cache unchanged. Since the write frequency typically is 10% compared to read frequency of 90%, this write through scheme does not seem to impose too much overhead. But, since the main memory is always updated (because of write through strategy), it has a correct copy of data all the time, and there is no need to transfer any data from the cache to the main memory. Also, if power is suddenly lost and the data cache

## 7.4 Cache for Minicomputers

might become invalid, there is no problem because the core always has the correct copy.

The set associative data cache of the PDP-11/70 is also designed with the capability of running in degraded mode if certain problems are detected in the cache. If one particular set is malfunctioning, the system has the capability of forcing all references to other sets. Also, the system has the capability of completely bypassing the cache and forcing all references to main memory, with some degraded performance. All these are achieved with the help of a programmable control register. It is also to be noted that switching from the two set modes to the one set mode does not necessarily decrease the performance by 50%, because of the statistics of read hit probability.

### PDP-11/60

A cache memory was also used later in the PDP-11/60, a midrange minicomputer (M7). The simulation results of Strecker, which had very strongly affected the cache design of the PDP-11/70, also affected the design of the PDP-11/60. However, several design tradeoffs were made, which were appropriate for the PDP-11/60 design and its goals.

First, the block size of the 11/60 was chosen to be one word instead of two since a 16-bit unibus was used as the memory bus for the 11/60. Even though the block size of one word resulted in a slightly lower hit ratio (87% compared to 92% for the 11/70), it was thought to be quite adequate for its goals. Also, with the goal of achieving mid-cost and mid-performance while exploiting the given memory technology, the cache was organized as a directly mapped one rather than a set or fully associative one. Because the 11/60 used a set size of one, the replacement strategy was quite simple. (In fact, there was no need for a replacement strategy. The PDP-11/70 on the other hand used a random one.)

To reduce time delays associated with synchronization and transmission on the unibus, and for ease of retrofitting existing memory subsystems to the unibus, the cache was located between the CPU and the unibus rather than between the unibus and main memory.

Utilization of denser memory chips and a slight sacrifice of performance resulted in a significant reduction in the number of components. The PDP-11/70 cache required 440 chips, whereas the PDP-11/60 cache required only 85 chips. Simpler cache organization and more dense memory chips primarily were responsible for this improvement.

As the 16-bit minicomputer evolved into 32-bit ones, it was evident that cache organizations would be essential to provide adequate memory speed for these high-performance minicomputers. Two examples of such machines are the PDP VAX-11/780 and the Data General MV/8000.

## VAX-11/780 System

The VAX-11/780, a 32-bit high-performance minicomputer, was introduced by DEC in 1978. This system served as virtual address extension (VAX) of the PDP-11 family and provided over 4 billion bytes of virtual address space (32 bits) mapped to over 1 billion bytes of physical address space (30 bits). Virtual to physical address translation was done by microcode, and the system provided three accelerating mechanisms, an instruction buffer, an address translation buffer (ATB), and a data cache to achieve high performance. An 8-byte instruction buffer provided enough look-ahead capability for the CPU and enabled the CPU to fetch and decode the next macro instruction while the current instruction was completing its execution. A 128-entry address translation buffer served as a cache for virtual address and associated protection information, and an 8KB, two-set associative cache provided high-speed access to frequently needed data (Figure 7.25) [D4]. The address translation buffer has the virtual address as the input and generates the physical address as the output, whereas the data cache takes this physical address (generated by the ATB) as the input and produces required data as the output.

Conceptually (and physically) both the address translation buffer and the data cache contain two separate entities: an address array and a data array (Figure 7.26). The address array is simply the tag store, and the data array is the corresponding data output. For the address translation buffer, the address array contains the tags associated with the virtual

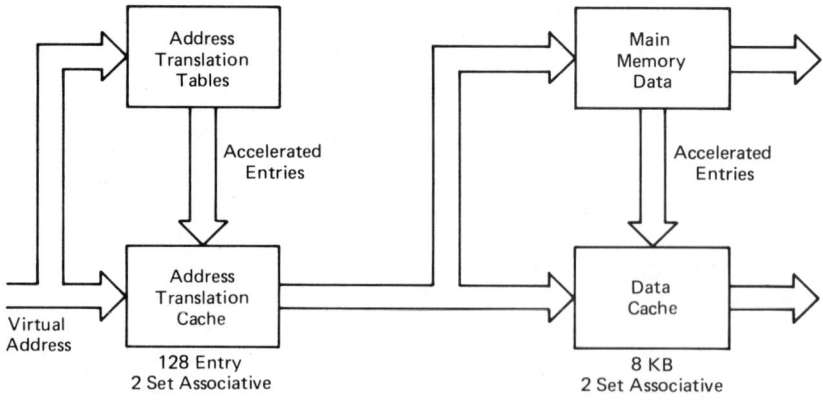

**Figure 7.25.** Address Translation Buffer and Data Cache for VAX-11/780

7.4 Cache for Minicomputers

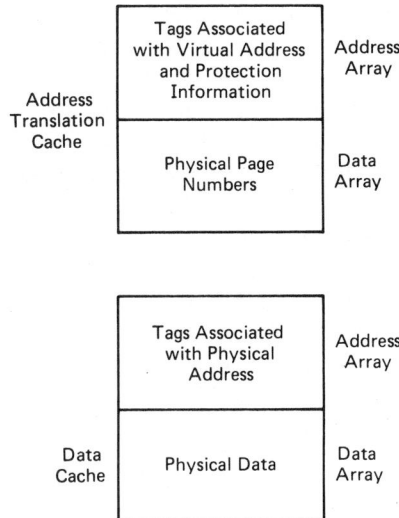

**Figure 7.26.** Address Translation Cache and Data Cache for VAX-11/780

address and the protection information; whereas for the data cache, the address array contains the tags associated with the physical address. For the address translation buffer, the data array contains the physical address (physical page from number), whereas the data array of the data cache contains the actual physical data.

*Virtual and Physical Address Space of VAX-11/780*

The virtual address space of over 4 billion bytes is defined by a 32-bit virtual address and extends from address 0 to FFFFFFFF. The total virtual address space is partitioned into two spaces: process space (extending from 00000000 to 7FFFFFFF over 2 billion bytes) and system space (extending from 8000,000 to FFFFFFFF, over 2 billion bytes). The per process space is further partitioned into two sections—the program space P0 (extending from 00000000 to 3FFFFFFF) and control space P1 (extending from 4000,000 to 7FFFFFFF). The highest quarter of virtual space (from C0000000 to FFFFFFFF) is currently unassigned [D4].

The entire virtual address space is divided into 512-byte pages whose boundaries are invisible to the programmers. The virtual address generated by the CPU specifies three things: (1) whether system or process space, (2) virtual page number, and (3) physical offset within a page. Maps of virtual page numbers to physical page number of main memory are stored in main memory as page tables. Besides containing the address translation information, each entry in the page table contains some protection information for the corresponding virtual page. Since these mapping page tables can be quite large, the address translation buffer essentially serves as an accelerator for page table entries.

The physical address space of the VAX-11/780 is 30 bits (over 1 billion bytes). The physical address space consists of two parts, primary memory space and I/0 space (Figure 7.27).

The virtual and physical memory space architecture has definite impact on the organization of translation buffer and data cache. To provide fast access to information for both system and process space, the address translation buffer consists of entries for both system and process space.

Partitioning of the address translation buffer into system and process space enables selective invalidation of only process page table entries for process swap. Since system space is shared by all the processes, these entries are not invalidated during process swap, thus improving the total system performance.

## Address Translation

As shown in Figure 7.28(a) and (b), the virtual address of the VAX-11/780 consists of three fields: byte offset within the page, an index portion, and some tag information. VA(0 to 8) specifies the byte offset within the page, VA(9 to 13) and VA31 (system and process space bit) serve as the index, and bits 14 to 30 of VA constitute the virtual page number. Six bits of index address (VA31 and VA13-9) serve as the index address or class address for the address and data array of the ATB. Both the address array and the data array of the ATB are organized as two-set associative

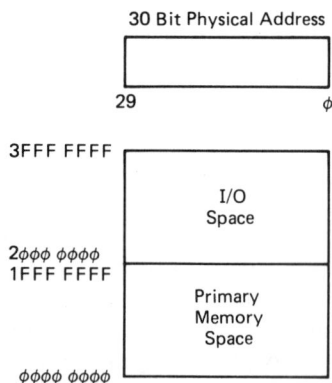

**Figure 7.27.** Physical Address Space

### 7.4 Cache for Minicomputers

cache. Each set of address array consists of 32 entries for system space and 32 entries for process space, a total of 64 entries per set.

The index field of the virtual address selects a location in both the sets of the address array and the data array. Once selected, the tags from both the sets of the address array are associatively compared against the tag of the virtual address. If there is a match between the VA tag field and either of the set tags, the reference is considered to be an address hit and the corresponding physical page frame number is obtained from the corresponding set of the data array. This physical page frame number is 21 bits. The byte offset from the VA field is concatenated with the physical page from number to generate the physical address of 30 bits. Also, during the address translation, the protection information for the virtual address is checked for any possible access violation. If there is some protection violation, some system software is invoked to handle it (Figure 7.29).

However, if there is no match between the VA tag field and either of the tag entries (of the address array), the reference is considered to be a miss and a microtrap is generated. The microtrap invokes a microprogram routine, which tries to update the entry in the address translation cache from a proper PTE entry (from main memory). If it succeeds in fetching the PTE entry (note that it can get a page fault, depending on if it is a process page table entry), it tries to update the ATB address array and the data array and tries the reference again. If the associated valid bit is set (that means the page is a valid page), it succeeds in the next try. If the valid bit is reset, it invokes a system softward routine, which would have the responsibility of locating the proper page, bringing it to the main memory (if necessary), updating the PTE, and then retrying the reference.

Since the address translation buffer contains a maximum of 128 entries, at a given time it can accelerate a maximum of 128 different virtual pages. Also, theATB generates a 30-bit physical address, which has to go through another level of translation before actual data are obtained. This mapping is provided by the data cache.

*Data Cache*

Like the address translation buffer (ATB), the data cache is also organized as two-set associative cache, set 0 and set 1. Each set, like the ATB, has two parts, an address tag array and a data array. Since a quad word (2 long words, or 4 words or 8 bytes) is the basic unit of information transfer between the cache and the main memory, each address array entry (of the data cache) corresponds to one data matrix entry consisting of a quad word. The address array entries provide the mapping from the physical address (generated by the ATB) to the physical address of the cache; and the data array entries provide the actual physical data.

For achieving the optimum hit ratio and given cost–technology considerations, the data cache (both the address array and the data array) is organized as two set associative, with 512 entries in each set. These 512 entries can be thought of as 512 different classes. Since each entry of data array consists of 1 quad word, the capacity of each set of data array is 512 quad words (or 4K bytes), and the total capacity of the data cache is 1K quad word or 8K bytes.

*Data Cache Operation*

The physical address generated by the ATB consists of three fields: bits 0 to 2 specify long word address and byte offset within the long word, bits 3 to 11 specify the index or class address, and bits 12 to 29 serve as the tag portion of the physical address. Note that the address array of the data cache has no protection information, and it is not partitioned into system or physical address data. The concept of system or process space is associated only with virtual address and not with data.

Also, note that even though each set of the data array of the data cache has 512 entries, each of its entries consists of a quad word or 2 long words. Hence each set of the data array really has space for 1024 long words. So the index address for the address array (512 reentries) and the data array (1024 entries) are of different size, and a mechanism has to be provided to address these. Whereas bits 3 to 11 of physical address (PA) serve as the index address of the address array, bit 2 of PA (long word specifies) is combined with bits 3 to 11 of PA to serve as the index address for the data array.

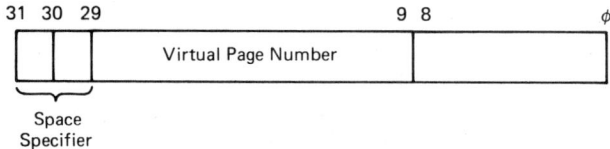

| Bits | | Space |
| 31 | 30 | |
|---|---|---|
| 1 | 0 | Program Space |
| 0 | 1 | Control Space |
| 1 | 0 | System Space |
| 1 | 1 | Reserved |

(a)

**Figure 7.28(a).** Virtual Address Format of VAX-11/780

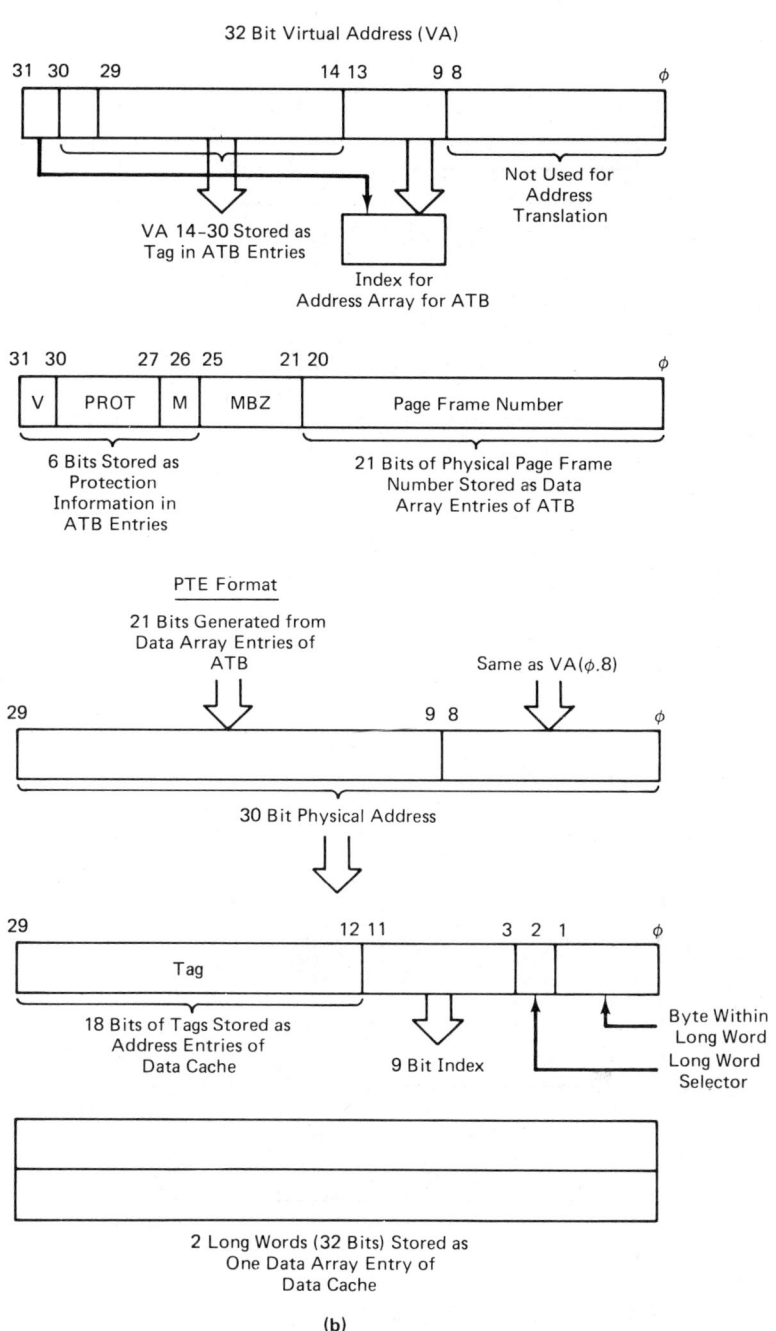

**Figure 7.28(b).** VA Format, PTE Format, Indexing of Data Cache and Cache Entry

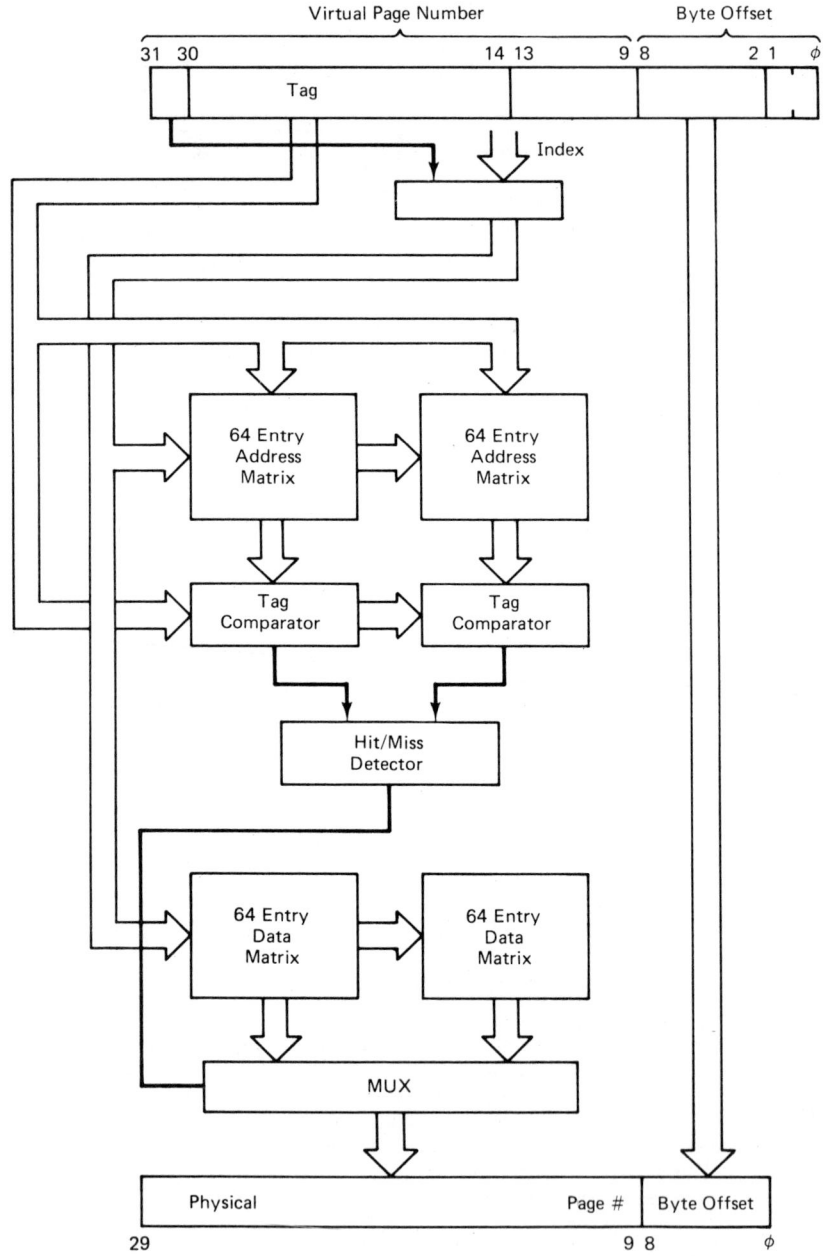

**Figure 7.29.** VAX-11/780 Virtual to Physical Address Translation

## 7.4 Cache for Minicomputers

The index field of the PA (bits 3 to 11), for the address array, specified a location in both sets of the address array. Once selected, the tags from both sets of address array are associatively compared against the tag of the PA. If there is a match between the PA tag field and either of the set tags, the reference is considered to be a data bit, and a corresponding quad word of data is obtained from the corresponding set of the data array (Figure 7.30). These physical data are 32 bits wide. The physical byte offset portion of the physical address can be concatenated with the output

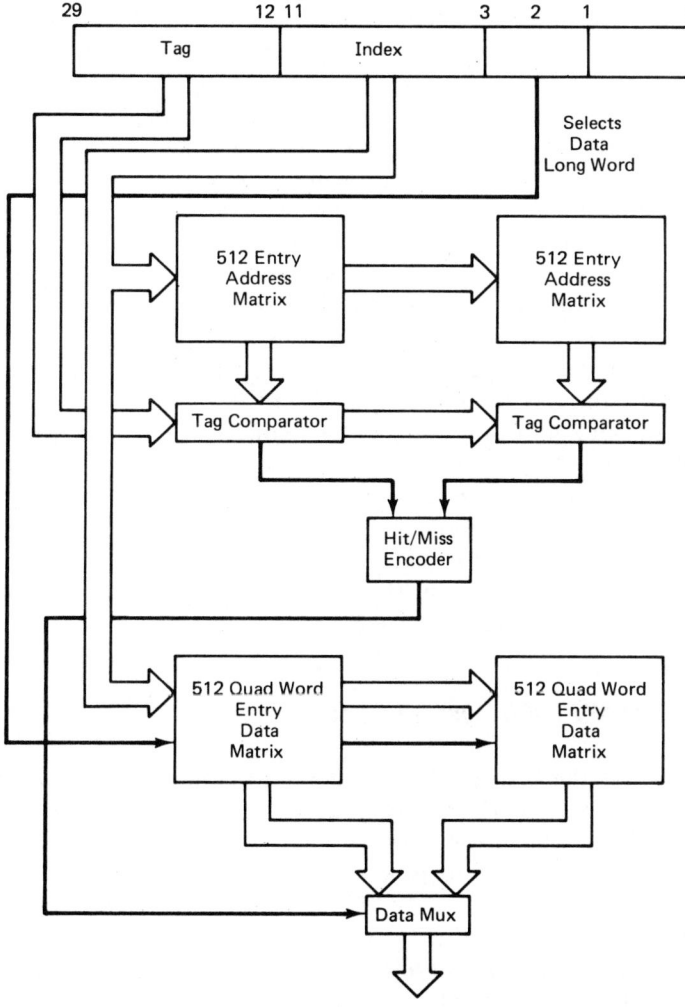

**Figure 7.30.** Data Cache of VAX-11/780

of the address array to select any specific byte of data desired. Also note that these data can be either the data desired by the CPU or may even be the instruction, which can be loaded into the instruction buffer. However, if there is no match between the PA tag field and either of the tag entries (of the address array), the data reference is considered to be a miss and a microtrap is generated to handle this.

For the VAX-11/780, for the data cache a distinction is made between read or write miss. If there is a read miss, the entire quad word (2 long words) has to be retrieved from the main memory and written into the associated set. If both sets are valid, some sort of replacement decision might have to be made to select the one to update.

The data cache uses a random replacement rather than LRU or FIFO strategy as its replacement strategy for updating the set. A flip-flop is essentially used as a random bit, which is complemented every cycle until a miss occurs. In the case of write miss, the referenced location is updated in main memory only. The data cache uses a modified write through scheme. For cache write hits, both the cache and the main memory are updated. However, no overhead is imposed on CPU to wait until the completion of the memory write cycle. Only for two successive writes or an instruction buffer miss followed by a write is the CPU forced to wait. This scheme also results in improved performance.

Note that the data cache serves as accelerator for long words of main memory and has the capacity of 8K bytes of data. Since each page contains 512 bytes of data, conceptually, the data cache can hold information of either 16 distinct pages (512 bytes each) *or* 64 bytes of information of 512 different pages.

The VAX-11/780 demonstrated the implementation of a full-scale cache concept for both address translation and the data cache on a high end minicomputer. Since then, these caches have become ubiquitous in all high end minicomputers.

## Data General MV/8000 System Cache

The MV/8000 is the high-performance 32-bit minicomputer of Data General, announced in 1980 [D5]. It offers complete hardware–software compatibility with the entire range of its 16-bit AOS based systems (Eclipse family). The MV/8000 architecture has a virtual address space of 4.3 billion bytes (32 bits) and a physical address space of 512M bytes. The first implemenation of this architecture supports a physical address space of 2M bytes. Virtual to physical address translation is done by microcode, and the system has provided three accelerating mechanisms: an instruction cache, an address translation buffer, and a data cache to achieve high

## 7.4 Cache for Minicomputers

performance. A 1K byte (64 blocks, 16 bytes) direct mapped instruction cache provides enough look-ahead and look-behind capability to achieve high pipelined implementation of the CPU for high performance. A 256-entry address translation buffer serves as a cache for virtual address and address protection information, and a 16KB (1K blocks, 16 bytes each) direct mapped cache provides high-speed access to frequently needed data, as shown in Figure 7.31. The address translation buffer has virtual address as the input and generates physical address as the output, whereas the data cache takes this physical address (generated by ATB) as the input and produces required data as the output.

The AOS/VS operating system of MV/8000 partitions the 403 billion bytes of virtual storage space into two exclusive spaces: individual user program space and system space. The user programs occupy the lower half of virtual address space (up to 2.15 billion bytes), and the system occupies the remaining half of the address space. These spaces do not overlap.

For managing this huge virtual address space efficiently, the total virtual address space is partitioned into eight smaller virtual spaces called segments. The virtual to physical address translation is done on a segment basis using either a one- or two-level page table structure. Both the logical and physical address space are partitioned into 2K byte paths, and the hardware supports the 2K byte page structure directly (Figure 7.32).

Since the logical address space is much larger than the physical address space, all the pages of the disk or secondary store cannot reside in the main memory. Hence, the system employs a mapping scheme using

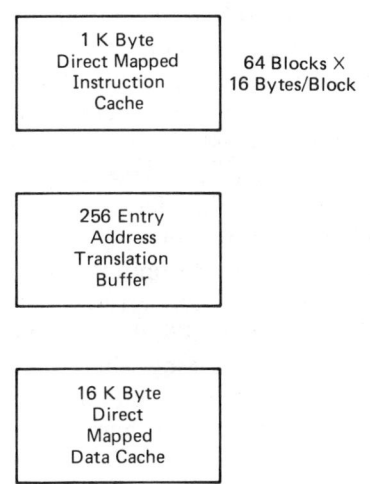

**Figure 7.31.** Information Accelerator Mechanisms for MV/8000

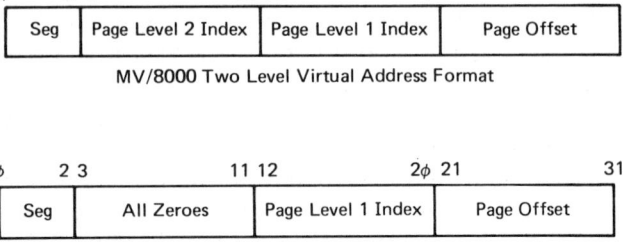

**Figure 7.32.** One- and Two-Level Virtual Address Format of MV/8000

a series of page tables to map logical pages to physical pages. This translation is done by an address translation unit (ATU). The page table entry provides status information about the page, whether it is valid and can be accessed, whether it is currently in the physical memory, and if so where does it reside in physical memory. Also, it has some access protection information associated with a page: whether it is used for read only or write, and so on. These page tables are kept in main memory and secondary store. Figures 7.33 and 7.34 show address generation mechanisms for the MV/8000.

For providing faster access to physical pages (and for avoiding access to page table entries), the hardware ATU accelerates up to 256 addresses of different logical pages that are potentially most frequently needed by the CPU.

Besides accelerating page table entries, the entries of ATU contain two extra bits of information to help the operating system to manage its pages more efficiently during page faults. These two bits are a modified bit and a reference bit. A page fault occurs when a reference is made for a logical page that is not currently in the physical memory. Each time a page fault occurs, the new requested page must be transferred from the backing store to the physical memory. Depending upon the room available in the physical memory, a page might have to be removed from the physical memory to make room for the new page. The operating system uses the modified bit information to determine whether the particular page selected for removal needs to be transferred or not. If the modified bit is 0, that is, the page has not been modified since it was last brought in from the disk, and the disk has a valid copy, there is no need to transfer this page to the disk. However, if the modified bit is 1, the page has been modified since it was brought last and there is a need to transfer this to the disk.

The reference bit information is also used by the operating system to determine the frequency of reference to individual pages. It helps op-

## 7.4 Cache for Minicomputers

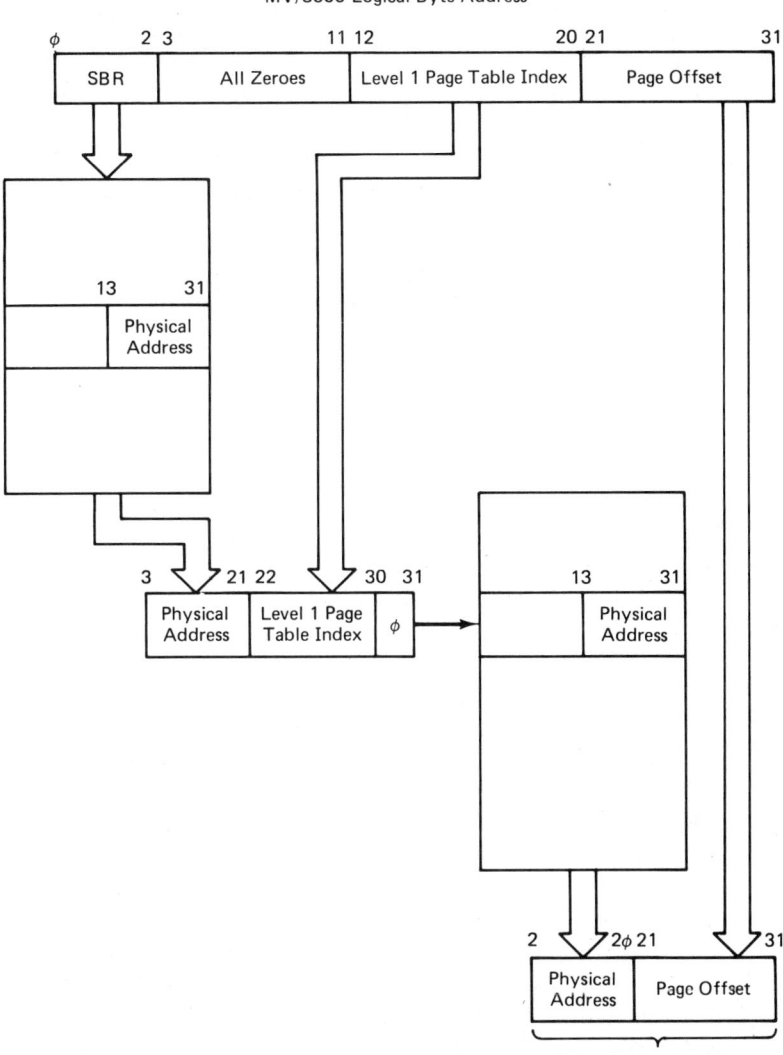

**Figure 7.33.** MV/8000 One-Level Page Table Address Translation

erating systems to replace the least frequently referenced page.

Besides this mapping, the MV/8000 uses a *demand page* swapping mechanism for improving its main memory utilization. Demand paging implies that logical pages are stored in disk rather than the main memory and are brought to main memory only when demanded. The page fault

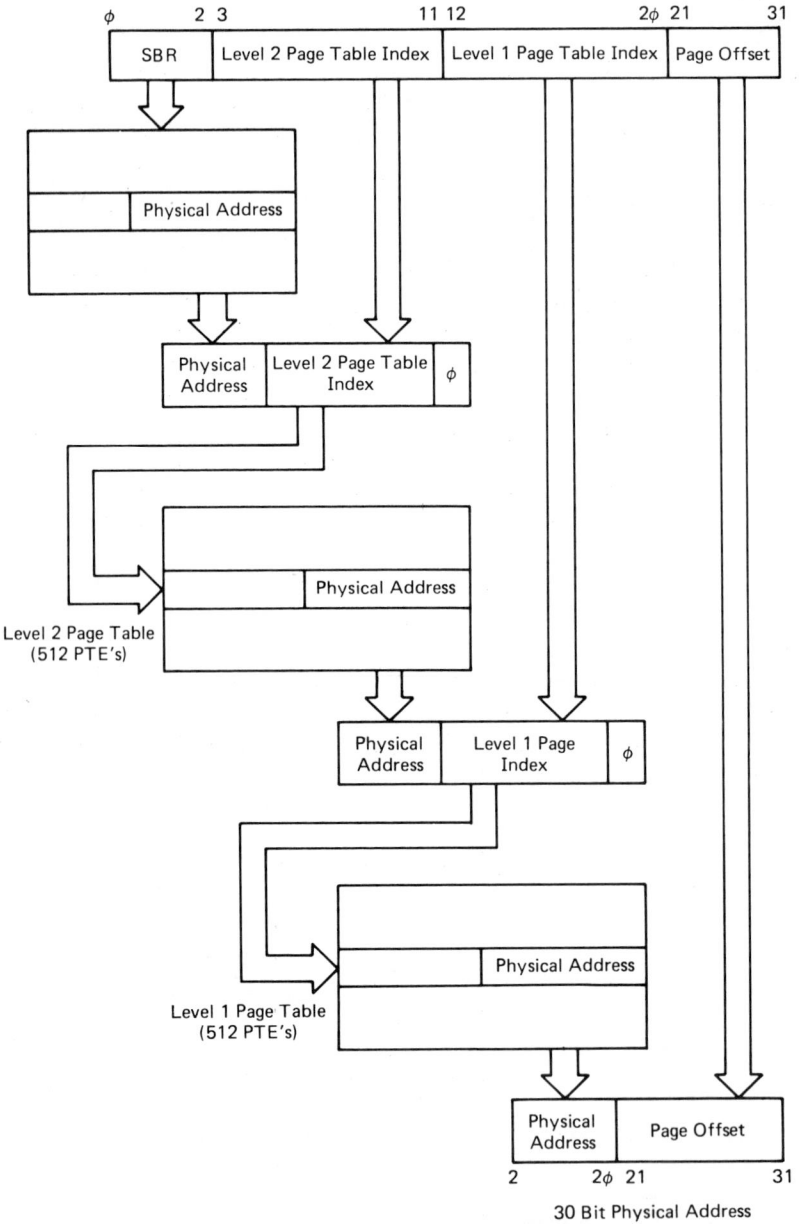

**Figure 7.34.** MV/8000 Two-Level Page Table Address Translation Mechanism

### 7.4 Cache for Minicomputers

handler of the paging mechanism handles the demand page operation. Upon detection of a page fault, the page fault handler is invoked, which initiates request for the appropriate page, brings in the page, and updates the appropriate page table entry.

The address translation buffer contains entries for 256 pages and is organized as 256-entry direct mapped cache. Besides the ATB, the MV/8000 also has a data cache.

*Data Cache*

The data cache (called the system cache) of the MV/8000 is a 16K-byte cache with a cycle time of 110 ns for accessing 4 bytes. The cache is designed in such a way that a fetch can be initiated by the CPU every machine cycle. The CPU can fetch 4 bytes of data from the cache in 220 ns and 8 bytes in 330 ns.

Both the main storage and the system data cache are divided into blocks of 16 bytes, and a 16-byte block is the basic unit of data transfer between the main storage and the cache. The cache is organized as a 1K 16-byte blocks, direct mapped cache. Any block in the system cache contains 16 contiguous bytes from main memory. However, since the cache is direct mapped, there is one-to-one correspondence between main memory blocks and system cache blocks. Even though MV/8000 architecture supports up to 512M bytes of physical address space, the first implementation of the MV/8000 has support for up to 2MB of physical space. For this the main memory can be visualized as partitioned into 128 units, each unit consisting of 1K blocks. The system data cache has a maximum space of one to three units. However, since the cache is organized on a block basis, a particular block of a particular unit can reside in a fixed location of the cache. For example, block 0 at unit 1, 2, 3, and so on, can reside in the block 0 position of system cache, and so on. This direct mapping scheme eliminates the need for an associative search for large number of blocks and also eliminates large numbers of comparators and multiplexers.

Because the first implementation supports physical address space of 2MB, only bits 1 to 31 (lower-order 21 bits) of the physical address are used by the cache as the effective address. This effective address consists of two fields: bits 28 to 31 (4 bits) specify byte offset within the block; bits 11 to 27 specify the block address. The block address actually consists of two subfields: an index field and a tag field. Since the cache is organized as 1K direct mapped, bits 18 to 27 (10 bits) serve as the index field and bits 11 to 17 (7 bits) serve as the tag field. Since the cache is organized on a block basis, the tag is associated with a block.

The data cache can be visualized as consisting of two entities: a tag array and a data array. The index field of the effective address (bits 18 to 27) specifies a particular block location of tag array and data array. Once selected, the tag entry of the tag array is compared with the tag field of the effective address (bits 11 to 17). If there is a match between the two, the reference is considered to be a data hit, and the byte offset of the effective address is concatenated with the index field to get proper data from the cache to CPU.

However, if the requested block is not found in the tag array, then the corresponding data block has to be fetched from the main storage, sent to the CPU, and stored in cache for future reference. The particular word requested by the CPU is the first one that is fetched from the main storage, and it is sent to the CPU first. The rest of the block is fetched from the main storage subsequently.

Since the cache is direct mapped, the replacement scheme is straightforward. There is only one place where the requested block can reside.

The system cache uses a write back strategy as its writing strategy. So it keeps a modified bit to keep track of whether the block needs to be rewritten to the main memory. Upon write hits, only the cache block is updated. Upon block removal, if the block has been modified, it is first rewritten to the main memory and then updated with the proper block.

## 7.5 MEMORY MANAGEMENT AND CACHE SUPPORT FOR MICROPROCESSORS

With persistent advancement in technology and rapid decline in the cost of hardware, microprocessors with the capability of high-end minicomputers are being produced. We have seen the growth of four generations of microprocessors from 4-bit simple microprocessors to most complex 32-bit CPUs. The perfomance and capability of the first two generations of microprocessors were quite limited. The address space was limited to 64K bytes, software development was done with the assembly language, and memory management was not a big issue. However, the memory addressing capability of third- and fourth-generation microprocessors has increased quite significantly. Memory addressing capabilities of some of the third-generation microprocessors are 1M bytes for Intel's 8086, 16M bytes for Motorola's 68000 and National's 16–32, and 8M bytes for Zilog and AMD's 28000. The memory addressing capability of some fourth-generation microprocessors, such as Intel's IAPX 432, is $2^{40}$ bytes. (This is much longer than most of the mainframes and high-end 32-bit minicomputers addressing space.)

With this large address space capability, the memory management problem—that of efficient allocation, reallocating memory space for optimization of overall memory usage, and protection of memory contents from unauthorized access—has been extended and applied to microprocessors. The memory management solution approach that has been applied to main memories has been adapted to microprocessors.

## 16-bit Memory Management Unit (MMU)

The need to provide support for high-level languages, sophisticated operating systems, large programs and data bases, and decreasing memory prices have accelerated the trend toward longer memory space for microprocessors. The concept of virtual memory management, which used to belong exclusively to mainframe and minicomputers, is becoming ubiquitous in high-performance microprocessors. Standard mechanisms for implementing virtual memory such as segmentation, paging, and segmentation with paging are being applied to microprocessors. In the 16-bit microprocessor field, two major camps have emerged in virtual memory implementation: AMD, Zilog, and Intel support segmented memory schemes, while Motorola and National advocate linear memory schemes.

## Zilog's Z8010 MMU

Zilog's Z8010 and AMD's AMZ8010 (the second source device) are the first-generation memory management units for 16-bit microprocesssors. This chip supports a segmented virtual memory management scheme similar to the ones developed for various mainframes and minicomputers.

The logical address space of the Z8001 CPU is partitioned into many linear address spaces each with a specified length or size, called segments. Each item of the segment is accessed by a two-component address; the first component specifies the segment number (segment selector), and the second component specifies the offset from the base of the segment to the item being selected (displacement selector).

The Z8001 CPU supports a segmented address space of 128 logical segments, each with 16K bytes, resulting in a total logical address space of 8M bytes. The Z8001 CPU generates a logical address that consists of a bit segment number and a 16-bit offset (Figure 7.35). Besides this, the CPU further generates status signals to indicate whether it is doing an instruction fetch, data fetch, or stack area operation and whether the address space is being used by user or by supervisor. So, conceptually, the total logical address space of the CPU is 48M bytes. This 48MB of

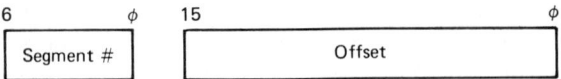

**Figure 7.35.** The 23-Bit Logical Address of Z8001 CPU

logical address space is equivalent to 768 logical segments, each being 14K bytes.

Transforming this logical address into a 24-bit physical address is the job of the MMU (Figure 7.36). A single MMU provides support for sixty-four 64K-byte logical segments (total logical address space of 4 MB) and maps these logical segments into 16MB physical address space (256 physical segments).

In the Z8001 system, memory segments are organized as sequential sets of memory locations (segments) varying in length from 256 bytes to 64K bytes. Segments are located at 256-byte boundaries (i.e., the least significant 8 bits of the segment base address are always zero). The mapping from logical to physical segments is done by a segment table that holds a segment description for each segment.

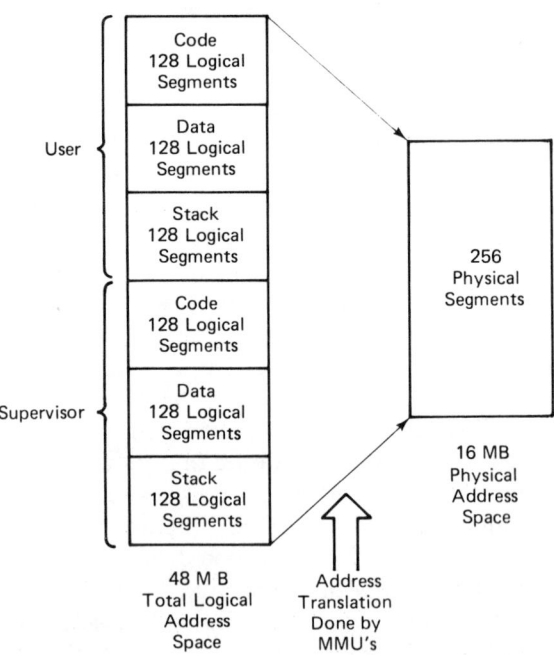

**Figure 7.36.** Z8001 Logical to Physical Address Space Mapping

## 7.5 Memory Management and Cache Support for Microprocessors

A segment description in the MMU is 32 bits wide and contains three fields: a 16-bit segment base, an 8-bit segment limit field, and an 8-bit segment attribute field (Figure 7.37). Since the eight least significant bits of the base address are zero, they are not stored in the segment description. The segment base field specifies the starting physical address of the logical segment. The limit field specifies the length of the segment size in blocks of 256 bytes. The attribute field contains eight attribute bits of the segment. Because each MMU supports 64 segment descriptors, two MMUs are required to handle all 128 logical segments that the Z8001 can manipulate directly. Each MMU can be programmed to handle either segments 4 to 63 or segments 64 to 127.

The transformation of logical address into a physical address, called memory relocation, is shown in Figure 7.38. The logical segment number component of the logical address is used as an index to select a particular segment description in the segment table. To generate a 24-bit physical address, the MMU adds the support bit of the offset address to the 16-bit segment base field of the corresponding segment descriptor. Since the eight low-order bits of the segment base are always zero, the eight low-order bits of the segment offset need not participate in the addition of base address to the offset. Rather, they are simply concentrated to the

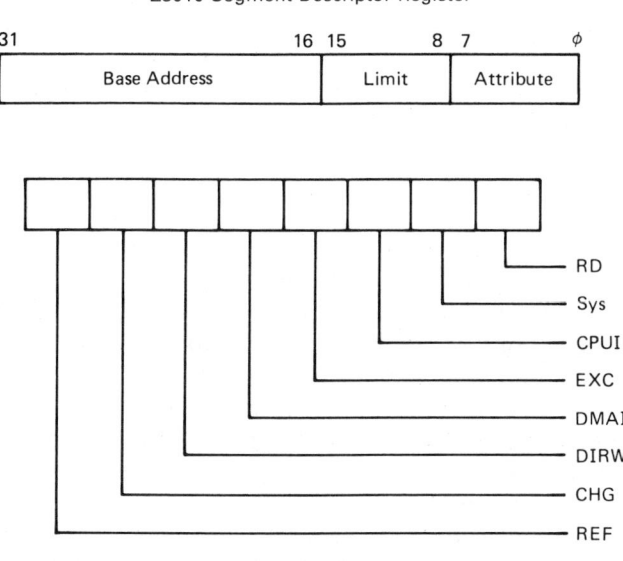

**Figure 7.37** Z8010 Segment Descriptor Register

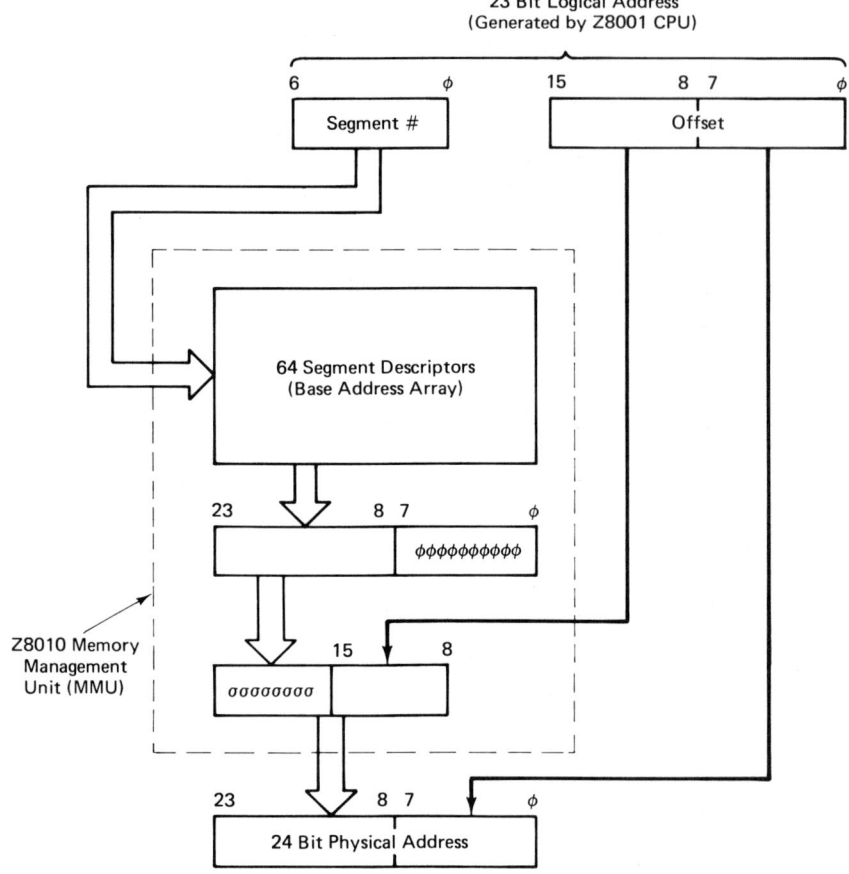

**Figure 7.38.** Generation of Physical Address for Z8010 MMU

result of the 16-bit algorithm (of the higher-order byte of the offset to the most significant 16 bits of the base address) to form the 26-bit physical offset. This process obviates the need for a 24-bit adder.

Besides address relocation, the other important tasks to be performed by the MMU are segment management and protection from unauthorized or unintended accesses (Figure 7.39). To provide safeguard to memory areas from unauthorized or unintended access, the MMU has an 8-bit attribute field with each segment. The CPU provides the nature of memory reference interaction to the MMU in the status lines. For every memory reference, these status lines are compared against the attributes associated with the corresponding segment. If there is a mismatch, the

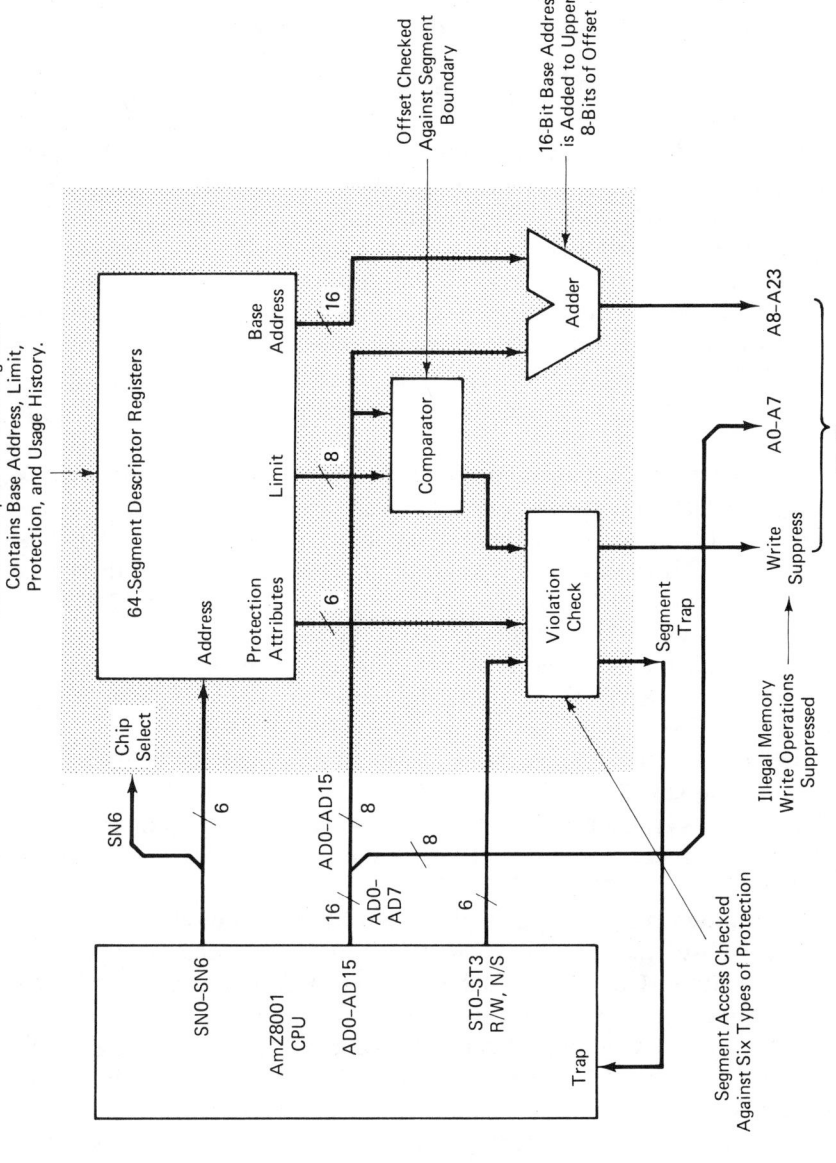

**Figure 7.39.** Protection checking of MMU and interconnection of AMZ8001 CPU to AMZ8010 MMU

MMU generates a trap, interrupts the CPU, and saves the corresponding status information, which can be interrogated by the CPU to determine the particular cause of the trap.

The MMU checks each memory reference for two major types of trap conditions: access violations and write warnings. Attempted reference in a mode not allowed by the read only, execute only, CPU inhibit, DMA inhibit or system only attribute of the segment or attempted memory reference outside allocated memory size of the segment constitutes an access violation. The write warning trap is generated by the MMU when the CPU makes an attempt to write into the last 256 byte locations of a segment that is used as stack. By generating this trap request, the MMU gives a warning to the CPU that the stack is in danger of overflow and invokes an operating system service routine to handle the trap. The operating system service routine, if desired, can increase the memory allocated in the stack and avoid a total stack overflow.

The MMU is designed to operate in three major functional states: the memory management state, the command state, and the quiescent state.

In the memory management state, the MMU essentially provides the memory management function of address translation and protection checking. In this state, the memory reference initiated by the CPU is checked by the MMU for access validity and then the logical address is translated to a physical address. In the command state, the MMU responds to 22 special I/O instructions from the CPU for loading base addresses, the limit register, and attribute register for the segment descriptor–segment table. Also in this state, the CPU can interrogate the MMU status information. In the quiescent state, the MMU address output lines remain tri-stated. The state of the MMU is determined by the status information in the status line of the CPU.

The address translation function of the Z8010 is very similar to that of PDP 11/34. Similarity between the two can be observed from Figures 7.40 and 7.41.

Even though the Z8001 CPU and Z8010 MMU provide support for a very large address space and excellent memory management capability, they do not support a true virtual memory. A true segmented virtual memory management system needs support for dynamic memory relocation and segment swapping. Segment swapping involves saving of the current status of the CPU (upon detection of a segment fault), initiation of a request for the appropriate segment, bringing in the required segment, and starting the CPU from where it left off. Saving the state of the CPU has to be done by the CPU. Upon detection of a segment fault, the Z8010 MMU generates a segment fault; however, the Z8001 CPU does not have

## 7.5 Memory Management and Cache Support for Microprocessors

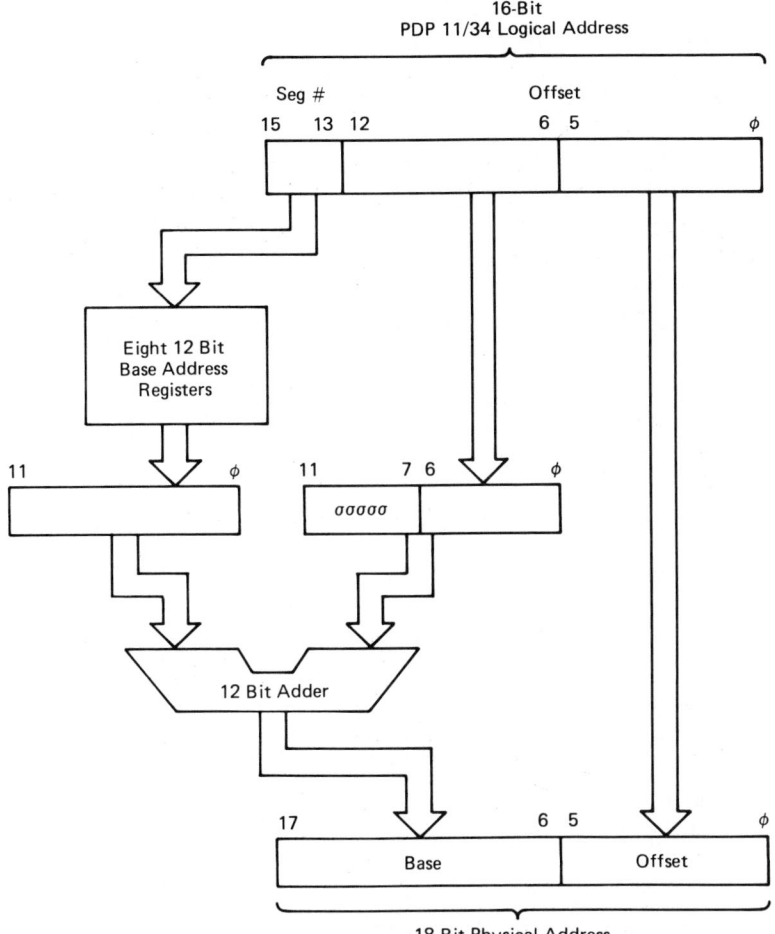

**Figure 7.40.** PDP 11/34 Address Translation Mechanism

the ability of interrupting the currently executing instruction and saving the state.

The second-generation 16-bit microprocessor Z8003 has the support for true virtual memory management [C9]. This chip absorbs the support circuitry for segment trap and also eliminates many software initialization routines. It includes an instruction abort pin to back up the CPU one instruction. This chip, along with the Z8010 MMU, provides a true virtual memory management scheme.

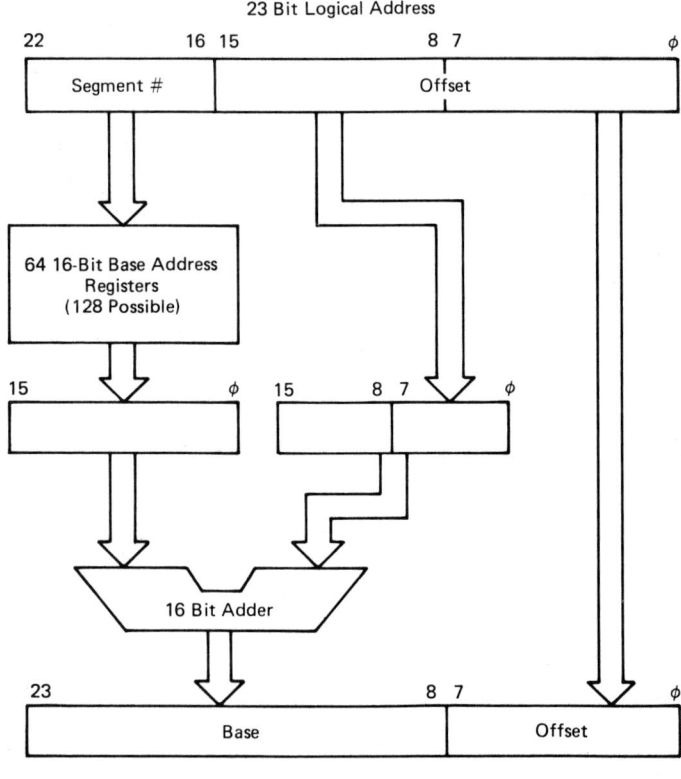

**Figure 7.41.** Z8010 MMU Address Translation Mechanism

## Memory Management for 8-bit Microprocessors

The concept of memory management first applied to 16-bit microprocessors has even been applied to 8-bit processors. Motorola's MC6829 is the memory management unit (MMU) for its 8-bit MC6809 microprocessor. By partitioning the memory into fixed-sized pages of 2K bytes, the MMU extends the 8-bit CPU's address limits beyond the bounds of 64K bytes to 2M bytes. It employs a very simple paged mapping scheme for converting the 16-bit logical address of the processor into a 21-bit physical address [R3].

The 16-bit logical address of the CPU consists of two fields. Bits 0 to 10 (11 bits) specify the byte offset within the page and bits 11 to 15 (5 bits) specify the logical page numbers. So, the logical address space consists of 32 logical pages, each page being of 2K bytes. The MMU employs

## 7.5 Memory Management and Cache Support for Microprocessors

a total of 128 mapping registers, partitioned into 4 sets of 32 registers, one per task. Each mapping register is 10 bits wide to provide the higher-order 10 bits of the physical address. So, at any particular instance of time, a task can access directly 64K bytes of memory on thirty-two 2K-byte pages. However, if the physical memory requirement of the task exceeds the 64K-byte space, the mapping registers for the corresponding task can be reloaded to provide a larger physical address space.

Even though the chip has 4 sets of 32 registers, only one set is active at a time. A particular set of registers is selected by an operating key, which selects one out of four tracks. However, the chip is designed in such a way that eight of those chips may be present in a system allowing a maximum of thirty-two 64K bytes (maximum of 2M bytes) to be supported directly in hardware registers.

### Address Translation

The logical to physical address translation is quite straightforward. The upper 5 bits of the logical address (bits 11 to 15) select a particular mapping register of the corresponding task (selected by the operating key task number). The corresponding mapping register generates the upper 10 bits of the physical address. The lower-order 11 bits of the logical address (bits 0 to 10) are appended directly with the 10 bits of the physical address generated by the mapping register to provide a 21-bit physical address. The MMU takes 110 ns to translate a logical address into a physical address (Figure 7.42).

The MC6829, however, does not have direct support for page protection and transparent page swapping. For page swapping, the programmer has to set up instructions for properly loading the mapping registers. The chip has good support for updating these mapping register contents.

### National's 16082 MMU

National Semiconductor's 16082 is the first memory management unit (MMU) to have support for 32-bit, demand paged virtual memory architecture [N3, K9, L6]. It uses a combination of segmentation with paging scheme to support the virtual memory architecture of the main CPU, 16032. The 16032 CPU provides a uniform addressing space of 16M bytes (i.e., both its logical address space and physical address space are 16M bytes each). Even though both the address spaces are the same, the mapping from logical to physical address space is done by the 16082 MMU. Besides the logic for address translation, the MMU chip supports memory protection.

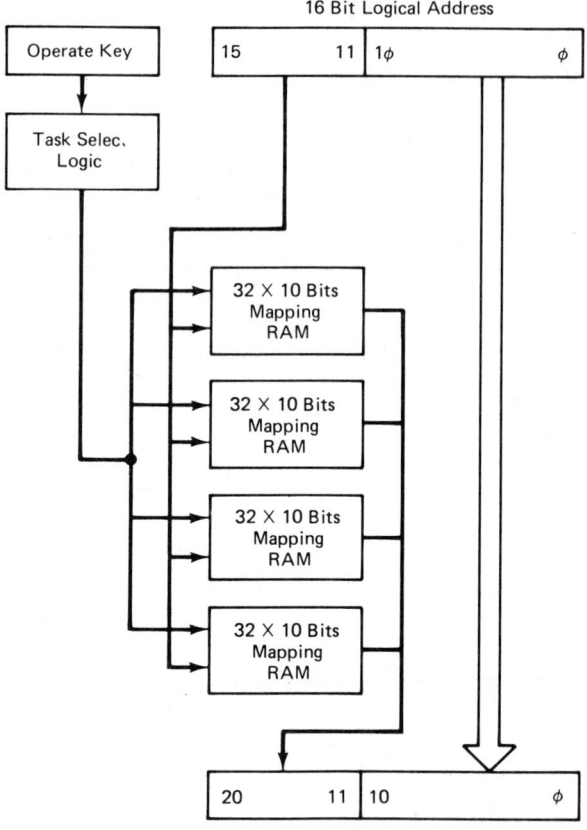

**Figure 7.42.** Address Translation Mechanism of Motorola's MC6829

## Address Translation

Both the logical and physical memory space of the 16032 CPU are partitioned into 512-byte pages. So for virtual memory management, both the address spaces are divided into 32,768 pages of 512 bytes each. To provide mapping of the logical address space to physical address space in a conventional scheme of page tables would necessitate a very large page table size. To minimize this mapping table size, a clever two-level approach is used by a combination of page table entries and pointer tables.

A logical address is generated by the 16032 CPU, which consists of two fields (as shown in Figure 7.43): bits 0 to 8 specify offset within the 512-byte page and bits 9 to 23 (15 bits) specify logical page address. This

## 7.5 Memory Management and Cache Support for Microprocessors

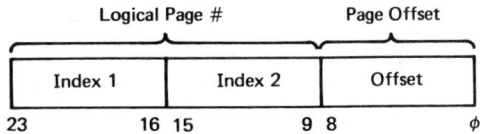

Figure 7.43. National's NS16082 Virtual Address Format

logical page address is partitioned into two subfields: an 8-bit page table entry address and a 7-bit pointer table entry address. The 8-bit page table entry address specifies an index address for the first-level page table, which has 256 entries, each entry being 32 bits. The MMU has two page table base registers, PTB1 and PTB2, one for the user and the other for the supervisor, which are manipulated by the operating system for manipulating the page table entries.

The top 8 bits of the virtual address are multiplied by 4 and added to the corresponding starting address of the page table base to point to one of the 256 page table entries. Each page table entry contains a 15-bit page frame number, which selects one of 256 pointer tables. Each pointer table has 128 pointer table entries. The next 7 bits of virtual address (bits 9 to 15) are multiplied by 4 and added to the page frame number to locate one of the 128 entries of the pointer table. Each pointer table entry is also 32 bits, and it generates a 15-bit physical page frame number.

The least significant 9 bits of virtual address are appended with this 15-bit physical page frame number to generate the 24-bit physical address.

The overhead of this scheme is not that much. The size of the page table is 1024 bytes or 2 pages; and each pointer table is 512 bytes or 1 page. Hence the system needs 2 pages for the page tables and 256 pages for the pointer tables. However, only the page table pages need to be resident in the main memory. The pointer table pages can reside on disk (secondary store) and can be brought to main memory as demanded. The page table entry format and pointer table entry format are shown in Figure 7.44.

The MMU has 32 entries (associative cache) in its translation buffer. When MMU receives a 24-bit virtual address, it compares associatively the upper 15 bits of its virtual address with its 32 entries in the translation buffer. These entries contain the most recently accessed virtual addresses with their translated physical address.

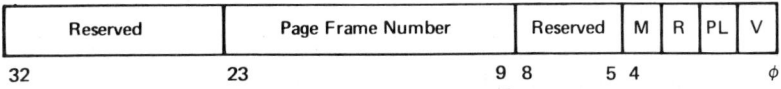

Figure 7.44. National's 16082 Page Table Entry (PTE) Format

If the associative compare results in an address hit, the translated address is generated and provided to CPU quickly. However, if there is no match, the MMU refers to the page table and pointer table in memory and tries to update the buffer. The MMU uses two page table base registers for accessing appropriate page tables. The address translation process is shown in Figure 7.45.

## Protection Checking

Besides address translation function, the MMU chip provides protection for memory for multitasking and multiprogramming environment. This protection checking is provided by two levels of page table entries. Index 1 page table has 256 page table entries and Index 2 page table has 128 page table entries.

Each page table entry and pointer table entry has 8 bits of access control information out of which, currently, 5 bits of information are used and 3 reserved for future purposes. These 5 bits are valid bit (V), referenced bit (R), modified bit (M), and two bits of protection level (PL). The meaning of these bits are as follows:

V bit: This bit of page table entry specifies whether the associated entry is valid or not.

R bit: Reference bit of page table entry specifies whether that particular page has been referenced.

M bit: This bit specifies whether the page associated with the Index 2 page table has been modified or not.

PL: Protection level bits specify the relationship between user, supervisor, and protection level bit.

| Mode | PSR 8 Bit | Protection Level Bits | | | |
|---|---|---|---|---|---|
| | | 00 | 01 | 10 | 11 |
| User | 1 | No access | No access | Read only | Full access |
| Supervisor | 0 | Read only | Full access | Full access | Full access |

Note that the modified bit is used by Index 2 page table entry only.

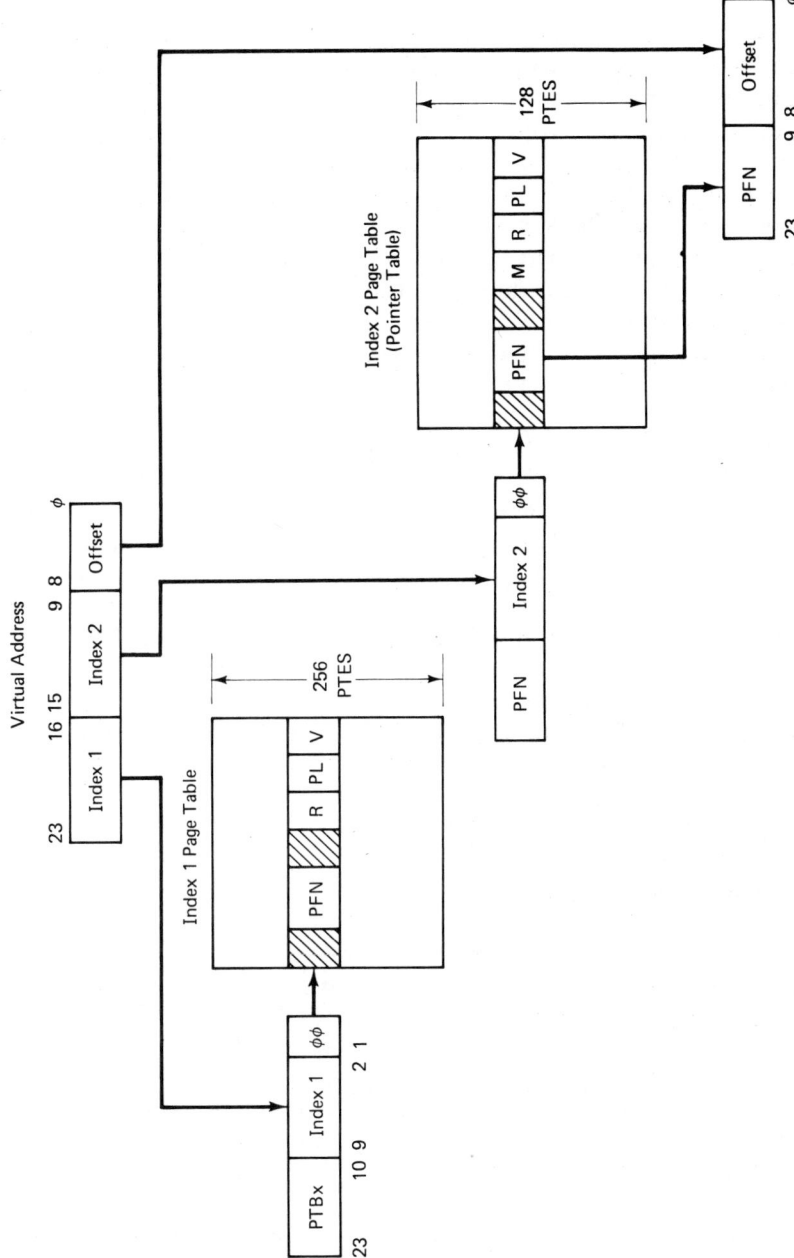

**Figure 7.45.** Virtual to Physical Address Translation for NS16082.

## Virtual Memory Support

To support true virtual memory architecture, the MMU interacts with the 16032 CPU with two separate pins—FLT (float) and abort. When the MMU determines that it must access a main memory page table entry to perform an address translation, it suspends the current memory cycle by asserting the float pin. This pin causes the CPU to float off the bus, making it available to the MMU.

When the MMU finishes accessing the information, it resumes the suspended cycle by deasserting the float pin. When the MMU decides that the requested virtual page is not in the main memory, it asserts the abort pin, which causes the CPU to stop the current instruction and traps to the operating system routine to handle this. The CPU state and status need to be saved to allow the instruction to be reexecuted at some future point. For supporting true virtual memory schemes, this reexecution feature is extremely critical, since the instruction must be reexecuted after an instruction abort when the references data have been properly transferred from the secondary memory to primary memory.

Besides this, the MMU chip contains a memory management status register (MSR) to specify the operational move and current processing status of the MMU. Provision of this register permits user control of address translation, breakpoints, and program tracing. This register maintains information such as error class flag, translation error trace flat, breakpoint number bit, error data direction bit, breakpoint direction bit, error status flag, breakpoint status flag, translate user bit, translate supervisor bit, and so on.

## Trends of Virtual Memory and Cache for Microprocessors

The concepts of virtual memory management with segmentation and paging and address translation and protection have been applied to first- and second-generation memory management units of 8- and 16-bit microprocessors. So far, in the microprocessor area, the total virtual memory management has been solved with a multiple-chip solution—one CPU chip and one MMU chip. However, with persistent improvement in technology, the future microprocessor's 8-, 16-, or 32-bit CPU's will move toward a single-chip virtual memory management solution with integrated instruction cache, address translation cache, and a data cache. Again, for the first generation of such chips, the same concepts that have been very well known in mainframe and minicomputers will be extended to microprocessors.

## 7.5 Memory Management and Cache Support for Microprocessors

On one side, efforts will be made to integrate these on one chip (for most solutions) and, on the other, bipolar fast building blocks like tag buffer and a data buffer will be developed to build bigger, faster, and cheaper mainframes and minicomputers. Here this approach will be taken for suitable cascadability of chips for building bigger and wider cache schemes. In the near future, caches and virtual caches will be ubiquitous in almost all microprocessors.

# References

[A1] Anderson, J. P., and E. L. Glaser, "Automatic Utilization of Hierarchical Memories," *Proc. Gigacycle Computing Systems,* AIEE Winter Meeting, Jan. 1962, pp. 124–132.

[A2] Agrawal, O. P., "Cache Memory Systems for Multiprocessor Architecture," *Proc. 1977 Nat. Compt. Conf.,* June 1977, pp. 13–16.

[A3] Agrawal, O. P., R. J. Zingg, and A. V. Pohm, *Proc. 14th IEEE Computer Soc. Int. Conf.* (IEEE, New York, 1977), p. 74.

[A4] Amstadter, B. L., *Reliability Mathematics Fundamentals: Practices, Procedures,* McGraw-Hill, New York, 1971.

[A5] Allen, C. A., "Design of Digital Memories That Tolerate All Classes of Errors," Ph.D. dissertation, Stanford University, Palo Alto, Calif., 1966.

[A6] Agrawal, O. P., "Applicability of Cache Memories to Unconventional Computing Structures like SYMBOL-ZR," Ph.D. dissertation, Iowa State University, Ames, Iowa, 1974.

[A7] Astrahan, M. M., and N. Rochester, "The Logical Organization of the New IBM Scientific Calculator," *Proceedings of the Electronic Computer Symposium* (IRE), Los Angeles, Apr. 30–May 2, 1952, paper xix (7 pp.).

[A8] Anderson, Judith A., and G. J. Lipoveki, "A Virtual Memory for Microprocessors," *IEEE 2nd Symposium on Computer Architecture,* 1975, pp. 80–84.

[B1] Bloom, L., M. Cohen, and S. Porter, "Considerations in the Design of a Computer with High Logic to Memory Speed Ratio," *Proc. Gigacycle Computing Systems,* Jan. 29–Feb. 2, 1962, AIEE Special Publ. 2-136, pp. 53–63.

[B2]   Belady, L. A., "A Study of Replacement Algorithms for a Virtual Storage Computer," *IBM Systems Journal,* vol. 5, no. 2, 1966, pp. 78–101.
[B3]   Bell, C. G., and D. Casasent, "Implementation of a Buffer Memory in Minicomputers," *Computer Design,* Nov. 1971, pp. 83–89.
[B4]   Bell, J., D. Casasent, and C. G. Bell, "An Investigation of Alternative Cache Organizations," *IEEE Trans. Computers,* vol. C-23, Mar. 1974, p. 346.
[B5]   Baum, A., and others, "Hardware Considerations in a Micro-Computer Multiprocessing System," *Compcon, 1975,* Spring Digest, Feb. 1975, pp. 27–30.
[B6]   Bhandarker, D. P., "Analysis of Memory Interference in Multiprocessors," *IEEE Trans. Computers,* vol. C-24, no. 9, Sept. 1975.
[B7]   Baer, J. L., "A Survey of Some Theoretical Aspects of Multiprocessing," *ACM Computing Surveys,* Vol. 5, No. 1, Mar. 1973, pp. 31–80.
[B8]   Baylis, M. H. J., D. G. Fletcher, and D. J. Howarth, "Paging Studies Made on the I.C.T. Atlas Computer," *Proc. Int. Federation Information Processing Congr.,* Edinburgh, 1968, North-Holland, Amsterdam, 1968, p. D113.
[B9]   Belady, L. A., and C. J. Kuehner, "Dynamic Space Sharing in Computer Systems," *Comm. ACM* 12, 1969, pp. 282–288.
[B10]  Barnes, D., and D. Bursky, "As Memory Density Quadruples Again, Designers Focus on Reliability," *Electronic Design,* Jan. 18, 1979, pp. 34.
[B11]  Brainerd, J. G., and T. K. Sharpless, "The ENIAC," *Electrical Engineering,* 1967 (Feb. 1941), p. 163.
[B12]  Buchholz, W., "Design Objectives for the IBM Stretch Computer," *AFIPS Proc. Western Joint Computer Conf.,* 1957, pp. 99–105.
[B13]  Basche, C. J., and others, "The Architecture of IBM's Early Computers," *IBM J. Res. Dev.,* vol. 25, no. 5, Sept. 1981, pp. 363–375.
[B14]  Bloch, Erich, "The Engineering Design of the Stretch Computer," *Proc. the Eastern Joint Computer Conf.,* 1959, pp. 48–56.
[B15]  Brooker, R. A., "Some Techniques for Dealing with Two Level Storage," *Computer Journal,* vol. 2, 1960.
[B16]  Beckmann, P. *Probability in Communications Engineering,* Harcourt Brace Jovanovich, New York, 1967.
[C1]   Conti, C. J., "Concepts for Buffer Storage," *Computer Group News* 2, Mar. 1969, pp. 9–13.
[C2]   Carter, W. C., D. C. Jessep, and A. Wadia, "Error-Free Decoding for Failure-Tolerant Memories," *Proc. IEEE Computer Group Conf.,* June 1970.
[C3]   Carter, W. C., K. A. Duke, and D. L. Jessep, Jr., "Lookaside Techniques for Minimum Circuit Memory Translaters," *IEEE-IC,* vol. C-22, no. 3, Mar. 1973.
[C4]   Cork, M. L., "Reliability with Error-Detecting and Correcting Codes in Semiconductor Memories," Ph.D. dissertation, University of Arizona, Tucson, 1975.
[C5]   Chu, W. W., and H. Opderbeck, "Performance of Replacement Algo-

rithms with Different Pay Sizes," *Computer*, vol. 7, Nov. 1974, pp. 14–21.

[C6] Censier, L. M., and P. Feautrier, "A New Solution to Coherence Problems in Multicache Systems," *IEEE Trans. Computers*, vol. C-27, no. 12, Dec., 1978, pp. 1112–1118.

[C7] Conti, C. J., D. H. Gibson, and S. H. Pitkowsky, "Structural Aspects of the System/380 Model 85: General Organization," *IBM Systems Journal*, vol. 7, no. 1, 1968, pp. 2–13.

[C8] Chow, C. K., "Determination of Cache's Capacity and Its Matching Storage Hierarchy," *IEEE Trans. Computers*, vol. C-25, no. 2, Feb. 1976, pp. 157–164.

[C9] Chow, W. M. "Central Server Model for Multiprogrammed Computer Systems with Different Classes of Jobs," *IBM Res. Dev.*, vol. 19, no. 3, May 1975, pp. 314–320.

[C10] Callahan, J., C. N. Patel, and D. Stevenson, "Bringing Virtual Memory to Microsystems," *Electronics*, June 30, 1981, pp. 119–122.

[D1] Denning, P. J., "The Working Set Model for Program Behavior," *J. Assoc. Computer Mach.*, vol. 1, May 1968, pp. 323–333.

[D2] Data General, "New Eclipse Handles Demanding Real Time Applications," *Data General News*, vol. 1, no. 1, Feb. 1975, pp. 1–4.

[D3] Data General, "Front-ending MOS Memories with Bipolar Cache: Best of Both Worlds," *Input/Output*, Data General Users Group, vol. 2, no. 2, 1975, pp. 6–8.

[D4] Digital Equipment Corp., "Translation Buffer, Cache, and SBI Control Technical Description," VAX-11/780 Implementation, EK-MM780-TD-001, 1978.

[D5] Data General, "Eclipse MV/1000 Principles of Operation," doc. no. 014-00E48, 1980.

[D6] Digital Equipment Corp., "Computer Engineering," 1979, pp. 263–266.

[D7] Denning, P. J., "Equipment Configuration in Balanced Computer Systems," *IEEE Trans. Computers*, vol. C-18, Nov. 1969, pp. 1008–1012.

[E1] Enslow, P. H., Jr., *Multiprocessors and Parallel Processing*, Wiley, New York, 1974.

[E2] Easton, M. C., "Model for Interactive Data Base Reference String," *IBM J. Res. Dev.*, vol. 19, Nov. 1975, pp. 550–556.

[E3] Eckert, J. P., and others, "Design of Univac-LARC System I," *AFIPS Proc.*, Eastern Joint Computer Conference, 1959, pp. 59–63.

[E4] Eckert, J. P., "Univac-LARC, the Next Step in Computer Design," *Proc. 1956 EJCC* (AIEE special publication T-107), pp. 16–19.

[F1] Fotheringhan, J., "Dynamic Storage Allocation in the ATLAS Computer Including an Automatic Use of a Backing Store," *Comm. ACM*, vol. 4, 1961, p. 435.

[F2] Ferris-Prabhu, A. V., "Improving Memory Reliability through Error Correction," *Computer Design*, July 1979.

[F3] Fuller, S. H., and F. Baskett, "An Analysis of Drum Storage Units," *J. Assoc. Computer Mach.*, vol. 22, Fall 1975, pp. 83–105.

[G1] Gibson, D. H., "Considerations in Block-Oriented Systems Design," *Proc. AFIPS Spring Joint Computer Conf.*, 30, 1967, pp. 75–80. Spartan, Washington, D.C.
[G2] Gibson, D. H., and W. L. Shevel, "Cache Turns up a Treasure," *Electronics,* Oct. 13, 1969, pp. 105–107.
[G3] Goldberg, J., K. W. Levitt, and J. Wensley, "An Organization for a Highly Survivable Memory," *IEEE-IC,* vol. C-23, no. 7, July 1974, pp. 693–705.
[G4] Goldstine, H. H., and A. Goldstine, "The Electronic Numerical Integration and Computer," *Math. Tables Aids Computers,* 2, July 1946, 97.
[G5] Glorioso, R. M., and T. D. Chase, "Design of Virtual Memory for Small Computers," *Computer Design,* vol. 12, 1973, pp. 67–72.
[G6] Gelenbe, E., "The Distribution of a Program in Primary and Fast Buffer Storage," *Comm. ACM,* vol. 16, no. 7, July 1973, pp. 431–434.
[G7] Gecsei, J., and J. A. Lukes, "A Model for the Evaluation of Storage Hierarchies," *IBM Systems J.,* no. 2, 1974, pp. 163–178.
[G8] Gecsei, J., "Determining Hit Ratios for Multilevel Hierarchies," *IBM J. Res. Dev.,* July 1974, pp. 318–327.
[H1] Hamming, R. W., "Error Detecting and Error Correction Codes," *Bell System Tech. J.,* Apr. 1950, pp. 147–160.
[H2] Hill, F. J., and G. R. Peterson, *Introduction to Switching Theory and Logical Design,* Wiley, New York, 1966.
[H3] Hellerman, H., *Digital Computer System Principles,"* McGraw-Hill, New York, 1973.
[H4] Haltfield, D. J., "Experiments on Page Size, Program Access Patterns, and Virtual Memory Performance," *IBM J. Res. Dev.,* Jan. 1972, pp. 58–66.
[I1] Inkol, R. J., and S. G. Chamberlain, "Design and Realization of a Two-Level 64K Byte CCD Memory System for Microcomputer Applications," *IEEE J. Solid State Circuits,* vol. SC-15, no. 1, Feb. 1980, pp. 131–135.
[J1] Joseph, M., "An Analysis of Storage Hierarchies in Digital Computers," Ph.D. dissertation, Churchill College, University of Cambridge, June 1968.
[J2] Joseph, E. C., "Innovations in Heterogeneous and Homogeneous Distributed Functions Architecture," *Computer,* Mar. 1974, pp. 17–24.
[J3] Juliussen, J. E., and F. J. Mowle, "Multiple Microprocessors with Common Main and Control Memories," *IEEE Trans. Computers,* vol. C-22, no. 11, Nov. 1973, pp. 999–1007.
[J4] Johnson, R. C., "Microsystem Exploit Mainframe Method," *Electronics,* Aug. 11, 1981, pp. 119–137.
[K1] Kroeger, J. H., and R. M. Meade, "Cache Buffer Memory Specification," *Proc. 1971 Computer Designers Conf.,* vol. 1, 1971.
[K2] Kaplan, K. R., and R. O. Winder, "Cache-Based Computer Systems," *Computer,* Mar. 1973, pp. 30–36.
[K3] Kurtzberg, J. M., "On the Memory Conflict Problem in Multiprocessor Systems," *IEEE Trans. Computers,* vol. C-23, no. 3, Mar. 1974, pp. 286–293.
[K4] Koppel, R., "RAM Reliability in Large Memory Systems—Significance of Predicting MTBF," *Computer Design,* Feb. 1979, p. 148.

[K5] Koppel, R., "RAM Reliability in Large Memory Systems—Improving MTBF with ECC," *Computer Design,* Mar. 1979, p. 196.

[K6] Katzan, H., "Storage Hierarchy Systems," *AFIPS Proc. Spring Joint Computer Conf.,* 1971, pp. 325–336.

[K7] Kilburn, T., and others, "Digital Computers at Manchester University," *Proc. IEEE* (London), 100, 1953, p. 487.

[K8] Kilburn, T., and others, "One-Level Storage Systems," *IRE Trans. Computers,* EC-11, 2, Apr. 1962, pp. 223–235.

[K9] Kuhn, L., "NSL6000 Brings Benefits of Virtual Memory to Microprocessors," *WOS Conf. Anaheim,* Sept. 16–18, 1950, pp. 1–7. Prentice-Hall, Englewood Cliffs, N.J.

[L1] Lee, F. F., "Project MAC Summer Study," Project MAC Report, Memorandum MAC-M-99, August 1963.

[L2] Lee, F. F., "Look-Aside Memory Simulation," Project MAC Report, Memorandum MAC-M-131, Jan. 1964.

[L3] Liptay, J. S., "Structural Aspects of the System, 360/65:11. The Cache," *IBM Systems J.,* vol. 7, no. 15, 1968.

[L4] Lee, F. F., "Study of Look-Aside Memory," *IEEE Trans. Computers,* vol. C-13, no. 11, Nov. 1969, pp. 1062–1064.

[L5] Lonsdale, K., and E. Warburton, "Mercury: A High-Speed Digital Computer," *Proc. IEE,* vol. 103, pt. B, suppl. 2, 1956, pp. 174–183.

[L6] Lavi, Y., and others, "A Bit Microprocessor Enters Virtual Memory Domain," *Electronics,* Apr. 16, 1980.

[L7] Lin, Y. S., and R. L. Mattson, "Cost Performance Evaluation of Memory Hierarchies," *IEEE Trans. Magnetics,* Sept. 1972, pp. 390–392.

[L8] Lin, S., *Introduction to Error Correcting Codes,* Prentice-Hall, Englewood Cliffs, N.J., 1970.

[M1] Meade, R. M., "On Memory System Design," *Proc. AFIPS Fall Joint Computer Conf.,* 1970, pp. 33–43.

[M2] Meade, R. M., "Design Approaches for Cache Memory Control," *Computer Design,* Jan. 1971, pp. 87–92.

[M3] Meade, R. M., "How a Cache Memory Enhances a Computer's Performance," *Electronics,* Jan. 17, 1972, pp. 58–63.

[M4] Mitchell, J., and others, "Multiprocessor Performance Analysis," *Proc. National Computer Conf.,* vol. 43, May 1974, pp. 399–403.

[M5] Mackinnon, R. A., "Advanced Function Extended with Tightly Coupled Multiprocessing," *IBM Systems J.,* vol. 13, no. 1, 1974, pp. 32–59.

[M6] Monroe, R. N., "Add-in Cache Memory Doubles Minicomputer Processing Speed," *Computer Design,* Oct. 1979, pp. 115–120.

[M7] Mudge, J. C., "Design Decisions Achieve Price/Performance Balance in Mid-Range Minicomputers," *Computer Design,* Aug. 1977, pp. 87–95.

[M8] Mattson, R. L., and others, "Evaluating Techniques for Storage Hierarchies," *IBM Systems J.,* vol. 9, no. 2, 1970, pp. 78–117.

[M9] Montgomery R. C., "Simple Hardware Approach to Error Detection and Correction," *Computer Design,* Nov. 1978, pp. 109–118.

[M10] Mattson, R. L., "Evaluation of Multilevel Memories," *IEEE Trans. Magnetics,* MAG-7, Dec. 1971, pp. 814–819.

[M11] Matick, Richard, *Computer Storage Systems and Technology,* Wiley, New York, 1977.

[N1] Nessett, D. M., *Aust. Computer J.,* vol. 7, no. 33, 1975.

[N2] Noguchi, K., L. Ohnisi, and H. Morita, "Design Considerations for a Heterogeneous Tightly Coupled Multiprocessor System," *Proc. National Computer Conf.,* vol. 44, May 1975, pp. 551–559.

[N3] National Semiconductor NS16082 MMU preliminary data sheet, 1982.

[P1] Peterson, W. W., and E. J. Weldon, Jr., *Error Correcting Codes,* MIT Press, Cambridge, Mass., 1972.

[P2] Pohm, A. V., "Cost/Performance Perspectives of Paging with Electronic and Electromechanical Backing Stores," *Proc. IEEE,* vol. 63, no. 8, Aug. 1975, pp. 1123–1128.

[P3] Pohm, A. V., O. P. Agrawal, and R. N. Monroe, "The Cost and Performance Tradeoffs of Buffered Memories," *Proc. IEEE,* vol. 63, Aug. 1975, pp. 1120–1135.

[P4] Pohm, A. V., O. Agrawal, and C. Cheng, "Fabritek Buffered Memory Study," Engineering Research Institute, Iowa State University, Ames, Iowa, 1973.

[P5] Pucknell, D. A., "A Preliminary Study of Cache Storage for the FM2000 CPU," Ferranti Digital Systems Division, Tech. Note C30/TN116.

[P6] Pucknell, D. A., "Costs Effectiveness Method for Speeding up Digital Computer Hardware," *IREE (Australia), International Electronics Convention,* Sydney, Aug. 1975, Convention Digest, pp. 7–9.

[P7] Papian, W. N., "High-Speed Computer Stores 2.5 Megabits," *Electronics,* vol. 30, Oct. 1957.

[P8] Pohm, A. V., and T. A. Smay, "Computer Memory Systems," *Computer,* Oct. 1981, pp. 93–110.

[P9] PDP 11/70 Processor Handbook, Digital Equipment Corporation, 1976.

[P10] Peterson, W. W., *Error Correcting Codes,* 2nd ed., MIT Press, Cambridge, Mass., 1961.

[R1] Rao, G. S., "Performance Analysis of Cache Memories," *JAC,* vol. 25, no. 3, July 1978, pp. 378–395.

[R2] Raphel, H. A., "Distributed Intelligence Microcomputer Design," *Comcon 75, Spring Digest,* 10th Annual IEEE Computer Society International Conference, Feb. 1975, pp. 21–26.

[R3] Rupp, E. J., "Memory Management Chip Extends Reach of 8 Bit Precisions," *Electronic,* Aug. 25, 1981, pp. 134–136.

[R4] Rhodes, C., "Caches Keep Main Memory from Slowing Down Fast CPU's," *Electronic Design,* Jan. 21, 1982, pp. 179–184.

[R5] Rhodes, C., J. Chun, and T. Herndon, "Computer Memory Functions Surface on VLSI Chip," *Electronic Design,* Feb. 18, 1982, pp. 159–163.

[S1] Scarott, G. G., "The Efficient Use of Multilevel Storage," *Proc. IFIPS Congress,* Spartan Books, Washington, D.C., 1965.

[S2] Searle, B. C., and D. E. Froberg, "Tutorial: Microprocessor Applications in Multiple Processor Systems," *IEEE Computer,* Oct. 1975, pp. 22–30.

[S3] Sastry, K. V., and R. Y. Kain, "On the Performance of Certain Multiprocessor Computer Organizations," *IEEE Trans. Computers,* vol. C-24, no. 11, Nov. 1975, pp. 1066–1074.

[S4] Sanyal, S., and K. N. Venkataraman, "Single Error Correcting Code Maximizes Memory System Efficiency," *Computer Design,* May 1978, pp. 175–184.

[S5] Lin, Shu, *An Introduction to Error Correcting Codes,* Prentice-Hall, Englewood Cliffs, N.J., 1970.

[S6] Sisson, S. S., and M. J. Flynn, "Addressing Patterns and Memory Handling Algorithms," *AFIPS Proc. Fall Joint Computer Conf.,* 33, 1968, pp. 957–967.

[S7] Strecker, W. D., "Cache Memories for PDP.11 Family Computers," *Proc. 3rd Annual Symp. Computer Architecture,* 1976, pp. 155–158.

[S8] Stevenson, D., "An Introduction to Memory Management," *Electronics and Power,* Apr. 1980.

[S9] Slutz, D. R., and I. L. Traiger, "Determination of Hit Ratios for Class of Staging Hierarchies," *IBM Research Report* RJ 1044.

[S10] Scherr, A. L., "Analysis of Computer Memory Performance," American Statistical Association Conference Session on Probability and Statistics in the Design of Computer Systems, Los Angeles, Aug. 18, 1966.

[T1] Takahashi, S. H., K. Nishino, and K. Fuchi, "System Design of the ETL MK-6 Computer," *Proc. IFIPS Congress,* 1962, North-Holland, Amsterdam, 1963, pp. 690–693.

[T2] Tucker, J. H., "Automatically-Loaded Scratchpad Memories in Digital Computer Memory Systems," Ph.D. dissertation, Churchill College, University of Cambridge, Feb. 1968.

[T3] Tang, C. K., "Cache System Design in the Tightly Coupled Multiprocessor Systems," *AFIPS Proc.,* vol. 49, 1976, p. 749.

[T4] Traiger, I. L., and R. L. Mattson, "The Evaluation and Selection of Technologies for Computer Storage Systems," *Proc. Conference on Magnetism and Magnetic Materials,* no. 5, part 1, pp. 1–12.

[T5] Tate, G., and W. Miller, "EDC Chip Boosts Memory Reliability," *Electronic Design,* Sept. 1, 1980, pp. 151–155.

[T6] Toshi, E. A., and T. Watanabe, "An All-Semiconductor Memory with Fault Detection Correction and Logging," *Hewlett-Packard J.,* Aug. 1976, pp. 8–13.

[T7] Tredennick, H. L., and T.A. Welch, "High-Speed Buffering for Variable Length Operands," *Symposium on Computer Architecture, IEEE Comp. Soc.,* College Park, Md. Mar. 1977, pp. 205–210.

[T8] Traiger, I. L., and D. R. Slutz, "One Pass Techniques for the Evaluation of Memory Hierarchies," IBM Research Report, RJ-892, 1971.

[V1] Von Neumann, J., A. W. Burks, and H. Goldstein, "Preliminary Discussion of the Logical Design of an Electronic Computing Instrument," in J. von Neumann, *Collected Works, vol. V.,* Pergamon Press, Elmsford, N.Y., 1963.

[V2] Aken, Jerry, "Match Cache Architecture to the Computer System," *Electronic Design,* Mar. 4, 1982, pp. 73–91.

[W1] Wilkes, M. V., "Slave Memories and Dynamic Storage Allocation," *IEEE*

*Trans. Electronic Computers,* Apr. 1965, pp. 270–271. Project MAC-M-164, MIT, Cambridge, Mass., June 22, 1964.

[W2] Whalen, M. W., "Speeding up Ferrite-Core Memories," *Electronics,* Oct. 13, 1969, pp. 108–110.

[W3] Weisbecker, J. A., "Memory Systems," U.S. Patent No. 3,601,812, Aug. 24, 1971.

[W4] Winder, R. O., "A Data Base for Computer Performance Evaluation," presented at IEEE Workshop on System Performance Evaluation, Argonne, Ill., Oct. 1971, and published in *Computer,* vol. 6, no. 3, Mar. 1973.

[W5] Wiesen, J. M., "Mathematics of Reliability," *Proc. 6th National Symp. Reliability Quality Control,* Jan. 1960.

[W6] Williams, F. C., and T. Kiliburn, "A Storage System for Use with Binary-Digital Computing Machines," *Proc. IEEE (London),* vol. 46, no. 3, Mar. 1949, p. 81.

[W7] West, J. T., "Lasting Computer Design Exploit Standard Parts," *Electronics,* Nov. 13, 1975, pp. 130–136.

[W8] Winograd, S., "On Parallel Evaluation of Certain Arithmetic Expressions," *J. ACM,* vol. 22, no. 4, Oct. 1975, pp. 477–492.

[Y1] York, K. D., "A Low-Cost High-Performance Alternative to Fully Associative Buffer Memories," Private Memo, Architecture Department, Burroughs Corp., Computer Systems Group, July 11, 1973.

[Z1] Zilog, *An Introduction to the Z8010 MMU Memory Management Unit,* Mar. 1981.

[Z2] Zilog, *Z8000* vs. *68000 Segmented* vs. *Linear Addressing,* concept paper.

# Index

Access time (s)
  average, 5
  effective, 9, 24, 50–56
  fast, 5
  IBM 360/95, 5
  ILLIAC IV, 2
  machine, 5
  memory, 5
  processor, 5
  shortest, 4
Address
  assignment, 27–28
  cache, 11, 18
  mapping, 24, 26–27
Addresses, associated, 18
Addressing pattern, 17
Agrawal, O. P., 187, 188–89
Algorithmic
  operation, 8
  source language, 6
Algorithms, 27–56
  single-swap, 20
  swapping, 27–33
Allen, C. A., 136
Allocation, storage, 6–8
AMD, cache support, for microprocessor
  AMZ 8010, 213–19
  28000, 212
Amdahl, 470V series, cache memories for, 12
Anderson, J. P., 157–58
Anticipatory rule, 24

Architectural innovations, improving performance by, 3
Arithmetic stack, 9
Associated addresses (entries), 18
Associative memory, 9, 20, 26
Atlas ICL computer, 8, 9, 146–52
Automatic storage allocation, 6–9, 23
  dynamic, 6–8
  static, 6–8
Auxiliary memory storage, 6, 10
  moving information from/to, 6–8

Backing store, 5, 10, 24
Bandwidth, 75–79
Behavior, program, predictability of, 6–8
Bell, C. G., 189–90
Bell, J., 189–90
Bipolar cache and core memory system, 5
Block
  cache store entries, 18, 20
  frequency of use, 57–65
  length, 19
  size, hit ratio dependence on, 65–68
Bloom, L., 9, 153, 154, 155, 156
Branches, and processor/main memory gap, 8
Bridge, transparent, between processor/main memory speed, 9, 18, 145
Brooker, R.A., 146

237

Buchholz, W., 146
Buffer
 filling, 68–74
 partitioning, 18–19, 26–27
Buffer/buffering (cache)
 concept of, 9, 10, 11
 see also Cache
Buffered memories
 elements of, basic, 17–22
 hit ratios in, 57–74
Buffered virtual memory system. See Cache virtual memory system
Buffered/unbuffered memory systems, cost/performance comparison, 20–22
Burroughs B6500 computer, 8
Bus performance in servicing multiprocessors, 90–92
Byte-addressable machine, 20

Cache (buffered) memory(ies), 3, 17
 philosophy of, 18
 sample cache memory, small, design of
  cost effectiveness, 19–22
  minimum requirements, 18–19
  performance effectiveness, 19–22
Cache memory systems, 3, 8–16
 elements of, basic, 17–22
 history of, 161–81
 transparent, 9, 18, 145
Cache virtual memory system
 defined, 10
 design of, 23–26
  buffer partitioning, 26–27
  comparative performances, 33–39
  effective cycle/access time, 50–56
  multimodule main memories, 39–59
  swapping algorithms, 27–33
Cache-based system
 defined, 9
 historical development
  cache for microprocessors, 212–27

Cache-based system (*Contd.*)
  cache for minicomputers, 189–212
  cache-related studies, 181–89
  IBM memory systems, 161–81
Cache/paged virtual memory system, compared, 10–11
Cache-processor, multiple, system, organization of, 81–90
Capacity
 of memory systems, 1–3
 historical development, 3–9
 of small memories, 18
Casasent, D., 189–90
CDC 7600 Computer, 8
Cells, memory
 high speed, 21
 slow-speed, 17
Censier, L. M., 80, 90
Cheng, C., 187
Chips
 memory, 3
 microcomputer, 11
 semiconducter, 119
Chow, C. K., 187–88
Chu, W. W., 112, 186
Circuit speed, 21
Codes, error detecting/correcting 119–43
Cohen, M., 9, 153, 155
Coherence, of cache information, 79–80
Commercial single bit error correction (SBEC) Circuits, 139–42
Component
 failure, 128–35
 speeds, 3
Computer system, historical development, 1–3
Conflicting usage writeback (CUW) algorithms, 29, 30–32
Conti, C. J., 181–82
Control logic, 18
Core and disk
 demand paging system, 5
 overlaying system, 5

Correcting (error) codes, 119–43
Cost
 of storage, 2, 4, 5
 /performance relationship, 5, 6–7, 18–22
 /speed relationship, 5, 6, 7, 11
 vs. speed, 4, 5, 6, 7, 17
Cost effectiveness, of buffered memories, 17–18, 19–22
Cost/performance comparison, buffered/unbuffered memory systems, 20–22
Current storage technologies, cost-performance characteristics, 6–7
Cycle time(s)
 effective, 9, 20–22, 23, 50–56
 IBM 360/95, 5
 memory, 2, 4, 5, 8
 system parameters affecting, 20–21

Data cache, 11, 18
Data General, cache memory systems for
 eclipse, 191, 206
 MV/8000, 16, 198, 206–12
Demand rule, 24
Design
 for cache virtual memory systems, 23–26
  buffer partitioning, 26–27
  comparative performances, 33–39
  effective cycle/access time, 50–56
  multimodule main memories, 39–50
  swapping algorithms, 27–33
 goal of, 6
 sample cache, for multiprocessor system, 97–103
 simple, for sample cache memory, 17–22
Detecting (error) codes, 119–43
Digital Equipment Corp., cache memory systems, for
 PDP-1, 160
 PDP-8/E, 189–91

Digital Equipment Corp. (*Contd.*)
 PDP-11/34, 218–19
 PDP-11/45, 8
 PDP-11/60, 11, 197–98
 PDP-11/70, 8, 11, 192–97
 PDP-VAX-11/780, 16, 198–206
Directly mapped buffer, 27–28
Directory, 18–19
 time to search, 20
Distance, Hamming, 121, 123
Dynamic storage allocation, 6–8
 system, 8
 user, 8

Easton, M.C., 58, 72
Economic reason for successful cache memory, 17
Effective
 access time, 9, 24, 50–56
 cycle time, 9, 20–22, 50–56
 performance, of buffered memory systems, 20–22
Electronic Numerical Integrater and Calculator (ENIAC), 145
Error detecting and correcting (EDAC) codes, 119–21
 check lists/circuitry, positioning, 124–27
 single-error detecting (SED) codes, 121–22
ETL-MK-6 computer, 9, 152
Extrinsic design parameters, buffered memory systems, 24–25

Failure, component, 128–35
Feautrier, P., 80, 90
Ferranti Atlas, 9
 Mercury computer, 146, 152
Fetching policies, 24, 40, 43
Filling, of buffer, 68–74
Flagged conflicting writeback (CUX) algorithm, 29, 32–34
Flagged register swap (FRS) algorithm, 29, 33, 35, 37–39
Flagged swap (FS) algorithm, 29, 32–34

Flagged swap (FS) algorithm (*Contd.*)
    timing, 37–39
Flat film memory, 5
Flynn, M. J., 58
Fraction of reads (FR), 33
Fujitsu FACOM M Series
    Mainframes, cache memories
    for, 15
Fully associative
    memory, 26
    store, 20

Gap between processor/main memory
    speed, 2–9
GE 645 computer, 8
Gecsei, J., 188
Gibson, D. H., 26, 159, 160, 161, 183
Glaser, E.L., 157–58

Haltfield, D. J., 186
Hamming, R. W., 120
Hamming codes, 120, 122–24
Hardware-managed hierarchy, 5
Hierarchies, high-speed memory, 3,
    5–16
    defined, 5
    historical development, 1–16,
    145–61
Hierarchy organizations, memory
    coherence of cache information,
    79–80
    multiple buffered modules, 75–79
    multiple cache-processor system,
    81–90
    multiprocessor system, sample
    cache design for, 97–103
    multiprocessors, bus performance
    in servicing, 90–92
    three-level, optimum allocation of
    resources, 92–97
    virtual memory systems, 10–17
High-speed computer memories,
    historical development, 1–16
High-speed memories
    commercial single bit error correction
    (SBEC) circuits, 139–42

High-speed memories (*Contd.*)
    error detecting and correcting
    (EDAC) codes, 119–27
    impact of EDAC codes on system
    reliability, 136–39
    reliability analysis of memory
    system codes, 127–35
Historical development
    cache systems, 161–81, 189–212
    cache-related studies, 181–89
    hierarchical memories, 145–161
    high-speed computer memories,
    1–16
Hit ratio(s) (HR), 20–21, 25, 33
    analytical models, 57–65
    buffer filling and cold-start miss
    ratios, 68–74
    dependence on block size, 65–68
    effect of multiclasses on, 26
Hitachi's HITAG M Series
    Highlights, cache memories
    for, 15

IBM systems, cache memories for
    303X, 176
    360/85, 8, 10, 11, 157, 161–67, 168,
    176, 181, 182, 184
    360/95, 5
    360/195, 8, 167, 176, 181, 184
    370/155, 167–72, 176, 181, 184
    370/158, 8
    370/163, 176
    370/165, 167, 172–176, 184
    370/168, 8, 176
    370/168-3, 176
    370/3033, 176–181
    4331, 16
    selective sequence electronic
    calculator (SSEC), 145
    stretch computer, 146
Identifier, 18
ILLIAC IV/UNIVAC 1, compared,
    1–2
Illusion, of
    an infinite memory, 145, 146
    large storage working at faster
    buffer speed, 10, 11, 17

Illusion (*Contd.*)
  single, large, one-level storage space, 8, 9
Inaccessibility, of cache, 9
Index registers, 9
Information
  managing of, 8
  moving of, 6–9
Instruction cache, 11, 18
Intel, cache support, for microprocessor
  8086, 212
  IAPX 432, 212
Interleaving
  buffering of interleaved modules, 75–79
  deeper storage, 8
  memory, 3
Intrinsic design parameters, buffered memory systems, 24–25
Invisibility of cache, 9

Kaplan, K. R., 68, 186–87
Katzan, H., 167

Large
  cache systems, historical development, 161–81
  high-speed memory systems
    error detecting/correcting codes, 119–27
    reliability analysis, 127–35
  main-frame systems, 2, 11–15
  memory, computing cost of, 20–22
  programs, and overlay problems, 6
Lee, F. F., 154, 156, 159, 160–61
Levels of memory, 10
  first, 5
  second, 5
  three, 9, 75, 92–97
  two, 5, 23, 75–92
Lin, S., 121
Lin, Y. S., 185–86
Linear memory schemes, 220–24
Liptay, J. S., 166–68
List structures, efficient, 8

Locality of reference, 25
Look ahead, 8
"Look aside" memory, 9, 153–56, 160
Loop, short program, 9
Lukes, J. A., 188

Machine-independent programs, developing, 8
Main-frame systems, large/super large, memory capacity, 2, 11–15
Manchester University, England, 145
Mapping
  address, 24, 26–27
  of buffer, 18–19
  policies, 24
Matching, of processor/main memory speed, 2–9
  buffering approach, 9–11
Mattson, R. L., 67, 112, 184–86
Meade, R. M. 183–84
Memory
  cache, 3, 10–11, 17–22, 23, 26–56
  capacity, 1–16, 17
  chips, 3
  cost, 2, 4, 5, 6, 7
  cost vs. speed, 4, 5, 6, 7
  hierarchy, 3, 5–16
    defined, 5
    organizations, 75–118
  speed, 1–16
  virtual, 3, 10, 11, 103–18
    history of, 8, 11, 145–227
Memory(ies), main
  address, size of, 20
  capacity, historical development, 6–9
  illusion of, 8, 9, 10, 11, 17, 145, 146
  multimodule, 39–50
  /processor speeds, mismatch of, 2–9
  resources, availability of, 8
  speed of, 1–3
    historical development, 3–4
  store, moving information to/from, 6–8

Microcomputer systems
  cache memories for, 11
  memory capacity, 2, 12–15
Microprocessors, 1–2
  caches for, historical development, 212–27
Microsecond-to-millisecond hierarchy, 8
Minicomputer systems, 1–2
  cache memories for, 11, 16
    historical development, 189–212
  memory capacity, 2
Mismatch, of processor/main memory speed, 2–9
Miss ratio (MR), 27, 29, 33
  cold-start, 68–74
Modularity, developing programs with, 8
Modules
  main memory, 23, 25
  multiple buffered, 75–79
Monroe, R. N. 188–89
Motorola, cache support, for microprocessor
  MC 6809, 220
  MC 68000, 212
  MC 6829, 221–22
Movement of information, automatic, 6–9
Multiclass buffer memory, 26–27
Multilevel storage system, 5–9
Multimodule main memories, 39
  module delays, 40–50
Multiple cache-processor system, organization of, 81–90
Multiple-error correcting codes, 120
Multiprocessing and processor/main memory gap, 8
Multiprocessor systems, 78–118
Multiprogramming/multiprogramming systems, 78–118
  and processor/main memory gap, 8

Name cache, 11
Nanosecond-to-microsecond hierarchy, 8, 23
  concept, development of 9, 10
Natick, Richard, 105

National semiconductor, cache support, for microprocessor AS models, 13–15, 16–32, 212, 221–22

One level
  memory device, lack of, 5
  storage space illusion of, 8
Opderbeck, H., 112, 186
Operations, speed of elementary, 3
Organizations, memory hierarchy, 75–118
Overlapping, 26, 33
Overlay problems/strategies, 6
Overlaying system, core and disk, 5

Paged/cached virtual memory system, compared, 10–11
Paging system, demand, core and disk, 5
Partitioning
  of buffer, 18–19, 26–27
  of processor-used memory, 83–84
PE, 3240 minicomputer, cache memory for, 16
Pennsylvania, University of, 145
Performance, memory
  cost relationship, 4, 5, 6–7, 18
  semiconductor memories, 119
  improvement, need for, 2–3, 17
  large increase of, at small cost increase 17–18
  system performance, computed using system parameters, 20–22
Performance effectiveness, of buffered memories, 19–22
Performance(s) of buffered memory systems, compared, 33–39
Peterson, W. W., 121
Pipelining, and processor/main memory speed gap, 8, 25
Pohm, A. V., 187, 188–189
Porter, S., 9, 153, 155
PRIME 750, cache memory for, 16
Priority update list, 18–19, 20
Processor
  access time requirements, 5, 6
  historical progress of, 1–3

# Index

Processor (*Contd.*)
 /main memory speeds, mismatch of, 2–9
 registers, speed of, 8, 9
Program
 behavior, predictability of, 6–8
 stack, 9
Programming
 costs, and overlay problems, 6
 reason for successful cache memory, 17
Pucknell, D. A., 191

Register
 index, 9
 processor, 8, 9
 shift, 20
Reliability
 analysis, of memory system codes, 127–35
 memory system reliability, impact of EDAC codes on, 136–39
 of semiconductor chips, in large memory systems, 119
Replacement policies, cache virtual memory systems, 24
Resources, main memory, availability of, 8

Sample cache memory system
 cost effectiveness, 19–22
 design, of simple, 17–19
 elements of, 18–19
 evaluation, of simple, 17, 19–22
 performance effectiveness, 19–22
Scarott, G. G., 158–59
Scherr, A. L., 66
Search
 memory, 18
 the directory, time to, 20
Segmented memory schemes, 213–20
SEL 32/77, cache memory for, 16
Semiconductor
 memories, 119–43
 monolithic memory, 10
Shift register, 20
Simple swap (SS) algorithms, 29, 30–32

Simple swap (SS) algorithms (*Contd.*)
 timing, 36–37
Single bit error correction (SBEC) circuits, 139–42
Single-error correction (SEC) codes, Hamming's, 120, 122–24
Single-error detecting (SED) codes, 121–22
Single-level memory device
 illusion of, 8
 lack of, 5
Single-swap algorithm, 20
Single-unit memory module case, 35–36
Sisson, S. S., 58, 160, 183
Size (capacity)
 main memory, early development of, 6
 of buffer, 18–19
 of memory capacity, 4–5
 of storage modules, 4–5
 vs. speed, 5
Slave memory, 9, 156–58
Slutz, D. R., 188
Small memories, speed/capacity, 18
Small-capacity, high-speed memory, 10, 17
Software-managed hierarchy, 5
Special (search) memory, 18
Speed
 circuit, 21
 ideal, of storage systems, 8–9
 mismatch of processor/main memory, 2–9
 of individual components, 3
 of main memory systems, 1–3
  historical development, 3–5
 of processors, early development, 1–3
 of small memory, 18
 ratios, 10
 theoretical limiting, 3
 vs. cost, 4, 5, 6, 7, 17
 vs. size, 5
Sperry UNIVAC, 110 Series, cache memories for, 15
Static storage allocation, 6–8

Storage
  cost of, 2, 4, 5
  cycle time, 2, 4, 5, 8, 9
  hierarchy, 4–5
    cost effectiveness of, 5–7
    multiple, 5
    single–level, 5
    size, early development of, 4
    space, illusion of large, fast, 8, 9, 10, 11, 17, 145, 146
  technologies, current, cost–performance characteristics, 6–7
Storage allocation strategies
  automatic, 6–9, 23
  dynamic, 6–8
  static, 6–8
  system, 8
  user, 8
Storage systems, speed of, 8
Store, cache, associated entries, 18
Store–through (ST) algorithm, 29–31
  timing, 36
Strecker, W. D., 67, 72, 76, 197
Subset addressing pattern, 17
Swapping algorithms, 24, 27–33
  definition, 27
Switching functions, controlled, 21
SYMBOL-2R, virtual memory for, 8
Synchronization of various activities, timing for, 18
System dynamic storage allocation, 8
System parameters, affecting cycle time, 20–21

Tag store, 18–20
Tang, C. K., 80, 90
Technology
  current storage, 6–7
  improvements in, 17
  lack of/limitations in, 3, 5, 9
Throughput, 3, 81
Time sharing, and processor/main memory gap, 8
Time sharing systems, virtual, 1
Traiger, I. L., 188
Transferability, developing programs with, 8

Transparency, of cache, 9, 18, 145
Tredennick, H. L., 91

UNIVAC 1/ILLIAC IV, compared, 1–2
Update list of buffer, priority, 18–19, 20
User
  dynamic storage allocation, 8
  managed hierarchy, 5

Very large scale integration (VLSI)
  microcomputer chips, 11
  systems, cache memories for, 11–16
Virtual memory, 3
  concept proposed, 8
  design of cache virtual memory, 23–56
  history of, 8, 11, 145–61
Virtual memory systems, 10
  balancing page service/request rates, 113–16
  organization/mapping, 103–11
  page fault generation rates/modeling, 112–13
  page fault ratio, 111–12
  page replacement strategies, 116–17
Virtual time–sharing systems, 1
von Neumann, 1

Welch, T. A., 191
Wilkes, M. V., 9, 156–57, 158
Winder, R. O., 68, 186–87
Words
  associated, with main memory entries, 18
  memory, size of, 19
  transferred between cache/main memory, 27–33
Write–through (WT) algorithm, 29–31, 44
  timing, 36

Zilog, cache support, for microprocessor
  28000, 212
  Z8010, 213–19